Even the
DEFEATS

Even the
DEFEATS

**How Sir Alex Ferguson Used Setbacks
to Inspire Manchester United's
Greatest Triumphs**

J O H N   S I L K

First published by Pitch Publishing, 2020

Pitch Publishing
A2 Yeoman Gate
Yeoman Way
Worthing
Sussex
BN13 3QZ
www.pitchpublishing.co.uk
info@pitchpublishing.co.uk

A CIP catalogue record is available for this book
from the British Library.

ISBN 978 1 78531 685 2

Typesetting and origination by Pitch Publishing
Printed and bound by TJ Books Limited, Padstow, UK

Contents

'I am not kidding. This isn't just a job to me. It's a mission. I am deadly serious about it – some people would reckon too serious … we will get there. Believe me. And when it happens life will change for Liverpool and everybody else – dramatically.'

Alex Ferguson, 1988

Dedication

I WOULD like to recognise the kindness of my stepmother, who had a big influence on my upbringing. None more so than in harnessing my passion for football, and for Manchester United in particular. Sadly she is no longer with us, but her generosity and interest in my hobbies as a child sparked an enthusiasm for the game and the club she encouraged me to support. The influence she had on me that day when she saw me pretending to play football without a ball in the garden would prove to be far more significant than I could ever have possibly imagined. Her intentional mispronunciation of my childhood favourite player, Jesper Olsen, to tease me, along with her generosity and thoughtfulness in buying me football stickers or the latest replica shirt, are just some of the fond memories I have of her.

Acknowledgements

THE IDEA of this book had been rattling around my head for quite some time, possibly as far back as 2002, though I didn't realise then that an e-mail conversation between friends would eventually turn into 80,000 words almost two decades later.

I always thought the theme was interesting, one that would appeal to fellow Manchester United supporters, and even fans of other clubs. Thankfully, the people at Pitch Publishing thought the same so I am grateful for their assistance. Without Jane and Paul Camillin, Alex Daley, Gareth Davis, Graham Hales, Duncan Olner and Dean Rockett, this book would not have got off the ground.

Huge thanks need to go to a number of authors, journalists and fanzine producers. Without the following, this project would not have been possible – Wayne Barton, Ryan Benson, Barney Chilton, Richard Connor, Michael Crick, Daniel Harris, James Mariner and Jim White. They gave up significant chunks of their time, tolerated my e-mails and phone calls during the editorial process, and provided me with excellent feedback.

Interviews with Sir Alex Ferguson's biographer, Paul Hayward, and ITV commentator Clive Tyldesley, gave me an invaluable insight into the workings of the former Manchester United manager. I appreciated their time, particularly in light of the fact they had never even heard of me before I got in touch.

ACKNOWLEDGEMENTS

Assisting me with contacts, helping with translations, fact-checking historical occurrences and simply offering advice that I sought, were all vital ingredients in bringing this project together. Therefore, there are special mentions for Michael Cox, Anna Dittrich, Roger Hannah, Simon Hart, Fatema Imani, Jamie Jubon, Nik Martin, Iain McCartney, Mark Ogden, Lewis Sanders IV, Emre Sarıgül, Rob Smyth and Alistair Walsh.

In addition, interviews with two of Ferguson's former henchmen – Archie Knox and René Meulensteen – gave me a priceless insight into how the club was run and how crucial decisions were made, particularly in the wake of a defeat. Their contributions enriched this book immensely. When he agreed to write the foreword for this book, René gave me the best news since Manchester United won the Premier League title in 2013.

I would like to express my gratitude towards former players John Curtis and Ben Thornley, who both gave up their time to talk about what it was like playing under Ferguson.

Nods also need to go to Bernhard Buntru, Rina Goldenberg and Dean Stewart. All three, inadvertently, helped me get this project up and running.

It would be remiss of me not to mention the central character of this account. As a fan of Manchester United for almost 40 years, Sir Alex Ferguson has provided me with some of the best memories of my life. For that, I will always be truly thankful.

Foreword by René Meulensteen

HAVING SPOKEN with John at length about my time at Manchester United, and what it was like to work alongside Sir Alex Ferguson, his knowledge and passion for the club shone through.

As a result, anyone who reads this book will enjoy reliving the amazing journey of Sir Alex's time at the club, especially as this account offers some excellent insights.

I also found the topic particularly intriguing. The boss mentioned in his retirement speech on the pitch at Old Trafford, 'Even the defeats are all part of this great football club of ours.'

His response to losing, both in the way he was with opposing managers and how he galvanised the team and staff around him, was a vital component in the make-up of British football's most successful manager.

I worked at close quarters with Sir Alex over several years and his reaction to a defeat comprised of three phases.

Firstly, there was the moment, directly after the defeat, when everybody got back in the dressing room. He always had some final comments. It could be something like, 'We played really well, you didn't get what you deserved.' Highlighting the good things with words of encouragement. No problem. Then there were other moments when he felt the team didn't meet the expectations, and he always had the highest of expectations – he could be very fierce. He would say forcefully, 'That wasn't right, this wasn't good enough, you need to step up' so that everybody got the message. And that was always immediately after the game, and would last three to five minutes, no more.

The second phase would begin with a moment where he always had a little bit of time for himself before he would confront the media. In that moment, with the press, I always felt he was in control, very collected, very measured, in the way he spoke about the result. Sometimes, after addressing the media, especially at home games, he would come into the dressing room and sit quietly by himself. Players and staff could see a defeat hurt him in this moment. They noticed how it really got to him.

But then, afterwards, there would be the third phase where he would always invite an opposing manager to his office for a glass of wine. I found that a remarkable quality of his. By then, that defeat was gone. He was back to his normal self. He wouldn't get into a strop or a mood, he would communicate normally with jokes and would be very accommodating for the opposing manager. Everything was really good. It was a great experience for me. It's an enormous quality to have, to walk tall with defeat, especially when you are winning so often, to remain humble if you do have a stumble.

The DNA of Manchester United

The principles, the DNA of Manchester United, how we want to play – Ferguson was very clear about that. I still remember the day when he brought me into his office, when he appointed Mick Phelan as assistant manager and me as first-team coach. He had a flip-chart with it all written down and said to me, 'Listen, René, I just want to share this with you because when I close my eyes this is what I want to see – United at our best.'

Each page of the chart would give more instructions on how Ferguson viewed the team and its style of play. Each page had different elements as to how he saw us playing. At times, we have to press really high and in numbers, aggressively.

Sometimes you want to drop a little bit deeper, press on a certain player, and then hit them in the spaces they leave. If you have to defend deeper, form a block, not giving chances away, but when we do gain possession can we counter? Can we break quickly through the lines? Then, next page – set plays. Then bang, the next page – possession.

Possession is key. It's where you get the initiative of the game, but the rhythm is also important. In the build-up it is different to when you are in congested areas where you need to switch to one-touch, and of course Paul Scholes and Michael Carrick were excellent at that. Possession must always have a purpose. And the players need to understand that purpose. Are we having possession to keep the ball? Are we trying to take the sting out of the game?

The most important thing was on the final page, which was all about the attacking style of United. He had written four words. 'This is what I want to see when we attack. Pace. Power. Penetration. Unpredictability. Those are the four things I want you to instil in that group every single day,' Sir Alex told me. Then he drew a line underneath all those and said, 'And if that doesn't work – we gamble!' And he smiled.

1

The final piece of the jigsaw

FOOTBALL FANS, even those of some of the most successful clubs, rue defeats almost as much as they enjoy the victories, sometimes more. Supporters of the big teams can be a greedy bunch, and probably lack the gallows humour of those further down the food chain.

Many will have an almost morbid curiosity with how the defeat came about. Others, and this applies to followers of all clubs, will take great pleasure in venting their anger at the manager, the board, the club mascot, the players (in that order), as they seek to apportion blame for the crumbling team they see before them. Manchester United fans, despite all the success through the Sir Alex Ferguson era, are no different.[1]

On Christmas Day 2009, my friends and I sat around the table asking each other questions as the year was coming to an end. If you could change one thing – what would it be? As some people jostled for position to express their thoughts, others seemed tongue-tied, not remembering the day before never mind the previous 360. 'Anything?' I asked. 'Anything,' they confirmed.

---

1 Ferguson's first three and a half years at the club included many dissenting fans. The grumbling returned during a fallow period between 2003 and 2006.

My mind was clear – 'I would change the result of the Champions League Final against Barcelona,' I blurted out. No one else at the table was a football fan. None of them could empathise. The fact that I had no control over the result didn't matter. I still wanted the power to change it.

In fact, if I could only alter one result as a United fan, that one would be it.[2] That match was a chance to establish a European dynasty as the first team to win back-to-back Champions Leagues.

We also lost the 2011 final at Wembley, but that one was far less painful. By then United's star was waning, largely due to the loss of Cristiano Ronaldo, and Barcelona were in a different stratosphere in footballing terms. But in the Eternal City there was a real opportunity. Ferguson knew it too, as will be detailed later in this book. United were at their peak, the Catalans had yet to reach theirs. The English champions and European Cup holders were favourites going into that final, and the opening passages of play reflected that, making the eventual defeat all the more difficult to take.[3]

Under Ferguson, United had a history of just falling short in Europe's premier competition. The knockout blows in the latter stages at the hands of Borussia Dortmund, Monaco, Real Madrid, Bayer Leverkusen and AC Milan all hurt to this day.

But those defeats were still a step or two short of the final, where heartache could still have arisen. The loss to AC Milan in 2007 at least meant we didn't have to face Liverpool in the final, a prospect many United fans were dreading. Some may think you could flip the scenario and imagine the bragging rights if you win. That *some* are not Manchester United or Liverpool fans. Supporters of neither club wanted that final,

---

2   There are numerous other teams with United in their title, but given the Old Trafford faithful's affinity for using it, and the fact that this book is principally about Manchester United, it is this club I am referring to when using this name.

3   All bookmakers gave shorter odds on a United victory. Barcelona had squeezed past Chelsea in the semi-finals. The London club were not at United's level.

and probably never will. The high from winning such a game is nowhere near as dramatic as the sense of despair should we lose.

Domestically, there are quite a few 'what if' moments too, as United followers desperately seek that one more trophy that would make their dreams complete. The final piece of the jigsaw, if you will. For me there are a couple. I would love to have just one more league title. Take your pick from 1995, 1998, 2010 or 2012.[4] The first three would have created an unprecedented series of championships, the last one because of the very nature of the defeat – in the last minute to our cross-city rivals.

But what if we did alter history, domestically at least, and manipulate it so that United win one of those league titles that slipped through their grasp? Be careful what you wish for. Take 1995, for instance. United win that title. Paul Ince, Mark Hughes and Andrei Kanchelskis stay, the Class of '92's emergence is stunted, and United do not win the treble in 1999. Or the arrivals of Arsène Wenger, José Mourinho and Roman Abramovich's cash do not provide the fly in the ointment that puts a stop to domestic dominance, and United stroll to a few more titles in the 2000s. But then Ferguson does not have a problem to solve; does not appoint Carlos Queiroz as his assistant; does not buy Ronaldo; and does not win the Champions League of 2008. A lot of ifs, buts and maybes, but you catch the point. Perhaps the defeats were necessary to inspire the club and Ferguson to greater things, the Barcelona 2009 defeat aside.[5]

With the exception of the latter years in the Champions League, where even so-called Fergie Time caught up with

---

4   There were other near misses, but they sit a little easier with me. Though the title loss of 1992 was my worst moment as a United fan, I do not yearn to change it in the way I do some other setbacks, as I think it helped inspire the club to greater things.

5   Spoiler alert: there is one chapter in this book that does not have a happy ending.

the great man, I noticed a distinct pattern.[6] The recurring theme involved some of the lowest points of the Ferguson era and yet on each occasion they led to eventual triumph. Some of the answers to how the success was achieved lie in the defeats that preceded them. From the thrashing at Maine Road and the 'Ta ra Fergie' banner in 1989 to winning the FA Cup the same season; from the haunting defeat at Anfield in 1992 to achieving the Holy Grail a year later; from 'you can't win anything with kids' to a youth-inspired double; from the crushing European defeats at the hands of Galatasaray and Barcelona to that glorious night at the Camp Nou; from appearing to be out of his depth after the arrivals of Wenger and Mourinho to overcoming the pair in style; from further European disappointments to winning the Champions League again in 2008; from last-minute title despair to going out on a high – every low was the beginning of a journey towards an eventual peak.

The more I looked into the subject, the more I discovered a clear relationship between the two – failure and success. This book goes some way to filling in the gaps en route from defeat to victory.

There have been many excruciating defeats but one stands out above all others – the loss to Liverpool at Anfield in 1992 that confirmed Leeds United as champions. I'm not old enough to remember the club's relegation in 1974 so that Sunday on Merseyside will always be the worst day I have ever endured as a fan of the club. And no matter what happens in the future, it always will be.

The clouds eventually lifted and United ended a 26-year wait for title glory a year later. The images of Ferguson and his assistant Brian Kidd celebrating on the pitch after a remarkable

---

6 Fergie Time was a phrase used to describe late goals. Ferguson had a tendency to look at his watch as his team piled forward, in desperate search of a goal. Steve McClaren once said, 'Manchester United never lose, they just run out of time.'

turnaround against Sheffield Wednesday, taking the team a step closer to the championship, will never be forgotten. But nor will Anfield '92.

Further success followed in the 1993/94 season, but a year later Ferguson had to deal with a series of issues that are difficult to ignore when analysing future glory. In the space of six days, the title was relinquished to Blackburn Rovers, followed by an FA Cup Final defeat to Everton. Both setbacks precipitated the sales of three key players – Mark Hughes, Andrei Kanchelskis and Paul Ince.

Within four years, though, United would go on to have arguably the greatest night of the Ferguson era, but just five of the 14 players in the matchday squad against Everton would be involved in that unforgettable night at the Camp Nou.[7]

When conducting research for this book, watching the team toil against Hereford United and Oldham Athletic en route to winning the FA Cup in 1990, it's almost impossible to comprehend that just nine years later United won the European Cup. Of course, the team changed entirely in that time, but as a fan it remains one entity.

During the journey from Wembley 1990 to Camp Nou 1999 there were numerous bumps in the road. The season after winning the FA Cup, United entered Europe for the first time in my life as a fan, having started supporting the club in 1985. Like Fergie, I became obsessed with conquering the continent.

Life goes on

Wednesday, 30 October 1996. Maybe not the most significant date in Manchester United's history, but for me, it was a memorable one.

There had been defeats before, many of which were more painful and had far-reaching ramifications. Several of these

---

7   Peter Schmeichel, Gary Neville, Denis Irwin, Nicky Butt and Ryan Giggs were the five. Roy Keane and Paul Scholes were involved at Wembley in 1995 but suspended at the Camp Nou.

will be highlighted in this book. But this one to Fenerbahçe in the Champions League group stage was different. United had more than just lost to a deflected shot from Elvir Bolić. It was the night they forfeited their undefeated home record in Europe.

This achievement had come under threat a few times during Sir Alex Ferguson's reign, most notably when a late equaliser from goalkeeper Peter Schmeichel preserved the record, salvaging a draw against Rotor Volgograd in the UEFA Cup a year before. But now, it was gone. Forever.

I went out that autumn night with friends, but was distracted the whole evening. How could I enjoy myself? And how could my pals expect me to have fun? All the time, I was wondering how Ferguson must be feeling. If it was bad for me, what on earth must he be going through? No manager had ever led United to defeat at Old Trafford in a European tie and now Ferguson had that unwanted record. Despite all his success at the club, he recognised in his first autobiography, *Managing My Life*, that it 'put a blot' on his copybook that he 'had always dreaded'.

For Ferguson, the burden of defeat was something he had to carry throughout his managerial career.

Meanwhile, as a fan, I was keen to discover what the reaction of the manager would be. From the initial post-match team-talk, to speaking to the media; from the changes he would implement to remedy the setback, to the long-term ramifications – his response was always fascinating.

I recognised how I was becoming obsessive about how Ferguson must be feeling and what he would do to fix the issue, if indeed an alteration was needed. Sometimes remaining calm and not overreacting was the crucial medicine required to cure the ills.

My curiosity with the manager's thoughts, both in the immediate aftermath of a defeat, and how he would rouse both himself and the club afterwards, was something that returned time and time again. The more painful the defeat, the more keen I was to hear what the manager had to say. I was often shocked, never disappointed. From the 'they got him sent off, typical Germans' raw comments after a Champions League exit at the hands of Bayern Munich, to tirades at journalists questioning his side's struggles – Ferguson's reactions were priceless. These remarks only endeared him to the United support even more. But the comments would also reverberate around the dressing room, often garnering the response the manager yearned for.

Ferguson acknowledged during one particularly sticky spell in the autumn of 1996, in the wake of three successive league defeats, to Newcastle, Southampton and Chelsea, that he was 'always a better manager in adversity'.[8]

Journalist Henry Winter explained his admiration for Ferguson's reaction to hard times, 'One of the things about Ferguson is that he used emotion very intelligently. He went through the gears. I ended up going to Ferguson's press conferences when Manchester United lost, that was Ferguson at his best. He would come out, he would blame the referee, he would blame the media, he would blame the temperature of the tea at half-time – anything to defend his players.'

In Ferguson's first few years at Old Trafford, a bad defeat appeared to be followed by thrown teacups rather than a tactical tweak; the hair dryer as opposed to a wily streak. However, the more you listened to him, and those close to him, you began to realise it was more than just a rousing speech that would help his team respond. Don't get me wrong, Ferguson was a great motivator and frequently reminded us that there is nothing wrong in losing your temper. And there was nothing more likely to push him to breaking point than a defeat. But it was his ability to pinpoint what was wrong and rectify it that was crucial to the success that followed.

---

8   The run included the aforementioned home defeat to Galatasaray, but was punctuated by a less meaningful win in the League Cup.

As the years went by, the Old Trafford faithful trusted the manager more and more. So much so that when he would use his go-to phrase 'no question about that' the supporters shared the Scot's conviction. They did not question. They knew he would get a reaction.

After one painful defeat – a 6-1 thrashing at home to Manchester City in October 2011 – I was desperate to know what Ferguson was thinking. It was troubling me all the way home after leaving the ground. His post-match interview explained a lot and it eased my worries. In the weeks that followed, my amazement and fascination grew further still. He reasoned the team were careless, that Jonny Evans's sending off had skewed the match terribly in City's favour. As fans we believed him. After 25 years he had earned our trust. Ferguson was angry at how his side had shipped so many goals with a gung-ho attitude. A succession of clean sheets was what Ferguson wanted, and the doctor got what he ordered. Unbelievable. In the wake of such a galling defeat, how could he just dictate the results of the following fixtures like that?

When he failed to appear for the mandatory press briefing after going out of the Champions League in 2013, as fans, we knew how he felt – because we felt the same. Crestfallen. Little did we know that it was his final match in the competition and therefore his last shot at lifting a third European Cup.

When news began to emerge of his impending retirement on social media one Tuesday night in May 2013, it was difficult to believe. There was plenty of evidence to suggest the rumours were untrue, such as his programme notes from the match against Chelsea just two days previously. Ferguson spoke of his excitement about leading the club for many more years to come with the current crop of players. His passion for the club and the sport remained undimmed, just like it had throughout that season. One such example was when he remonstrated with referee Mike Dean at half-time against Newcastle United. He was as demonstrative that day as any of the previous 9,548.

Ferguson himself, no doubt, would be dismissing any suggestions of retirement the next day, in his usual inimitable style:

'Yous lot are full of … ' he would surely say.

'Retirement is for young people. I'm too old to retire. I would have nothing to do.'

'As long as my health is good I will carry on. My family will make this decision.'

'Making up stories again.'

'Your job is to tell the truth.'

The club's future was in safe hands – Ferguson's hands. It made the rumours all the less credible. Early the next morning, Paddy Crerand was on the radio, dismissing the suggestion that Ferguson was about to retire. 'Rubbish,' he told Irish radio station News Talk. 'I don't think there's a word of truth in this. When the club say something, that's when I'll believe it.'

Within half an hour of Crerand's interview, Sir Alex Ferguson's retirement was confirmed in an official club statement. Ferguson, who likes a gamble and built a close friendship with Crerand over the years, has almost certainly never taken his compatriot's advice on which horse to back.

There was no dismissal of the rumours, no turnaround, no remonstrations. He was going, bringing down the curtain on 26 and a half remarkable years as manager of Manchester United.

People often say they remember where they were when John F. Kennedy was shot. I was not born at the time of his assassination in 1963 but I remember the scene on 6 November 1986, sat at the breakfast table as news broke of Alex Ferguson's arrival. Little did I know then the effect that news would have on the rest of my life.

The 'remember where you were' moment was repeated more than a quarter of a century later when the news of Ferguson's retirement was confirmed on BBC Radio Five Live. I slumped down on the couch, and tears rolled down my cheeks. I had not cried over football since the aforementioned loss at Anfield in 1992.

Ferguson would often ask for just one more player in order to reach the Promised Land, much to the exasperation of the United board. 'The favourite line when I want to buy a player is to tell them it's the last piece of the jigsaw,' Ferguson wrote in *Six Years at United*, published in 1992. And board member 'Mike Edelson is fond of reminding me,' Ferguson continued, 'it's the biggest jigsaw in the world.'

For me, that final piece came on Sunday, 12 May 2013, shortly after a late winner from Rio Ferdinand had secured victory over Swansea in Ferguson's last home game as manager. As Fergie took the microphone to address the crowd, I looked around the stadium. I saw many in tears. I started to weigh up the age of the people around me. 20? 25? Some in their early 30s? Most had never known another manager of their club. In the 26 and a half years that Ferguson was at the helm, Manchester City had 21 managers. Real Madrid had changed their head coach 25 times. When he took over, Manchester United had won seven league titles. Almost four years into the Ferguson era, Liverpool led the title-count 18-7.

Fast forward almost a quarter of a century and Ferguson had reversed that trend, winning 13 titles without reply, knocking Liverpool off their perch. By the time the Scot left the Old Trafford building, United led 20-18.

Back in 1994, shortly after Ferguson claimed his first title as United boss, a banner was unfurled at Anfield by the home fans, reminding the team from just an hour up the M62 that Liverpool were still Kings of England. 'Come back when you've won 18,' it said. United supporters responded after their club's 18th and 19th titles, unfurling flags at Anfield, pointing out to Liverpool fans that it was the Old Trafford club who were now on top of the perch from which they once reigned supreme. Ferguson loved it, declaring after the second flag had been on display at the home of their rivals, 'I wish I had taken that banner to Liverpool.'

The United manager searched hard to find answers. He once said he viewed the game like chess, often waiting for the opposing manager to make the first move. Now he had made his last move. Checkmate.

All that was left was for him to make a speech, to give fans one last opportunity to experience what it must have felt like to be in the changing room with the boss.

'I've absolutely no script in my mind, I'm just going to ramble on and hope I get to the core of what this football club has meant to me.' Ferguson never needed a script.

'First of all, it's a thank you to Manchester United; not just the directors, not just the medical staff, the coaching staff, the players, the supporters, it's all of you. You have been the most fantastic experience of my life. Thank you,' Ferguson said, and the crowd erupted as loudly as it did for any of the late winners he would soon reference. By now the welling up of the tears had reached breaking point, where volume and then gravity took over.

'I have been very fortunate. I have been able to manage some of the greatest players in the country, let alone Manchester United. All these players here today have represented our club in the proper way. They have won a championship in a fantastic fashion. Well done to the players,' Ferguson continued to more applause.

'My retirement doesn't mean the end of my life with the club. I will now be able to enjoy watching them rather than suffer with them,' he joked.

'If you think about it, those last-minute goals, the comebacks – even the defeats – are all part of this great football club of ours.'

Now I had the final piece of the jigsaw. 'Even the defeats,' I thought. Yes – even the defeats are what made United, and Ferguson in particular, so successful.

2 (i)

From Maine Road massacre ...

AFTER AN FA Cup quarter-final home defeat to Nottingham Forest in the spring of 1989, Alex Ferguson was 'angered and embarrassed' by his team's lack of commitment to the cause. 'Where was the passion that was supposed to run through Alex Ferguson teams?' the Scottish manager questioned in his first autobiography, *Managing My Life*.

By the summer of the same year, after almost three years at the helm, Ferguson needed a proper overhaul. 'I resolved that I had to change everything round and gather a squad around me capable of winning the league.' When he looked at his team he realised it didn't mirror its manager 'in any way, shape or form'. A key to a successful club, he reasoned, is that the team should resemble some of the characteristics of the person who shaped it, something that would become obvious much later in the Ferguson tenure. So he acted.

But not everyone would be happy with the upcoming change, and Ferguson knew that better than anyone. The sales of Old Trafford favourites such as Norman Whiteside and Paul McGrath, who left within days of each other, along with Gordon Strachan, who was disposed of just after that cup defeat to Forest, was a bitter pill for many supporters to swallow. Strachan was heavily criticised after the loss to

Forest, where Ferguson compared his performance to that of a 'triallist'. There was more sympathy for Whiteside, who was described by Ferguson as 'one of the most talented footballers I have known'. McGrath, meanwhile, had been a stalwart at the heart of the United defence yet was shipped out to Aston Villa for just £400,000. The decision to sell Whiteside and McGrath, however, was not about ability. The manager felt the pair's 'drinking Olympics' was impinging on their fitness as injuries began to take their toll. The United boss received an avalanche of letters from supporters, heavily criticising him, and even questioning his sanity.

Their departures were, at least in Ferguson's eyes, more than offset by the incomings of Neil Webb for £1.5m and Mike Phelan for £750,000 to herald a new beginning in the summer of 1989.

Less than 18 months previously, the club had finished second, albeit nine points off winners Liverpool. But that runners-up finish told you more about the quality of the division that season than United's prowess. A truer reflection of Ferguson's team lied in the goal difference gap between the top two teams, with United's 30 worse off than Liverpool's. In addition, United were never within touching distance of the top from the autumn onwards.

In the 1988/89 season United reverted to type, finishing 11th. Further evidence of United's demise was provided in their average attendance, which had slipped below arch-rivals Liverpool's. Crowds as low as 23,368, 26,722 and 30,379 had watched United's final three league games of the season against Wimbledon, Everton and Newcastle.

In slightly better news, the perch Liverpool were sitting on looked increasingly vulnerable. Kenny Dalglish's side missed out on the championship that campaign after Michael Thomas scored a last-gasp winner for Arsenal when the two teams challenging for the title met at Anfield on the last day of the season.

As for United, further purchases in 1989 gave Ferguson added belief. Midfielder Paul Ince arrived at Old Trafford for an initial £800,000, winger Danny Wallace for £1.2m, and Gary Pallister from Middlesbrough came in to shore up the defence for £2.3m, a record fee between two British clubs. Pallister was the expensive alternative to Glenn Hysén, the classy, silver-haired defender who had slipped from United's grasp and into the clutches of bitter rivals Liverpool for a mere £250,000, much to the chagrin of Ferguson. The initial comparisons between the two defenders was painful, both in terms of performances and price, as Hysén, who later reasoned United were no more than a mid-table team at the time, got off to a successful start to life at Anfield.

With increased expenditure comes increased pressure. Ferguson had spent in a few months almost as much as his predecessor Ron Atkinson had done in five years at the club. This was now very much a Fergie side. Almost three years into the job, and a revamp of the squad complete, there would be no more excuses. This was a team built to resemble its manager.

The season began in jovial, almost comical, style. Michael Knighton, who wanted to buy chairman Martin Edwards's majority stake in the club, came on to the Old Trafford pitch prior to the opening game against Arsenal. Knighton juggled the ball, hit it into an empty net, and blew kisses to the crowd. No sooner had he arrived than his empty gestures, much like his wallet, disappeared. According to some, he had neither the money nor the wherewithal to back up his claims.

These are suggestions that Knighton has denied. He said it was his decision to pull the plug on what looking back, would have been a bargain £20m deal at £10m for Edwards's share and £10m for rejuvenating the Stretford End of the ground. Some 30 years later, in May 2019, *Forbes* said the club was worth £3bn, 150 times the 1989 valuation.

Where Knighton's suggestion falls flat is that he boasts he saw how rich the future was for both the club and football; that his commercial ideas were guaranteed winners and eventually deployed by the club; that he predicted the riches soon to be on offer from satellite television. The problem is, that for all this to be true, one question remains unanswered – why did he pull out?

Either way, the only etching he had on Manchester United's history was that brief cameo prior to the season opener against the Gunners.

In *GQ* magazine, Martin Edwards recalled the moment vividly, 'I didn't actually see Knighton's shenanigans – I was still in the directors' room entertaining visiting guests – but I caught it later on the news. It's become an iconic moment, but at the time I was fuming. The deal hadn't been finalised yet. He was jumping the gun. That was really the first sign that something wasn't quite right about Knighton – it was reckless and his decision-making really worried me; others felt the same way. The fans loved it, but it was one of the worst possible moves he could have made. Even Knighton himself, in hindsight, has admitted it was a mistake. Why did he do it? Who knows? Maybe for publicity purposes. Whatever the reason, it raised huge questions in my mind, such that I now had severe doubts.'[9]

What should not be forgotten is the result that day, a 4-1 thrashing of the reigning champions, Arsenal. The result gave the supporters a boost of confidence regarding the season ahead and many hoped the win would be a marker ahead of a title pursuit. It would prove to be, much like Knighton, a false dawn. For now, though, the summer acquisitions aligned with the opening day pummelling of the Gunners, meant nothing could quell the optimism around the club.

Nothing, that is, except successive 2-0 defeats, the second of which was Pallister's debut against Norwich City at Old

9 It is worth remembering that in 1984 a proposed £10m offer from Robert Maxwell was rejected by Martin Edwards and the board. It is impossible to imagine the turmoil the club might have suffered had they accepted the offer.

Trafford. To make matters worse, the record buy hardly covered himself in glory, being caught out of position for the first and recklessly giving away a penalty for the second. Suddenly United's season was unravelling and the pressure on Ferguson was increasing.

A third successive loss, away at Everton, left the club lying in 16th, which was somewhat negated by an impressive 5-1 home win against Millwall, that left United in mid-table. However, concerns remained over a leaky defence that had yet to keep a clean sheet all season. Pallister had been purchased at such great expense in the hope that his strength and pace would help shore up the back line. However, the defence was anything but watertight. It looked like it was missing the recently sold Paul McGrath, who was excelling at Aston Villa. Next up, though, was the Manchester derby, and a chance for the red half to exert their authority.

Manchester City 5 Manchester United 1

A summer spending spree aligned with not losing to City in almost a decade meant United started as clear favourites for the derby.

Ferguson's starting XI, though shorn of the services of Steve Bruce and Bryan Robson through injury, still had an impressive look to it. Despite enduring a shaky start to life at Old Trafford, Jim Leighton was Scotland's number one, and regarded by Ferguson as 'the best goalkeeper in Britain'. Viv Anderson was a solid right-back and an England international. Alongside Gary Pallister at the heart of the defence was the reliable Mike Duxbury, who earned ten England caps. At left-back was the promising Lee Martin, while across midfield, Russell Beardsmore, Mike Phelan, Paul Ince and Danny Wallace cost six times what City had paid for their quartet. Perhaps more tellingly, though, City's midfield consisted of three who had come through the ranks, while United's had just one – Beardsmore.

Despite their undoubted individual talents, the strike force of Brian McClair and Mark Hughes never truly flourished. Hughes appeared to stifle his partner. McClair was prolific in Scotland, and was mirroring that form south of the border until Hughes's arrival. It was highlighted in 1989/90 with the Scot scoring just eight goals in all competitions, having found the back of the net 31 and 16 times respectively in his first two years at Old Trafford. In scoring the first of those tallies, McClair became the first player to net more than 20 league goals for the club in one season since George Best two decades before. It was also notable that it was at a time when Hughes was not at Old Trafford.

McClair had not missed a game for United since signing from Celtic, though he had to be patched up to start the derby. He incurred a head injury in the League Cup win at Portsmouth just three days before, meaning he wore a red and white headband for United's biggest match of the season so far. As unorthodox as the new addition to his kit appeared, at least it was in the club's principal colours, unfortunate though it was that one of those was red given that some may have mistaken it for blood.

As for Hughes, his uncanny ability to turn impossible situations into incredible goals helped him become part of Old Trafford folklore, as well as a mainstay of the first team.

Of the front two, it was Hughes who had the better technique, and he displayed it again at Maine Road. The outside-of-the-foot pass was an under-appreciated element of the Welshman's game. It was on show that September day, giving us a sneak preview of maybe the most famous assist of the Fergie reign at Nottingham Forest that would occur just a few months later. What an all-round player Hughes was, and a pity that relations between him and United never seemed smooth after he left in 1995.

The gulf in class between the clubs was obvious, as City full-back Andy Hinchcliffe recognised, 'On paper, we shouldn't have had a chance against United and nobody actually gave us a chance. We had struggled to adjust after promotion and the First Division was proving to be quite daunting.'

Nevertheless, City still had talent within their ranks. Hinchcliffe had a deadly left foot, and would go on to represent England, albeit seven years later. Ian Bishop was a cultured midfielder who would join Trevor Morley at West Ham in a joint deal just weeks after both featured in the derby. David White was a forward with electric pace who was tipped for international stardom, though he would only earn a solitary cap, on the same night that Paul Ince won the first of 53.

The pick of the bunch for City was Paul Lake, as Daniel Taylor wrote in *The Guardian*, 'Lake was already being spoken about as a future England captain. At Manchester City he was the most cherished young asset, the classic local boy done good, living the dream of every schoolboy who has longed to play for the club he supports. Lake had been exceptional all through his youth. "I didn't quite know how, or why, I found football so easy. I just did," Lake said.'

His career would be cut cruelly short at the age of 27. A reunion with Manchester United was organised in 1997 for his testimonial, featuring a couple of the players who played in the match eight years before. Lake came out for the exhibition match wearing 'a leg brace to stop my knee from falling apart', he documents in his autobiography *I'm Not Really Here*.

The classy midfielder recalled a moment en route to the ground on the morning of the game, 'Halfway through my journey to Maine Road I pull up to the traffic lights. And stood there at the bus stop is a City fan in his 30s with his arm around his young son, both of them kitted out in replica shirts and the old-style blue, white and red scarves. Having clocked me sitting there in my car, this fella nudges his lad and then does something that will stay with me forever. Pressing his palms together as if in prayer, he looks at me beseechingly and simply mouths "please ... please ... please".'

United began the match brightly, at least in terms of the kits – Ferguson's side resplendent in their Adidas outfit of red shirts, black shorts and sparklingly clean white socks. Despite their team's unconvincing start to the season, the away support were in full voice just seconds before kick-off, with chants of 'United, United' that could even be heard above the noise of the home faithful.

As the game commenced, commentator Clive Tyldesley, who was working for Granada Television in what was his TV debut, chillingly reminded United fans of some home truths, 'It's 21 years since the First Division title belonged to Manchester, when City succeeded United as champions in 1968. The trophy has spent the majority of that time on Merseyside.' The away supporters were well aware of that, and they were not thinking of Everton, who had also won the title on two occasions in the 1980s. An hour and a half of football later, the notion of United winning the league championship seemed further away than ever.

Speaking about that game more than 30 years later, Tyldesley feared his big day in the commentary box was going to be spoiled by events off the field. At the game's outset trouble was already brewing. 'A sickening display of crowd violence, which resulted in the game being halted for eight minutes,' was how *The Times* reported an early interruption to proceedings.

Once play restarted after the crowd trouble, it was the away side that were the more sprightly, spreading the play with confidence, belying their league position and justifying the expensive outlay on Messrs Phelan, Pallister, Ince and Wallace.[10]

Despite the questions over the United defence, in the early exchanges it seemed up to the task at Maine Road, Pallister flying in with some excellent tackles, giving little clue as to what was about to come. One challenge in particular, on City

---

10 Neil Webb, Ferguson's other summer buy, had snapped his Achilles tendon while playing for England and would miss the majority of the season.

striker Trevor Morley after a long kick upfield from goalkeeper Paul Cooper, was particularly vital.

City, though, began to seize control. An inkling of what was to come occurred when David Oldfield fed White, who spurned the opportunity to score, shooting well wide when Morley was better placed.

A few minutes later Hinchcliffe's trusted left foot picked out White before the winger dragged the ball back for Oldfield to hit home, Leighton helpless in goal. Poor Gary Pallister, though, was left on his backside as he tried to intercept the cross. Not a good look for Britain's most expensive defender.

Proceedings went from bad to worse for United when more calamitous defending led to Morley prodding home to make it 2-0. His leg beat both the away side's defenders and his own protruding moustache to the ball.

United were in a state of panic and there was little sign of instruction from the touchline to calm things down. That uncertainty was beginning to show itself on the pitch in the form of misplaced passes and mistimed tackles. Even Hughes's radar was malfunctioning.

At this stage, someone had to take charge for United. 'In the absence of Robson,' Tyldesley reminded us in commentary, 'you wonder who it's going to be.' United were missing Steve Bruce too, another leader, both in terms of personality and ability at the heart of the defence. On another day some of the players might have turned to the tough-tackling Paul Ince for inspiration. But the former West Ham midfielder was still a newbie at the club. Moreover, against City he could not even connect with his opponents when he tried to take them out in frustration, never mind retrieve the ball or seize the initiative.

Midway through the first half the home crowd taunted Ferguson with chants of 'Fergie, what's the score? Fergie, Fergie what's the score?'

Pallister was now playing as though he had won a competition to represent United for the day. Oldfield easily evaded the defender's challenge before setting up Bishop to head home his first goal for the club to make it 3-0.

More gleeful chants from the City support followed, 'What a waste of money!' This appeared to be directed at Mark Hughes after he missed an opportunity to score towards the end of the first half. The striker had returned to United a year before for the princely sum of £1.8m, though it was difficult to be sure who the Maine Road fans were directing their mirth at, such was the ineptitude of United's expensively assembled squad.

At the beginning of the second half Hughes responded to the taunts from the home crowd, giving his side a glimmer of hope as he scored with a trademark scissors-kick. If that goal had been scored in the latter part of the Fergie era, fans would have held the belief that this could be the beginning of a sensational comeback. However, this was the United of '89, not '99.

Any hopes of a glorious comeback were extinguished in the 58th minute when Oldfield restored City's three-goal advantage, tapping home after yet more calamitous defending. Ferguson had had three years to organise a defence, yet here they were, looking as shambolic as the day he took over, in the wake of a 4-1 defeat to Southampton in the League Cup.

As United subs Lee Sharpe and Clayton Blackmore began warming up on the touchline, Tyldesley commented, 'Alex Ferguson's got to do something.' But the manager and his team were short of ideas.

Manchester City had not scored four goals in a derby for 20 years, but it was soon five. In the 62nd minute Andy Hinchcliffe scored what he described as the best goal of his career, though the full-back had to be referring to the euphoria and the build-up play, rather than his finish, which was a simple header. Hinchcliffe later admitted that 'everything just fell right' that day. Conversely for Jim Leighton, nothing seemed to be going his way. As bad as this was for Scotland's number one, who was enduring a torrid time between the sticks, the concession of five goals would not even come close to the lowest point in his season.

City manager Mel Machin felt he had the key. 'We played with passion,' he said.

The home crowd mocked their opponents as the game ended 5-1, singing, 'Fergie must stay.' Almost three years after replacing Ron Atkinson, progress was painfully slow and the sands of time were running out for Ferguson. Losing like this to a City team consisting largely of journeymen and unproven youngsters was as bad as it could get and the United fans were beginning to lose faith.

Leighton had not kept a clean sheet all season but the defence were equally culpable for that statistic, particularly at Maine Road. Ferguson said he had never witnessed a worse defensive display in his entire managerial career. 'It was like climbing a glass mountain,' he said after the game.

Assistant manager Archie Knox spoke of how deeply affected Ferguson was by the mauling. He said, 'I think Alex said he felt like going home and putting his head in the oven. It was a disaster. It affected him. He says he became a bit of a hermit and he went into his shell round about that time. We weren't maybe as close socially as we had been. I was trying to get him out for a drink but he didn't want to.'

Defensive stalwart turned expensive misfit Pallister wrote in his autobiography, 'The funny thing was that we started off really well, playing lovely football, but then there was trouble behind one of the goals which spilled over to the side of the pitch, and the players were taken off. After that, everything City hit went in. I'd say it was the lowest point of my entire career.'

Pallister described Ferguson as being 'in shock after the game, practically speechless' and remembers returning to training on the Monday at the Cliff after spending the weekend in Middlesbrough with his family. 'There was no security and when I walked from the dressing room there were four burly United fans waiting for me outside the door. They told me I wasn't fit to wear a United shirt, we shouldn't have sold Paul McGrath, I was a "disgrace" to the club, the whole treatment. I thought it was just me but it turned out that all the lads had got abuse from these guys. They really ripped into us and it was quite frightening.'

Meanwhile, McGrath was part of an Aston Villa side that were in a title race with Liverpool. The only pursuit Ferguson was a part of was the sack race as the odds on him losing his job continued to shorten with every excruciating loss.

If supporters and media were baying for blood after Manchester United's most humiliating moment since they were relegated 15 years before, then it was Ferguson who felt it most. He described the 5-1 defeat as the 'most embarrassing' of his managerial career. 'After the game I went home, got into bed, and put the pillow over my head. A sense of guilt had engulfed me and I knew I was going to have to dig deep into my resources.' It is the last comment that is the most significant. A soul-searching exercise was necessary when in a dark place, brought about by poor results or tricky periods, but he would recover from the depths of despair. Ferguson would step up to the challenge. This included a colder, more analytical approach, learning from the mistakes, and not merely tub-thumping in response to a setback.

Ferguson continued the self-examination, 'Injuries had taken a toll but that could not be the entire explanation. Was I doing something wrong? I was convinced the training was fine and the general fitness was good. Analysing my team selections, my preparation for matches and my tactics, I couldn't see a major fault. I had worked hard at making sure my worry was not manifesting itself in the dressing room and I felt my demeanour was good.' Note here Ferguson the political animal, the actor even, aware that his own despondency could have an impact on his squad.

Analysing the various aspects of what went wrong, from tactics to fitness regime, is something almost all managers do regularly. What Ferguson did so brilliantly was pinpointing the mistakes rather than overreacting and trying to correct something that didn't need to be fixed.

In the months that followed the Maine Road massacre, it was City who would suffer more. Manager Mel Machin – who had become a close ally of Fergie's – was out of a job two months later. Ferguson recalled that friendship in his second autobiography as he said, 'In my early years in Manchester I grew friendly with Mel Machin, who was fired not long after they beat us 5-1. The reason given, I seem to recall, was that Mel didn't smile enough. I would have been sacked a long time ago had that logic been applied at United.' But that September afternoon at Maine Road was no laughing matter and if you had said that one of the two managers that day would be out of a job within a few weeks, your prediction would not have been the one sat in the home dugout.

Ferguson had eradicated some of the issues at the club. By selling McGrath and Whiteside the drinking culture was now largely gone, though interestingly Robson stayed, despite his fondness for a few pints. Ferguson knew the captain's value. He knew he could rely on him when it mattered most.

Other developments were appreciated by the powers that be, none more so than the structure to attract young players, which was in the midst of an overhaul. Ferguson said he had inherited 'a shower of shit' in terms of the youth policy when he arrived. At least his predecessor, Ron Atkinson, had recruited Eric Harrison, the coach behind the Class of '92. However, it was Ferguson who would be the key to its overall success, as Harrison acknowledged. Without Ferguson's influence United 'would definitely not have signed all our superb youngsters', Harrison remarked.

John Curtis and Ben Thornley, two former players who came through the youth ranks, have both said that Harrison and the man at the helm were cut from the same cloth. If Ferguson's team had yet to resemble its manager, his backroom staff certainly had reached that stage.

The manager said that prior to his arrival, and even during his early years at the club, 'Oldham and Crewe were doing better than us' in acquiring the region's best young talent. United had 'to show intent, that we'd arrived, and we were going to do something about it'. The appointment of Brian Kidd as the head of the club's main school of excellence was perhaps more crucial than any of Ferguson's early transfer moves. Kidd would be in charge of recruiting the best young players around. Harrison would shape them, assist them into being good enough and strong enough, both mentally and physically, for the first team.

Michael Crick in his book, *The Boss – The Many Sides of Alex Ferguson*, emphasises both Ferguson's and Kidd's roles in probably the most important acquisition of a youngster in the club's history, 'Brian Kidd had been doing community work for the Professional Footballers' Association in Salford and ran the main United school of excellence. One of Kidd's first tasks was to go and watch a 13-year-old Salford schoolboy who'd been recommended to Ferguson, not by a United scout, but by a ground steward at Old Trafford called Harold Wood. Kidd reported back that, while the dazzling youngster was a United fan, he was training with Manchester City. The boy's name was Ryan Wilson, though he would later adopt his mother's surname, Giggs. He took part in a United trial, but continued training with City. In November 1987, on his 14th birthday, the doorbell rang. It was Alex Ferguson.'

Giggs signed for United just a few days later.

Ferguson recalled Giggs's first practice match, 'He ran across the pitch and he was so light I don't think his feet touched the ground. It was like watching a cocker spaniel chasing a bit of silver paper in the wind. We were all like, "wow". When he got to 15 we put him against Viv Anderson in training. Viv was going, "Boss, what are you doing? He's a small kid, you can't do this." Then Ryan got the ball – bom, bom, bom – and Viv's going, "Jesus Christ!" That's Ryan – he was a phenomenal kid.'

When the Welsh winger broke into the first team, Harold Wood, who worked as a steward at the training ground as well as at Old Trafford, made what turned out to be an expensive promise. 'When I was in the first team he'd give me £1 every time I scored,' Giggs said of Wood. 'He started it when I was younger and then he carried it on and by the time I was like 19, 20, I was saying, "Harold, come on give it a rest" but he said, "No, here's your £1." He was a great character.' Asked if this continued through to his late 30s, Giggs confirmed, 'Yeah, he would still be giving me it.'

Ferguson knew that significant steps had been taken in terms of youth development and that in years to come they would reach fruition. But the manager didn't have years. He may not even have had months after the shocking nature of the defeat to Manchester City. After United were 'slaughtered' (Ferguson's description) at Maine Road, recovery was far from immediate. He was still searching for the remedy from late November until the end of the year, when his team didn't register a single victory. The Scot recognised that the pressure was on. For someone who said he had stopped reading the papers (on the advice of Sir Matt Busby), Ferguson would always seem to know about the rumours swirling around the club, or accusations he felt were unjust, all of which stemmed from the media. He said in his first autobiography, 'There was speculation that I was about to be fired, some of it going as far as to link Howard Kendall with my job. Obituaries of my regime at Old Trafford were plentiful in the sport pages.' Ferguson's use of the words 'my regime' is interesting. At this stage, he recognises that he *is* Manchester United.

As for Kendall, United dodged a bullet. He was a marvellous manager for Everton in the 1980s but he would never recreate that success elsewhere, including mediocre spells at Athletic Bilbao and Manchester City.

Perhaps for the only time in his tenure at United, the pressure of getting the sack was beginning to get to Ferguson. He admitted at the season's outset that his future was 'at stake'. Now, after a miserable first half of the season, his mood was as gloomy as the winter of discontent in which the club was mired. 'The lowest, most desperate point ever in all my years of management,' was how he described it. 'In those grim days I was, for the first time, beginning to feel uncomfortable about my position.' He was not the only one. After a 3-0 League Cup defeat at home to Spurs, part of the crowd chanted 'Bryan Robson's red and white army' in a clear reference to who they thought should be at the helm.

United didn't win a league match for almost three months. But Ferguson and the board knew that progress was being made, it just had yet to manifest itself on the pitch. The problem is that results are everything in football, and telling the fans that the ship was heading in the right direction was like saying the captain of the *Titanic* was doing a great job despite a few mishaps at the beginning of the journey.[11]

---

11 As the *Titanic* left the Southampton docks it came within two feet of crashing into another liner.

2 (ii)

... to the first trophy

THE PRESSURE was cranked up further still by the prospect of a tricky FA Cup third-round tie at Brian Clough's Nottingham Forest, cup specialists and the team that had knocked United out of the competition at the quarter-final stage a year before.

The BBC had chosen this tie as the one for their live coverage from the 64 options.[12] Prior to kick-off, moustachioed pundit Jimmy Hill suggested that even United's warm-up was unimpressive. Ferguson and Hill never enjoyed a great relationship, summed up a few years later when Hill received Fergie's wrath. The United boss labelled him a 'prat' over the pundit's criticism of an Eric Cantona tackle. Ferguson would go on to regret the comment and he sent Hill a letter of apology.

As for the game at Forest, the United manager would have few regrets, despite the jibes of 'Fergie, Fergie on the dole' from the home fans in reference to the vulnerability of his position. United turned in their best performance of the season, just when their manager needed it most. Ferguson's injury-ravaged side won 1-0 thanks to a headed goal from Mark Robins.

---

12 At the time just a handful of games would be shown on live television throughout the season.

Many will remember the game for the knives being out for Ferguson, as well as for the landmark goal from young Robins, but it was the pass from Mark Hughes that assisted the striker that should live longest in the memory.

United were in the hat for the next round but those knives were merely put to one side, rather than shoved in the drawer for good. The utensils would be sharpened quite a few times throughout the cup run as United teetered on the brink.

But Ferguson's assistant Archie Knox recalls chairman Martin Edwards giving some reassuring words as the team got off the bus upon arrival at the City Ground. Knox said, 'I remember when we were getting off the bus at Nottingham Forest and Martin said to Alec, "No matter what happens today you'll be Manchester United manager on Monday."'

The win at Forest had a couple of strokes of fortune, though. Firstly, in the build-up to Mark Robins' winner Lee Martin managed to keep the ball in play by millimetres. Secondly, the home side had a perfectly good goal ruled out after uncertain goalkeeping from Jim Leighton.

The cup run was just up and running. There would be several twists and turns over the next five months. This was long before anyone knew the meaning of squeaky bum time, but there would be plenty of those moments along the way.[13]

It will always remain a mystery for how much longer Edwards and the board would have remained loyal to the United manager, as the former chairman recalled in an interview in 2017, 'Although I supported him, if we'd gone out of the cup that game I don't know for how long I could have gone on supporting him.' And it was like that for 'the whole cup run really', Edwards added. Indeed, Clayton Blackmore often jokes that it was he, and not Robins, who saved the

---

13 Squeaky bum time refers to nervous moments in a sporting contest. It was coined by Ferguson during the final stages of the 2003 Premier League season, when Arsenal and Manchester United were both in contention to win the league.

United manager from the sack, as he scored the 86th-minute winner in the fourth round at Hereford United as Ferguson's side toiled. Though he jokes, Blackmore may have a point, particularly given those Edwards comments. Losing to Forest would have been one thing but if United had gone out to Hereford, who were lying in 21st in the old Fourth Division at the time, it would have been the club's most embarrassing cup exit in their history and one from which even Ferguson would surely never have been able to recover.

While the club's league struggles endured, ultimately ending the season in 13th place, the FA Cup was bringing light relief as well as respite for Ferguson and his team. Narrow wins over Newcastle United and Sheffield United meant the club were now in their first FA Cup semi-final of the Ferguson era.

Again, you wonder if the Scot would have survived if United had gone out at any stage of the competition, and they came dangerously close to doing so in the semi-final against Oldham Athletic. At the first time of asking, the topsy-turvy match ended 3-3 after extra time, but Oldham were within inches of success in the dying stages of the game. It led Rob Smyth in *The Guardian* to recall on the match's 30th anniversary that Ferguson had 'the expression of a man who has just been told his firing squad are stuck in traffic' at the final whistle.

He would show a similar expression of relief as his side won the replay, 2-1 after extra time, with once again Robins getting the winner and sealing United's passage to Wembley.

Crystal Palace 3 Manchester United 3

FA Cup Final days were so much better in the past. The whole day would be consumed with excitement; even *Going Live*, the BBC's flagship Saturday morning children's entertainment programme, was full of cup references. Back in those days there was little live television coverage of domestic football, save for around seven or eight league games a season on ITV, plus seven FA Cup matches on the BBC, one for each round plus both semi-finals. This heightened the sense of excitement surrounding what used to be the biggest day in the English football calendar.

United legend Denis Law, who was a frequent contributor to ITV's football output, visited the BBC studio in the build-up to the game. The former goal-getter's words to presenter Des Lynam were particularly prescient, though given Law's cheeky smile the comments were clearly tongue-in-cheek. He was drawing comparisons between the United cup-winning side of 1963 and the crop of 1990. Law scored in that final against Leicester City and hoped Ferguson's current side could not only go on to win the final against Crystal Palace, but also begin a period of league success like the side he played in under Sir Matt Busby. Law told Lynam, 'In '63 it was similar to United at the moment, they've had a poor time in the league. We nearly got relegated in '63, but then we won the cup. That gave us tremendous confidence. And then we went on to win leagues. Now the same could be with United today. Beat Palace today and then go on to win league after league.'

Law was looking away from both Lynam and the camera, smiling, as he said this, in almost dream mode, rather than expectation. He laughed at his own conclusion, knowing how unrealistic it was. In classic Lynam style, the smooth-talking presenter joked, 'The thing about you, Denis, is you're always so down and depressed.'

Law's powers of prediction, inadvertent or otherwise, were to evade him, however, as he expressed his confidence in goalkeeper Jim Leighton.

There were plenty of narratives going into the final.

Ian Wright's will he, won't he play, due to several injuries he'd sustained during the campaign. Eventually Wright had to settle for a place on the bench.

Palace manager Steve Coppell became the youngest to ever lead a side out for an FA Cup Final at the age of 34. More significantly he had already enjoyed success in the competition as a player, winning the trophy with United in 1977.

Both finalists finished on exactly the same number of points in the league, with only goal difference separating them meaning United ended up in 13th and Palace in 15th. Ironically, it was Manchester City who were sandwiched in between the two teams but with a far worse goal difference than United, despite the Maine Road thrashing they inflicted on their rivals earlier in the season.

However, the biggest narrative was whether Leighton could salvage his United career after a turbulent season. Indeed, in the league fixture between United and Palace at Old Trafford in the December of 1989, Fergie's side came a cropper with a 2-1 defeat after two goals from Mark Bright. The Palace striker mentioned one of the goals was 'helped in by Jim Leighton'. Palace were still reeling from a 9-0 defeat to Liverpool, and here they were a few weeks later, beating Manchester United – at Old Trafford.

The home defeat to Palace will also be remembered for the '3 YEARS OF EXCUSES AND IT'S STILL CRAP … TA RA FERGIE' banner held aloft by United fan Pete Molyneux, who later described the loss that day as Ferguson's 'nadir'. His bed sheet with the painted words was nowhere to be seen at Wembley, and would never be seen at a stadium again. Pete does not possess the original, having had it taken away from him by Stretford Police, who relieved him of it in the ensuing tussle after he had made his feelings known.

As for Manchester United's goalkeeping dilemma, the club had reached the final in spite of their man between the sticks, not because of him. Clean sheets in the opening two rounds were quickly forgotten as mistakes against Newcastle United in the fifth round and Oldham Athletic in the semi-finals put United under needless pressure. The one against Newcastle left you almost feeling sorry for him as he stumbled over an opposing player trying to claim a cross. He appealed to the referee, but it was awkward. It felt like a desperate plea as the official just ignored him. Leighton knew he was in trouble. It was even worse against Oldham in the semi-final, as he made two separate errors that led to the opening goal. Leighton would concede three that Sunday afternoon that had begun so dramatically as Palace knocked out heavy favourites Liverpool. Once regarded by Ferguson as the best keeper in Britain, the Scottish number one was under pressure going into the final.

Leighton and record purchase Gary Pallister were the two signings that had given Ferguson's detractors most traction, the latter due to the £2.3m transfer fee yet remaining unable to fix United's defensive woes. The former's problems ran deeper, verging on the cruel at times. Leighton, like his manager, was Scottish, and therefore some felt he got special treatment from Ferguson. But the goalkeeper struggled with the expectation, frequently suffering from migraines and stomach ulcers. The goalkeeper became the butt of many jokes on the terraces and in the fanzines. *Red Issue* ran a joke advert entitled 'The Leighton Condom' and with it you will be 'guaranteed to catch nothing'. The ad continued, 'Leighton condoms ensure you score comfortably.' Cup final day was set to be another uncomfortable moment for the man in charge of keeping the ball out of the net.

An annual part of the build-up on television would include going to the hotels of the respective teams before following the subsequent journey to Wembley, often with a camera in a helicopter above, monitoring the route. This year was no different and as Ferguson got off the bus at the stadium, Jimmy Hill, now alongside Des Lynam in the BBC studio, joked, 'Every time we've been on before there's been talk of him being sacked.' Ferguson's team had been on television, either live or as part of a highlights package, for all of their ties en route to Wembley, not least for the trickiness that each round posed.

United did not play a single FA Cup match at Old Trafford that season.

The final kicked off with United in all white. Who knows why they were not wearing the black shorts that were normally a part of their away attire. Palace were in their traditional red and blue stripes, having won the toss and chosen their home kit.

After a fairly equal opening to the game, Steve Coppell's men won a free kick, just after the quarter-hour mark, in a dangerous place to the right of the area as they attacked. It was particularly menacing due to their attacking prowess from set pieces but also because of United's defensive vulnerability. Such was the team's anxiety regarding their ability to defend, all 11 United players were in the box.

Perhaps it was the congested penalty area, maybe it was the nerves – either way, Leighton was about to make another calamitous mistake. He hesitated before deciding he was going to come for the cross, a pause that was to prove fatal as Palace defender Gary O'Reilly beat Leighton and Pallister to the ball, heading it over the stranded goalkeeper, who was in no-man's land due to his indecision.

To Leighton's relief United were on level terms shortly after thanks to a Bryan Robson header, aided by a deflection. Relief would turn to joy midway through the second half thanks to a left-footed strike from Mark Hughes following the most inadvertent assist of all time from Neil Webb's blocked challenge.

Throughout the opening stages of the second half the Red Devils were dominant, were stronger in the tackle and creating chances. Robson, unsurprisingly, was leading the way, winning the 50-50s that seemed to inspire his team-mates, in particular Paul Ince. And now even Webb, not known for his tough tackling, was getting in on the act. If his assist for the second goal was fortunate in its execution, it was brought about through determination.

Ferguson's side's superiority was beginning to show, and only an Andy Thorn defensive clearance prevented a third United goal.

The jitters in United's defence soon returned, however, as Leighton came to claim a cross and Pallister cleared. The centre-back gave his goalkeeper a glare.

United's nervousness was about to be ramped up a notch with a fired-up Ian Wright ready to come on. The striker had not started due to doubts about his ability to cope with the rigours of a Wembley final having just recovered from a shin injury. Wright would later recall his thinking during this spell of United dominance, as he sat on the bench, twisting with desperation to take part. When Wright did eventually enter the fray, on just shy of 70 minutes, he said he was 'so angry' with frustration at not having come on earlier, as he was convinced he could make an impact.

That grievance was about to be taken out on the United defence. Wright's first touch was to prod the ball forward having received it from his strike partner, Mark Bright. His second and third were used to turn inside Pallister with consummate ease, and his fourth was to slot the ball past Leighton. Four touches since coming on as a substitute and he had announced himself on the world stage.[14] Leighton could have been forgiven had he chosen to glare at Pallister this time as the defender was now the one most culpable. No matter. At 2-2, Ferguson was staring both at extra time and down the barrel.

The gun became fully loaded in the first half of the additional 30 minutes as Wright unleashed once more. If Ferguson's United career was under threat, the striker was about to end Leighton's once and for all. John Salako collected possession down the left before gaining an inch on makeshift right-back Mike Phelan, enough space to enable him to cross

14 The FA Cup Final would attract a global audience. Players from around the world would often reference the match when moving to England.

a hopeful ball into the box. Leighton's positioning can only be described as awful, far too close to his near post, which meant he had to scamper across goal, but was yards away from Wright's outstretched leg which volleyed into an unguarded net. How Ferguson on the bench must have squirmed. As Leighton saw the ball hit the back of the net he slumped to the floor as if he had just taken a right hook from Mike Tyson. It would later turn out to be the knockout blow for the goalkeeper.

For the immediate future, Ferguson had to act, but in an attacking sense. In footballing terms at least, Ferguson was never afraid to gamble. He threw on striker Mark Robins immediately after Wright had given Palace a 3-2 lead, and brought off defender Pallister. The new attacking threat would pay dividends with just minutes left on the clock as Hughes equalised, latching on to a through ball from Danny Wallace before finishing with aplomb. In the build-up to the final, Hughes had been criticised by BBC pundit Jimmy Hill for not scoring this type of goal, now 'Sparky' had responded in the perfect way, producing the exact kind of finish Hill thought he didn't score enough of. The game ended 3-3 after a thrilling 120 minutes.

Ferguson's managerial bravery was about to go up a notch. He once said, much later in his career, the most important characteristic of any great manager was having the courage to take a decision. And a decision over his goalkeeper had to be made.

Leighton was Ferguson's fourth signing and someone he was keen to get in. And at £500,000 he appeared to be excellent value given the goalkeeper's standing within the game. Now, two years after joining, the purchase had been an unmitigated disaster, and the cup final had crystallised everything that was wrong during Leighton's Old Trafford spell. His confidence was shot to pieces.

Ferguson would often seek a second opinion in these moments, and this time was no different. He wanted to know what his assistant, Archie Knox, thought of the matter. To this day Knox is of the same opinion. 'I would have kept him in,' he said in support of Leighton. But Knox, who had been alongside Ferguson at Aberdeen as well as United, was also aware of his position. He said, 'As assistant manager you give your point of view, and Alec would always want your point of view. You would never get me saying "oh well, we should've played Leighton" as I'm not that type of person. Whenever a decision is made, whether I agreed with it or not, I backed him to the hilt.'

Ferguson's gambling instincts came to the fore, despite the advice of his assistant. He dropped Leighton for the replay, to be played on the Thursday night, five days after the original match. His non-selection is something Leighton was never able to forgive his manager for. The goalkeeper described the next 19 months he spent at the club as 'purgatory'. He would only play one more time in that period before returning to ply his trade north of the border in 1992.

Crystal Palace 0 Manchester United 1

If the first match was to be the death knell on Leighton's United career, Ferguson's apparent Midas touch at crucial times was about to be witnessed for the first time in charge at Old Trafford. In Leighton's place came Les Sealey. Technically not as good a goalkeeper as Leighton, Sealey had the presence and strength of character the Scottish number one was sorely lacking.

Des Lynam, in the BBC studio once more for the replay, described the decision as 'extraordinary' and in many ways it was. Sealey was on loan from Luton Town and was about to make only his third appearance for United. Six years prior to the final, he was between the sticks for Luton when United scored five past him at Kenilworth Road. Yet here he was, walking out at Wembley for the biggest match of his career in such remarkable circumstances.

In hindsight, the truly extraordinary decision of the night was Palace manager Steve Coppell's reluctance to start with Ian Wright up front. The scourge of the United back line in the first meeting was once again on the bench. Oh how Wright must have been boiling up inside at his manager's judgement, not to mention the relief among Pallister et al in United's defence. Both the omission of Wright and the selection of Sealey were to prove decisive. Palace were toothless up front, United more solid at the back.

In addition, Sealey made three important saves, one of which was from a free kick where the goalkeeper barked seconds before, 'I can't see.' It mattered not. Sealey managed to get his legs in the way, clearing it to safety. It may have been a little unorthodox, but the memory of it is as clear for many United fans as the eventual winner, which arrived courtesy of Lee Martin on the hour mark. What is often forgotten is the role Neil Webb played in it. Webb had been signed amid much fanfare the year before as someone who could add silk to Robson's steel in the centre of the park. He made a promising start to his Old Trafford career before rupturing his Achilles tendon on England duty. Nevertheless, he recovered in time to play a crucial role for United at the business end of the season, scoring in the semi-final against Oldham Athletic and now spreading a beautiful diagonal pass into the path of Martin, to enable the right-back to score. Martin's run was described as 'inspired' by commentator John Motson at the exact moment the player chested it down, before half a second later prodding it into the roof of the net. Six players joined in the celebrations, but Webb wasn't among them, despite playing such a key role in what ultimately proved to be the winner.

Sealey made a couple more saves with his feet as the game progressed, the last of which, late on, was greeted with chants of 'Sealey! Sealey! Sealey!' from the Manchester United support which must have made Leighton feel even lower. Sealey offered his winner's medal to the man he had replaced between the sticks, such was the warmth between the two goalkeepers. But Leighton politely turned down the offer. 'I had been fortunate enough to win quite a few medals up to that time and, unless I could walk up the stairs and wear the hat and the scarf and lift the cup, then I didn't want anybody's charity,' Leighton told the BBC in 2018.

The game never lived up to its predecessor, but that didn't bother the United support, who were gleeful at the final whistle.[15] The troubled first three and a half years of the Ferguson tenure were at an end, and for the next 15 years, few would question his stewardship.

The road to victory in 1990 was littered with moments where you wonder what would have happened should Lady Luck have not been shining on Ferguson's side. Forest's unfairly ruled out goal in the third round, narrow wins in the next three ties that could so easily have gone the other way, and then the humdingers against Oldham Athletic and Crystal Palace where United were so close to defeat in both.

As fantastic as it was to get that first trophy under his belt, Ferguson knew that it was the title both he and the United supporters craved. Not least as Liverpool were back on their perch having just won their 18th league title. United had only won seven in their entire history and Ferguson was desperate to move that balance of power away from Anfield and towards Old Trafford.

---

15 The 1990 FA Cup-winning team was the last one where all the players, including substitutes, hailed from the British Isles.

3 (i)

From Anfield agony ...

THE FA Cup-winning side still had a makeshift feel to it. The goalkeeping issue remained as Les Sealey was only ever going to be a stopgap, albeit a capable one. Mike Phelan and Paul Ince, both midfielders by trade, were regularly filling in at right-back during the 1989/90 campaign. The combination of Brian McClair and Mark Hughes up front had largely malfunctioned, with the former eventually retreating to midfield or wide positions. Nevertheless, progress was obvious over the next year or so. The following season a sixth-place finish and a memorable European Cup Winners' Cup success, enabled by the previous year's FA Cup win, were evidence of significant improvement. Players such as Hughes, McClair, Bruce and Pallister were either at or coming to their peaks. The issue over full-backs was partially resolved by the arrival of Denis Irwin in the summer of 1990, who was equally adept on both sides of the back line. Younger players with great potential were being blooded with immense success, such as flying wingers Lee Sharpe, Ryan Giggs and Andrei Kanchelskis.

The European adventure was one to behold, particularly as English clubs had been banned from competing on the continent for five years after rioting at the Heysel Stadium in Brussels in 1985, leading to the deaths of 39 Italian and Belgian fans.

United easily negotiated the first two rounds of the Cup Winners' Cup, knocking out Pécsi Munkás of Hungary and Wrexham of Wales. Next up were French side Montpellier in the quarter-final. They were tricky opponents including future United player Laurent Blanc, as well as Colombian legend Carlos Valderrama, though the midfielder didn't feature in the first leg at Old Trafford. After a 1-1 home draw a disappointing exit loomed, especially due to the away goals rule. However, a passage through to the next round was secured in the second leg thanks to a long-range free kick from Clayton Blackmore – which rightly had the asterisk of a dreadful goalkeeping error attached to it – and a Steve Bruce penalty.

Legia Warsaw were seen off with consummate ease in the semis, meaning United would face Barcelona in the final, albeit as massive underdogs. However, after two Mark Hughes goals, the second driven in from a prohibitive angle with both feet off the ground after rounding the goalkeeper,[16] Ferguson had matched the European success he had achieved at Aberdeen. Indeed, the continental accomplishment with the Scottish outfit played a huge part in him securing the United job. With this latest triumph, Ferguson had also given himself some more breathing space in his current employment. On the eve of the Cup Winners' Cup Final, the Old Trafford supremo had described it as the biggest match of his United career, and for the supporters it was another step forward. The victory over Barcelona in Rotterdam was given further credibility when Johan Cruyff's team went on to win the European Cup a year later.

---

16 The Barcelona goalkeeper in Rotterdam was Carles Busquets, who was playing in place of the injured Andoni Zubizarreta. Busquets was made fun of by commentators for having a name that sounded like biscuits. He was culpable for both goals in the final. The Busquets family would go on to have the last laugh, though, with Carles's son, Sergio, playing a prominent role in the Barcelona team that dominated Manchester United in the Champions League Finals of 2009 and 2011.

It is important to note that in 1991 winning a European trophy, of any sort, was extremely prestigious, much more so than today where the Europa League plays a distant second fiddle to the Champions League. It was only when the Champions League expanded, particularly when the top leagues gained four entrants, that the other European competitions began to lose their lustre.

Despite the cup triumphs, a genuine title challenge had yet to occur, never mind the Holy Grail of winning the championship itself. Ferguson was well aware that winning the league was what United had hired him for. His predecessor, Ron Atkinson, won cups but his inability to turn United into title winners was what cost him his job. Still, mid-table in 1990, plus winning the FA Cup, followed by sixth the following year and securing a European trophy, meant Ferguson's side were on the right path. He believed his team were now ready for a title tilt. On the day after the final against Barcelona, he was in 'optimistic fervour', he said, before telling the gathering hordes 'we are going to win the league'. David Meek, who had been writing about United for many years for the *Manchester Evening News*, questioned the necessity of Ferguson's assertion. But the manager retorted, 'David, if Manchester United can win a European trophy, why can't we win the league? It's about time I raised the stakes at this club.'

The manager began to look for answers as to why the club had not managed to attain the consistency necessary to win a league title, something United had not achieved since 1967. Answers that eluded Wilf McGuinness, Frank O'Farrell, Tommy Docherty, Dave Sexton and Ron Atkinson. Some of Ferguson's predecessors commented on United's chances of winning the title for the first time in a quarter of a century after a decent start to the 1991/92 campaign. Some were optimistic while others urged caution. McGuinness said at the time, 'I think this could be our year.' Sexton was even more effusive, 'They're in a great position. Consistency is the key.' Docherty, who always seemed bitter about his United experience after getting the sack for having an affair with the physiotherapist's wife, was impressed with how the club had started the season. However, he feared the worst if the club wasn't able to achieve the Holy Grail this particular season. He said, 'I think this is the best chance they'll ever have because they've made a very good start. I think with the squad that they've got and the start they've made, if they don't win it this year, it could be quite some time before they win it again.' Atkinson had his doubts too, particularly if captain Bryan Robson had a sustained absence. 'I wonder what might happen if Robbo gets an injury,' Big Ron said. But the man who last led United to a league title, in 1967, Sir Matt Busby, was in a more jovial mood. 'It's 25 years since they've done it. But it's the right time to do it,' Sir Matt laughed. He was a supporter now, and the pressure was off him and on another Scot's shoulders.

Ferguson, meanwhile, was in bullish mood come the beginning of December 1991, with United a point off table-topping Leeds United and with a game in hand. He said, 'It's a challenge. We are not certain to win the league this year but I think we're getting closer. I think we have a really good chance and if they weren't to do it … it would be really disappointing. But I know they'll go to the wire. They've got the bottle, they've got the endurance, they've got the ability. And it could be decided by goal difference. It could be decided by one bad performance. We've one or two obvious challengers and we accept that. I really do feel that we have a great chance and it would be a tremendous feat by the players to get rid of the whole thing.'

This is the Ferguson of late 1991, an obvious step up from the anxious version we saw at Maine Road in 1989, sitting uncomfortably on the bench, and just wanting to stick his head under the pillow afterwards hoping it would all go away. Yet this Ferguson was still not quite there in terms of the utter self-belief he would exude later in his reign at Old Trafford. Note the talk of possible bad performances costing them, almost prophetically as it turned out. And perhaps most significantly he said 'to get rid of the whole thing', by which he meant the albatross of not winning the league in such a long time, knowing this had been plaguing both the club and his predecessors. Nevertheless, as United headed into the New Year, confidence was growing.

The new arrivals at the club from the previous summer had bedded in well. Peter Schmeichel had given the back line added confidence. Long gone were the nervy days when Jim Leighton kept goal and Ferguson described the purchase of the big Danish goalkeeper as 'a real snip'. At £500,000, Ferguson was not wrong, as Schmeichel would go on to stay at the club for eight years and become recognised as the world's best goalkeeper. Paul Parker had arrived to give added defensive security. In addition, given that Parker was English, it meant UEFA's four-foreigner rule at the time in European competitions could be dealt with a little bit better. Add to that the fact Parker was England's best right-back, after some sterling displays in the 1990 World Cup, and it made the deal a no-brainer.

The improvement at the back was evident on the pitch. Save for a crazy 4-1 home defeat to Queens Park Rangers on New Year's Day, featuring sloppy defending and a hat-trick from Dennis Bailey, Parker and the rest of the United defenders had performed stoutly as the club headed into the final stretch of the season.

What strikes you at this juncture is the success rate of Ferguson's buys. Gone are the days of misfiring in the transfer market with flops like Jim Leighton, Mal Donaghy and the man who Fergie described as his worst ever purchase, Ralph Milne. In quick succession came Irwin, Schmeichel, Parker and Kanchelskis. All were huge successes and first-team regulars. Also, these four signings were bought with value in mind.

Only Parker cost more than £1m, and without exception each one enjoyed their best years at the club.

The confidence coursing through the team in the winter months of 1991/92 was exemplified in the away thrashings of Arsenal, 6-2 in the League Cup, and Oldham Athletic, 6-3 in the league. The former included a Lee Sharpe hat-trick. In both matches United's forward play was mightily impressive and it is no exaggeration to say they could have scored ten each time, given the ease with which they created chances. In the match at Oldham's Boundary Park every time the Latics fought back with a goal or two, threatening to derail United, Ferguson's team would respond with interest, putting the game further beyond the reach of their opponents. Interestingly, Denis Irwin celebrated a goal against his former club, a much-missed element in the game of today, where players often posture.

If Ferguson could have bottled that confidence, and protected it until the season's end, United would have been champions.

Another 'if only' must come from three titanic tussles with Leeds United, the other protagonists in the title chase, and also a side trying to restore their glory days. Two of the matches against Leeds came in the cup competitions and Manchester United prevailed in both. The one in the league saw Ferguson's team only draw at Elland Road, having led for most of the second half. This three-point swing, with the Old Trafford outfit dropping two points late on and Leeds gaining one, would prove costly. But not nearly as much as the cup runs that ensued from the two victories. Those wins meant United went on to play a further four games in the season, including an energy-sapping loss on penalties in the FA Cup to Southampton, rendering their victory against Leeds in the previous round meaningless. What was significant, though, was the League Cup run, as United maintained their run of trophies in each of the last three seasons, winning the final against Nottingham Forest to lift the trophy for the first time in their history.

United were on Leeds' coat-tails come mid-April, and had two games in hand due to their cup exploits. Ferguson's men, however, were about to embark on a run of five games in ten days. Four points from the opening two matches of that spell meant they had replaced Leeds at the top of the table with the finish line in sight. They were two points clear, with a game in hand, and the Yorkshire side had just four games left to play.

Next up were Nottingham Forest, at home, on what was becoming a 'cabbage patch of a pitch' at Old Trafford, according to Ferguson. An Ian Woan strike opened the scoring for Forest. If any further evidence was needed to demonstrate United's fraying nerves, goalkeeper Schmeichel, who had had an excellent first season in English football, fumbled the ball, letting it squirm below his body for the opening goal. Almost 50,000 home fans fell silent, and even Denis Irwin, known for his calm demeanour, expressed his despair, clutching his head as the ball hit the back of the net. Brian McClair got United back on level terms but Scot Gemmill delivered the winner for the away side ten minutes from time.

Barney Chilton from United fanzine *Red News* recalls the game vividly, 'That Forest defeat on the Monday was brutal. With Neil Webb trudging off … that was a point where he [Ferguson] started losing control.' Webb was criticised by Ferguson in his book for a having a poor attitude around this time.

Leeds had leapfrogged their bitter rivals into top spot, but it was still in Manchester United's hands as they had played a game less than Howard Wilkinson's side.

Games in hand do not necessarily mean points in the bag, especially at this stage of the season where having jelly legs was not going to help win games, something United so desperately needed to achieve.

Next up was West Ham away, but the Hammers had already been relegated, making United's task seemingly easier.[17] Once again, commentator Clive Tyldesley struck a chord, just like he did at Maine Road three years before during the 5-1 mauling at the hands of City. 'Manchester United have always had their title destiny in their own hands,' Tyldesley told the viewers as the away side kicked off at Upton Park on that Wednesday evening, just two days after the defeat to Forest. 'If they win their games, the rest are fighting over the scraps. It's been their saving grace these last few, nervous weeks, but they must win tonight to stay in control. Anything less, and Leeds United would not only be in front, they'd be in charge too. West Ham are resigned to their fate, Manchester United still in command of theirs.'

Further evidence of the fading confidence at the club became apparent in striker Mark Hughes's form, which, according to Ferguson, was a 'major worry'. The striker had been dropped for the Forest game, though restored for the trip to Upton Park. For a player for whom 'confidence was everything', Ferguson said, going 14 games without a goal showed that Hughes had 'difficulty hoisting himself out of bad spells'.

He was not the only one. United were in the mire against West Ham and the game was on a knife edge when Kenny Brown scored 'the luckiest goal imaginable', Ferguson claimed in his autobiography. 'It hit him flush on the knee.' After Brown's strike 'you could see the hope draining out of us. In the last minutes of the match, a well-dressed man with a trilby called out to me, "Alex, Alex! Fuck you!"' Ferguson would never forget those kinds of incidents, those that crossed him, or insulted him. And he would use it as fuel for both himself and his players.

---

17 West Ham still had a mathematical chance of staying up, but the goal differential to their relegation rivals was so massive that they were down in all but name.

The loss at West Ham left the players despondent, summed up by Schmeichel's reaction to the goal. There was no hurry to retrieve the ball from the net as he just sat, legs crossed, dumbfounded. Pallister, who was partly culpable with a sloppy, tired-looking clearance straight to Brown, also put his hands on his knees, like a marathon runner who had just run out of gas. 'The realisation that our chance of the title had almost certainly gone made our dressing-room like a funeral parlour,' Ferguson said.

The players and staff were not the only dejected ones, as Barney Chilton remembers, 'Upton Park is a great stadium, and they always seemed to raise their game against us. And their fans went ballistic. It was painful and there was a deflated look on the faces of the United fans. It was almost like, "This is gone now."'

Fergie reacted in typically defiant style, describing the effort United's opponents had put in as 'obscene' and 'almost criminal' in light of the fact the Hammers were already relegated.

For all Ferguson's complaints about fortune and circumstance, West Ham had been the superior side, creating numerous chances. In the commentary box Tyldesley recognised, 'The better team won on the night.'

United's anxiety became all too apparent. At the final whistle, Pallister brought his shirt to his face, almost wishing the ground would swallow him up, such was his disappointment.

The last time United had won the league, in 1967, they did so in emphatic fashion thanks to a 6-1 win at Upton Park. Now, 25 years later, they had probably lost it at the same venue.

Manic Sunday

Manchester United's rivals for the title, Leeds, were now in the driving seat as they topped the league by a point with two games to play.

A glimmer of hope lay in the upcoming Yorkshire derby Leeds would have to negotiate against Sheffield United at

Bramall Lane. For the first time it was Leeds who appeared jittery, going a goal behind after 28 minutes before equalising on the stroke of half-time with what can only be described as the most bizarre goal of all time. The goal included so many freakish ricochets that it made the magic bullet theory almost plausible. The momentum now in their favour, Leeds took the lead in the second half only to be pegged back once more meaning it was 2-2 with less than 15 minutes remaining.

But the performance of Melvyn Rees in the Sheffield United goal had been so poor you half-expected him to be wearing 'I love Leeds United' underwear. If the first Leeds goal was freakish, their winner was just as weird, as a mix-up between goalkeeper and defender led to Brian Gayle heading over Rees, who had inexplicably gone for the ball when there was no need to do so. Fortune was certainly with Leeds at this most crucial stage of the season.

Liverpool 2 Manchester United 0

That victory for their rivals, and in such outlandish fashion, must have hit United hard. The title race was not completely over but United needed to win both their remaining games to stand any chance of claiming the crown. Having watched Leeds fortuitously win earlier in the day, the pressure cooker was almost at explosion point as they faced the daunting prospect of playing their bitterest rivals, Liverpool, at Anfield, knowing only victory would suffice.

If nerves had been their undoing in the previous two matches, now despondency had taken over as United put in a lacklustre display that portrayed a lack of hope rather than anxiety.

The match was beamed live to living rooms across the country on ITV.

Barney Chilton from *Red News* remembers the build-up all too clearly as he sat along with other fans in the Punch and Judy pub, near Liverpool Lime Street railway station.

Chilton described the atmosphere among the supporters as news filtered through of Leeds' victory, piling on the pressure, 'It was awful. Some fans were already crying.'

Anfield was packed to the rafters as the home support were desperate to see United fall on their sword and miss out on the prize that had resided in the Liverpool trophy cabinet for much of the last two decades. Liverpool had won it 11 times since United last had that honour.

Ian Rush opened the scoring, with his first goal against Manchester United at the 25th attempt, to add another storyline to what was turning into a horrible day for Ferguson and his team. The home supporters celebrated deliriously as if they had won the championship themselves, such was their desperation to prevent United from achieving just that. It is impossible to overstate the intensity of the dislike between the two clubs. Sure, there is a rivalry between Manchester United and City. Likewise there is an enmity with Liverpool and city rivals Everton. But among the fans from Old Trafford and Anfield it is so much more.

There were chances for both teams throughout the game but when Mark Walters sealed victory for Liverpool late on, making it 2-0, their supporters once again celebrated in emphatic style. At that exact moment, the ITV cameras cut to Leeds United striker Lee Chapman's living room, in the corner of the screen. Chapman was joined on the sofa by team-mates Eric Cantona, Gary McAllister and David Batty, who congratulated each other when Walters scored. Immediately after the game, the players were interviewed, bunched up on Chapman's couch as they sipped champagne. When asked if he could actually believe that Leeds were champions, Chapman said, 'It's a bit of a shock.' Cantona, whose English at this stage was virtually non-existent, seemed somewhat perplexed at proceedings, but Chapman spoke on behalf of his French colleague as he said, 'He's got bags of skill and I'm sure he's going to settle down even more next season.'

Following the defeat, former Liverpool defender Alan Hansen suggested United may never win the league, having come so close. Despite the rivalry between the two clubs, Hansen's prediction was understandable, and many fans at Old Trafford were beginning to fear the same.

'The feeling among the supporters, the feeling among all of us at Anfield that day, was that Manchester United would never win the league in our lifetime,' recalls Chilton. 'It was a horror show that day, it was awful. There's nothing that will compare, nothing in football will be that bad.'

There were some silver linings to the obvious clouds a week later after finishing the season with a 3-1 win at home to Spurs, and Mark Hughes finally getting back on the scoresheet with a brace. In what was to be the last ever match at Old Trafford in front of standing fans in the Stretford End due to the all-seater legislation coming in for the following season, the end of term walk round the pitch included cheers from all four corners of the ground. The team may have fallen just short in the title race, but Ferguson and his side had the fans on board, a far cry from the jeers and 'Ta ra Fergie' banners of two and a half years before.

There was plenty for Ferguson to mull over too. He had to decide what had gone wrong and what to change. The manager was well aware the gruelling schedule, combined with United's loss of nerve, had cost them dearly. It was the third time in the fallow period that the club had been odds-on to win the title, only to fail in their quest.

Once again, just like the torrid period towards the end of 1989, it was time for Ferguson to show his mettle, and inspire United out of the doldrums. When Ferguson is down certain characteristics come to the fore.

The fighter's instinct begins to emerge from the depths of despair. Perhaps from a feeling of being wronged, that what had happened was not deserved.

Various motivational tactics were employed, using the end-of-season collapse, both to help Ferguson and his staff, as well as the players. This was initially achieved, inadvertently, by some opposing fans at Anfield that April afternoon. Ferguson told his players to never forget incidents such as when some Liverpool supporters asked Lee Sharpe and Ryan Giggs for their autographs.[18] The two players obliged only to see the spiteful fans respond by tearing them up. 'Remember this day and just how important you are at Manchester United,' Ferguson told the pair. 'What has just happened should tell you how much people envy you. They wouldn't have done that otherwise. It proves how big we are.'

There was more. The following season Ferguson pinned up in the dressing room a photo known as 'Dante's Inferno' showing the devastated faces on the United bench during the crucial Easter Monday defeat at home to Nottingham Forest.[19] Once again, the mantra was to always remember, 'to make sure it never happened again'.

There were other issues for Ferguson to remedy, not least the lack of goals during the run-in. Two-thirds of the team's league goals came in the first half of the season and there was a distinct drop-off when it mattered most. Pressure played its part, as did fatigue. The Old Trafford pitch, which had become almost unplayable for a passing side like United, was also a factor. The impact of the surface was such that Ferguson regretted not purchasing the lofty Luton Town striker Mick Harford. He would have given the team a more direct option when going forward so they could avoid the inconsistencies the turf would throw up. Nevertheless, keeping the ball off the wretched playing surface at Old Trafford was an unusual assertion for a manager who was always proud of playing football in the right way.

---

18 Some have suggested that Paul Ince was also a victim of this prank.

19 *Inferno* is the first part of Italian writer Dante Alighieri's 14th-century epic poem *Divine Comedy*. The *Inferno* tells the journey of Dante through Hell, guided by the ancient Roman poet Virgil.

Come the season's end, Ferguson rued not finishing teams off. The 'goals dried up' and the team were 'left to suffer. We needed a passing pitch, hopefully next season will be better.' But an admission that 'we've thrown the league' clearly hurt.

However, there were plenty of rallying calls and upbeat messages too. 'We'll find a way, they're young enough to accept the challenges. We're going somewhere.' What is most apparent is Ferguson's confidence, he is now saying things with complete conviction, gone are the days of self-doubt that had troubled him during the early part of his tenure. Now he was 'philosophical' in defeat and that confidence was evident as he 'thanked the players and assured them next season's challenge would be successful.'

The message quickly filtered through to the players with Peter Schmeichel predicting title success in the near future as he believed there was 'so much talent in the squad'. Those words could so easily have come from the manager – further evidence that Ferguson's desire for his team to be a mirror representation of the boss was beginning to take shape.

Brian McClair was also picking up on the vibes. The Scottish striker said that the feeling in the dressing room at the end of the season was not despondent as they were desperate to right the wrongs, 'We couldn't wait to get back for pre-season because we thought we were close [to winning the league]. We got so close that we were ready.'

These remarks and the feelings within Old Trafford were in stark contrast to the comments of Alan Hansen, and previously Tommy Docherty. The fans, like Hansen and Docherty, also believed this was a big opportunity missed and one that might not arise again for a long time.

3 (ii)

... to title relief

WHEN LOOKING at the following season, it is impossible not to recognise the effect the previous term had on it. The fact United failed to win the league in such an excruciating manner was not lost on either the manager or the team. The fuel that it would provide, as well as the knowledge, cannot be ignored when analysing future successes.

'I knew,' Ferguson said, 'if we were to reach confidently for the title, I had to add another element, an extra dimension to the team. At least I had all summer to find the remarkable footballer I needed.' Prescient words indeed. But here, once again, was Ferguson's ability to analyse at its very best. He had identified that the side needed an injection, something different. Not merely a player to improve the side but someone to transform it.

The theme of defeats inspiring greatness could even be found in the transfer market throughout Ferguson's tenure. The first clear example of this came in the summer of 1992 when he recognised United needed to improve the team's strike rate, given how it had 'plummeted' in the second half of the previous season, according to the manager. Identifying the problem was not difficult, anyone could see the issue, but finding the answer is something Fergie was capable of doing time and time again, which explains his unprecedented longevity at the club.

Ferguson's initial reaction to United's failing front line was to turn to Alan Shearer, someone whose ability and mental strength had impressed him, first-hand, when the Southampton striker performed so impressively at Old Trafford in the past.

Ferguson first earmarked Shearer as a potential United striker when he scored three times over two League Cup ties in 1991. The manager was particularly impressed with his temperament and 'identified him as a player with great confidence in himself', the boss remarked in his first autobiography, *Managing My Life*. The United manager thus 'marked him down as someone we would be watching very carefully over the next season'. Now the United boss made his move, just over a year on from those Southampton fixtures. Shearer, however, rejected Ferguson's overtures, electing to play under Kenny Dalglish at Blackburn Rovers, much to the chagrin of the United manager, who was not slow in airing his frustrations: 'I found him very hard work and quite surly. The conversation suggested he was definitely going to Blackburn.'

In one last-ditch effort to change Shearer's mind, Ferguson dug deep into his closet of persuasion. 'Would Kenny have signed for Blackburn when he was a player?' he asked the striker. 'I know what he'd have done if United and Blackburn had both come in for him.'

Shearer was having none of it. 'I'm not interested in what Kenny would have done,' he snapped back. 'It's about what I want, not Kenny.' Mission failed.

But Ferguson can take failure on the chin, no matter how difficult it can be to swallow. Accept it, learn from it, move on. Just like the title defeat had initially felt 'like a death in the family' to Ferguson. 'But you have to get over it.'

If United had won the league in 1992, would they have searched so desperately for a striker? More pertinently, would the search have looked for someone to take the club in a different direction? Arguably not. There may not have been the soul-searching, detailed analysis that Ferguson brought to the table, as he looked for a way out, in order to scratch the title itch that had irritated him and the club for so long.

That new 'dimension' would come about in slightly fortuitous circumstances. At the beginning of the following season, after similar issues in front of goal had continued to plague the team, the fresh angle of attack had yet to be found. Dion Dublin had been signed after the failure to land Shearer but his broken leg, incurred in just his third outing, meant Ferguson had to delve into the transfer market once more. Whether he would have done so without Dublin's injury remains to be seen. What was to follow would become the stuff of legend at Old Trafford.

Come November, the team that had denied Ferguson's team title glory in the previous campaign, Leeds United, made an enquiry about full-back Denis Irwin, which got short shrift from the manager. While the Leeds chief executive, Bill Fotherby, and his Old Trafford counterpart, Martin Edwards, chatted on the phone, Fergie quickly jotted down the name of Eric Cantona on a piece of paper and pushed it into his chairman's view. Edwards brought the striker's name into the conversation and got some encouragement that a deal could be done. Ferguson recalled how his defensive pairing of Steve Bruce and Gary Pallister were 'raving' about Cantona after the two sides met at Old Trafford a couple of months before. Thus an agreement was reached and 'one of the most extraordinary periods in the history of Manchester United was about to begin', Ferguson wrote in his autobiography.

How this deal came about has been disputed by Edwards, who says Ferguson was not in the room at the time of Fotherby's phone call. The former chairman also says it was he who initially mentioned Cantona's name. The two versions do not quite marry, but given that Ferguson's dates back to within hours of the deal being concluded, while Edwards waited almost 30 years to tell his account, it is more likely that the manager's recollection is more accurate.

No matter how the transfer materialised, once more we can see the effects of the stars aligning, brought about by losses and setbacks. The title collapse, the new dimension that Ferguson so desperately sought, followed by missing out on Shearer and the loss through injury of Dublin, sparked the arrival of a new talisman at Old Trafford.

The fact that Cantona had contributed to United's downfall the previous season was another example of how failure could be used to trigger success.

The Frenchman's impact was immediate. His dedication to training inspired his team-mates to do the same. 'Many have justifiably acclaimed Cantona as a catalyst who had a crucial impact on our successes while he was with the club but nothing he did in matches meant more than the way he opened my eyes to the indispensability of practice,' Ferguson said. 'Practice makes players.' It can make managers too.

Ferguson, through a combination of circumstance, nous and learned experience, had acquired the player that was going to add the new dimension he craved. 'His presence illuminated Old Trafford,' Ferguson purred. 'I knew that when I had found myself longing in the previous summer for someone who would lift our already formidable qualities on to another plane I had been imagining a footballer very much like Eric Cantona.'

Prior to the Frenchman's arrival United's impotence in front of goal had been apparent. They began the new campaign, like they finished the last, struggling for form and scoring goals was the obvious problem – 17 in the opening 16 games of 1992/93 was a paltry return for a club with championship ambitions.

Cantona came on for his debut in the Manchester derby, replacing the injured Bryan Robson at half-time. The striker emerged, as the players came out for the second half, with a spring in his step that would remain for much of the next five years. A few windmills with his arms, a couple of jumps to get the muscles warmed up, and he was ready. The only question was whether Old Trafford was ready for him.

We soon found out whether Cantona could provide the dimension Ferguson craved. United's form, particularly in terms of strike rate, showed a significant surge, doubling in output from what it was prior to Cantona's arrival. The forward was often both scorer and provider, best demonstrated in a marvellous 4-1 win against Tottenham Hotspur that included a goal from the Frenchman but also contained one of the most memorable assists in the club's history. Cantona, with the outside of his foot, perfectly laid the ball into the path of Denis Irwin. As he made the through ball, John Motson in commentary immediately said, 'Oh! Look at that pass!' After Irwin had struck the ball into the net, Motson added, 'The return ball was one of the passes of the season. This man is playing a game of his own.'

Cantona's effect on the team was obvious. He scored valuable goals, rather than being prolific, and that remained the case throughout his time at the club. His impact was most noticeable in how others were playing better, as the Frenchman orchestrated play. In a purple patch over Christmas and New Year, 11 different players scored in four games. Now that's the dimension Ferguson was looking for.

Momentum was firmly with United and lessons were being learned from last season's failures too, not least a newly acquired fortitude, exemplified in a victory at Anfield as the season entered a crucial phase. That win at the scene of least year's final nail in the coffin, convinced both the players and the manager that this season's version had the wherewithal to win the title.

It convinced striker Brian McClair too, who got the winner that day, albeit aided by a foul he committed that he escaped censure for. A crucial game was 'winning at Anfield,' McClair explained. 'I scored the winning goal, and it was actually a foul. I gave Stevie Nicol a nudge.' McClair knew the significance, though. 'Having lost there the year before, to go there and win 2-1 ... was three more points than last year.'

To the United fans, it was so much more, with the memories of less than 12 months before still fresh in their minds. Now they were watching their team, spurred on by last season's demise, head inexorably towards title glory, reeling off victories against tricky opponents that had caused them such angst in the previous year's run-in.

In the spring of 1993, there was to be no repeat of the stumbles against Nottingham Forest, West Ham and Liverpool.

One of the most impressive performances came away at Norwich City, who were themselves still in title contention, making it a three-horse race along with Ron Atkinson's Aston Villa. But United blew Norwich away in an opening 20-minute salvo that had the commentary team at Sky gushing over the performances of Cantona, Ince, Kanchelskis and Giggs. Mark Hughes was suspended but it certainly didn't blunt United's attack. What was also striking was Ferguson's demeanour on the bench. Extremely calm, as though he expected it to happen, in stark contrast to a year earlier when his anxiety and tea-cup throwing moments were cited by some as to why they missed out on title glory. In that 3-1 victory over Norwich at Carrow Road, United's second was an example of what would become a trademark of Ferguson's sides over the next two decades – the counter-attacking goal.

United had been scoring quite a few over the previous 18 months thanks to the pace and skill of Sharpe, Giggs and Kanchelskis. But now here they were in front of a live television audience on a Monday night, in a clash against a rival for the league title, scoring a goal less than 12 seconds after they were at risk of losing one. Pallister managed to clear the danger just yards from his own goal. In doing so he found Cantona, whose first-time pass deep in his own half was probably the most impressive of the entire move, volleying it to Ince. The midfielder, first time, to Giggs, first time to McClair, first time through ball perfectly weighted for Kanchelskis, who rounded Bryan Gunn to score.

United ripped Norwich apart that night, thanks largely to Sharpe, Kanchelskis and Giggs, who would make a very handy attacking trident in the modern game. United's third that night was more about Ince, though, driving through from midfield, before teeing up Cantona to stroke home. The reaction of Sky commentator Ian Darke said it all, 'You can't believe this. We have mayhem here. Manchester United, incredibly, are three-nil up, and Alex Ferguson is the calmest man in Carrow Road.'

Bryan Robson also noted an air of calmness around Ferguson during the title run-in, so much so that he even penned a newspaper article saying that he thought the difference between the savage disappointment of losing out in 1992, and the triumph a year later, was down to the United manager's more relaxed approach. Ferguson was less sure of this but did add credence to the notion that he had learned from the previous year's travails. 'I do know I devoted more attention to my observation of players. Watching certain individuals carefully during pressure periods, recognising those who needed reassuring, enabled me to handle the preparation for each game more effectively.'

Ferguson had discovered over the crucial 12-month period that 'it is only when you focus on one or two players at a time that you get a real insight into them'. The Scottish manager also noticed how his 'management methods were evolving. For years I did everything on the training field myself. I did the coaching, the organising of the training programmes, the pre-season schedules, the warm-ups, the lot.' Maybe Ferguson had burdened himself with too much the year before, causing United to eventually blow up, handing the initiative to Leeds, and with it the league title. Now a year on, he 'realised that the art of observation had to play a bigger part'.

If Ferguson was calm on the Monday at Carrow Road, the following Saturday, he completely lost it, as delirium took over him and all who saw it, not least his assistant Brian Kidd. United, 1-0 down until the dying moments, scored with two late goals from Steve Bruce, the second of which came in the sixth minute of injury time, to take all three points and move a step closer to title heaven.

Once again, the team were evolving and beginning to embody the manager's approach, particularly in terms of never giving in.

Whereas 12 months previously, at the same stage of the season, United were struggling, now they were exuding confidence. The players had learned, and so had the manager, from the pitfalls of the year before. Add the vital new ingredient of Cantona to the mix, and you have the team quenching a 26-year thirst, displaying imperious form in winning their last seven league games.

Some have suggested that winning the title by virtue of Aston Villa losing at home to Oldham Athletic diluted the feeling. Not a bit of it. United fans spilled on to the streets to savour the moment. The players joined in with the celebrations too, enjoying a spontaneous party at Steve Bruce's house that carried on into the early hours, something Ferguson picked up on the following evening as Paul Parker yawned in the dressing room just before playing at home to Blackburn Rovers. The match became a title celebration more than a fight for three points. United won the game all the same, the crowning glory coming from a Gary Pallister free kick. The defender was nominated to take the kick as he had been the only outfield player not to have scored all season.

As United finally got their hands on the Holy Grail, the sight of Sir Matt Busby smiling in the crowd will be forever etched on the memory of all Old Trafford supporters.

Ferguson described this as 'the day I truly became manager of Manchester United'. But it was more. He added, 'There was a sudden, overwhelming realisation that now I was a master of my own destiny.'

4 (i)

From summer sales ...

THIS MANCHESTER United side under Alex Ferguson was never going to be a one-season wonder but it would take another painful knock to elevate the club further still.

Some may argue, in terms of quality, the level was never bettered from the 1994 team that had all the class and skill of the '93 version, but with the added experience, steel and confidence from the year before, plus Roy Keane, who had been signed from Nottingham Forest. Keane would arguably go on to have an even bigger influence on the team than Eric Cantona. For now, it was all about taking a step forward, and improve they certainly did.

The acquisition of Keane was aided and abetted by the failure to land Alan Shearer a year before. This time, Ferguson managed to woo his target by inviting him to his house for a game of snooker at a time when Blackburn Rovers were sniffing around once more. Ferguson was not going to miss out for a second successive summer. 'I made it clear how vital I felt his role could be in the successful years I was sure lay ahead of Manchester United. I was determined to avoid a repeat of what happened with Alan Shearer.'

A disappointing early exit in their first foray in the European Cup for almost a quarter of a century was the only serious blip in an otherwise mightily impressive season. It ended with winning both the title and the FA Cup in the same year for the first time in the club's history.

There was also the failure to win the League Cup, despite getting to the final, which provided a minor setback. That Wembley loss to Ron Atkinson's Aston Villa still grates some fans today. United were within a whisker of becoming the first club to win all three domestic trophies in one season.

Nevertheless, this was comfortably Ferguson's best team to date. It had solidity at the back, power and strength in its spine, and pace and skill in attack. Some feel this was the best Ferguson side of them all, even better than those that went on to win the Champions League, but a failure to turn that ability into European success ultimately undermines the argument.

The aforementioned strength, both in body and mind, would occasionally boil over. None more so than in March 1994 when United had a player sent off four times in five matches, including Eric Cantona – twice. But it was not enough to unhinge the unstoppable express that won the league at a canter, and beat Chelsea 4-0 in the FA Cup Final.

Two league titles, two FA Cups, one League Cup and a European Cup Winners' Cup was an impressive haul of trophies over a four-year period that seemed unimaginable at the turn of the decade.

There's good reason for the great esteem in which the 1994 collective are held. Ferguson even described it thus, 'Claims that the class of '94 were the greatest Reds could be severely questioned but I have no doubt they would stand up well to any comparison.'

From back to front, the team that started the FA Cup Final against Chelsea read: Schmeichel; Parker, Pallister, Bruce, Irwin; Kanchelskis, Ince, Keane, Giggs; Cantona, Hughes. Winning was coursing through their blood, and the statistics back it up. That starting 11 played together in 12 games throughout the course of the season and won every one.

However, it was never to start as a unit again. Over the course of the next 12 months the side would be broken up, largely on the basis of the 1994/95 campaign, which would become the club's first without a trophy in five seasons. It was a campaign Ferguson described as 'a leap into misery'. That anguish led to Ferguson axing three of his most significant lieutenants. It resulted in having even the most loyal of fans questioning the manager's sanity come the summer of 1995.

Paul Ince

At half-time in a Champions League group match at the Camp Nou, and with United already trailing 2-0, Ferguson's wrath was about to be directed primarily at one player – Paul Ince.

Ferguson was already annoyed with Ince for losing the mercurial José María Bakero in a 2-2 draw at Old Trafford, resulting in a goal for Barcelona, before travelling to Catalonia for the return match two weeks later.

Now the manager was becoming increasingly frustrated with the midfielder's tendency to go forward, when he preferred him to hold, stationed closer to the defence, particularly in Europe. He felt that Ince's ego was getting the better of him, causing him to get nearer to the opposition's box as the player thought he could exert a greater influence in attacking areas. Right-back Gary Neville spoke about what occurred in the bowels of the Camp Nou, 'At half-time the boss ripped into Incey. At one point, Brian Kidd half stood up to intervene, thinking it was about to go off.'

On the bench for United that night, and also in the dressing room at half-time, was reserve goalkeeper Kevin Pilkington. He described the incident in more detail. 'It was as close to a fist fight as you can get without it kicking off. Barcelona played the most devastating football I've ever witnessed, but the gaffer came and let rip, as if the lads hadn't tried. The boss ripped into Incey,' Pilkington said, backing up the words of Neville. Ferguson described the midfielder as a 'bottler', before adding,

'You can't handle the stage, can you?' The former West Ham player, clearly offended by the accusation, responded, 'I'm not a bottler. Don't you dare call me a bottler, gaffer. Don't you dare.' Ferguson was having none of it, this time shouting right in Ince's face, 'You're a fucking bottler!'

To the casual observer, Ince didn't seem more culpable than anyone else for what turned out to be a 4-0 defeat to a side that included the attacking talents of Hristo Stoichkov and Romário. But then Ferguson was no casual observer. He said, 'My anger in the dressing room at half-time was a response to the naivety we had shown in midfield. There was the vital need for Paul Ince to make sure he was always checking the forward runs of Bakero or Guillermo Amor. The way Paul was responding to such instructions had been causing me concern. I sensed that he no longer wanted to be the anchor man in midfield, where there was none better at the job. It was clear to me that he now saw himself as an attacking midfield player, which was a hopeless misreading of his strengths.'

Maybe a harsh assessment, given that Ince's attacking runs, movements and occasional moments of inspiration in the final third had brought vital goals in the previous couple of years, including a fundamental role in the equaliser against Barcelona at Old Trafford a couple of weeks before. Ferguson didn't see it that way, though, 'Players who can continually make energy-sapping runs from penalty box to penalty box are rare gems. I had brought Roy Keane to Old Trafford because he was one of them, a man whose reserves of stamina put him in the Bryan Robson category. Paul did not have anything like the physical endurance of those two. His strong suit was defending but he refused to embrace that reality.'

To compound the tension between the two, Ince's ill-discipline was not just evident in his untimely runs forward, or in a perceived lack of concentration. It was also manifesting itself in anger and frustration. An outburst at the referee in Gothenburg in the penultimate game in the group stage of the

Champions League resulted in a red card for the midfielder, again to the displeasure of his manager.

Ferguson was beginning the path to dismantling the side, citing the performances in painful, significant defeats as a good enough reason for doing so.

He would continue to chip away at Ince throughout that season as he became increasingly frustrated with the midfielder's antics. Ferguson said that Ince lacked 'humility' and was getting 'carried away' with his own ego, epitomised by the nickname the player had given himself – 'the Guv'nor'. Ince even bought a car with the letters 'GUV' on the number plate. For Ferguson this was an example of his golden rule being broken – his control was under threat, something he found unbearable. Of course, it was always in defeat that Ferguson's frustrations with Ince would come to the fore.

In his biography of the manager, *Fergie the Greatest*, Frank Worrall suggests that the final straw came when the two men arrived at Old Trafford at the same time and the door staff called Ince, not Ferguson, 'Guv' – eliciting a knowing wink from the midfielder.

Mark Hughes

Mark Hughes was not always someone Ferguson felt sure about during his tenure as United manager. During the striker's second spell at the club there were occasional bouts of impotency in front of goal, like his run of not scoring at the end of 1991/92, something Ferguson cited as a reason for the title slipping away from their grasp that season.

Indeed, even his transfer, which was welcomed by the fans who saw it as a return of the prodigal son, was one that Ferguson was less convinced about. After taking over as manager, the Scot made it a point to have lunch with Jimmy Murphy, Sir Matt Busby's trusted assistant. Murphy was a proud Welshman and was a big fan of his compatriot Hughes. During that meal, Murphy urged Ferguson to re-sign the striker from Barcelona.

Hughes had had a difficult time in Spain, where he scored just four times in 28 appearances. Once Ferguson made his interest known, Hughes jumped at the chance to return to the club where he was so adored by supporters.

At the beginning of 1995, United trailed Blackburn Rovers at the top of the table by three points. They had also scored fewer goals from more games, with the Rovers strike force of Alan Shearer and Chris Sutton firing on all cylinders. Cantona was still performing at the level expected of him but Ferguson was becoming concerned with his Welsh marksman. 'Hughes was 31 and we had to think about the future,' Ferguson said of his striker.

Following the acquisition of Andy Cole for a British record £7m in what was probably the last true 'surprise' transfer in British history, the writing was on the wall for Hughes. However, he was given a stay of execution towards the end of January by virtue of something that he had nothing to do with.

The night of 25 January 1995 became a date indelibly marked on the history of Manchester United Football Club due to the immediate aftermath of Eric Cantona's dismissal for a kick at Crystal Palace defender Richard Shaw. The centre-back had been niggling at the French striker all match and Cantona lashed out in response. A red card and an early bath ensued. That was not the main talking point of the evening, though. As Cantona walked down the touchline he received abuse based on his nationality from Palace supporter Matthew Simmons. The French striker responded with a kung-fu kick at the fan, as well as throwing a few punches before being dragged away by United kit man Norman Davies.

It was a remarkable scene, and one that would eventually see the Frenchman banned for eight months, but commentator Clive Tyldesley closed his evening's work with the following words, 'Nothing will keep the name of Eric Cantona out of the morning headlines. Sent off again. Alex Ferguson knows all the after-match questions will be about the fifth red card in the Manchester United career of Eric Cantona.' Why was Tyldesley not talking about the altercation with the fan? Simple really. 'I hadn't seen it,' he said. 'Not my finest hour, as I missed it. I knew he'd been sent off, and referenced how Manchester United were down to ten men, but it wasn't until after I left the ground I realised the magnitude of what Eric had done.'

Ferguson seemed oblivious too, as he stared into the abyss while Cantona was leaping into the crowd. It was only when he got home that Ferguson realised the magnitude of what had taken place. His initial reaction was to get rid of the Frenchman. He ultimately changed his mind, a decision he would not regret.

The consequence of Cantona's actions and subsequent ban were that in the immediate future, at least, any plans to sell Hughes had to be shelved.

Hughes was the perfect foil for Cantona, and Ferguson hoped Cole could be a similarly effective partner for the Frenchman, but with added goals. However, due to Cantona's lengthy ban, the manager was left with a marriage of inconvenience involving Hughes and Cole. The former was someone who could hold the ball up and bring others, particularly midfielders and wingers, into play. Cole was someone who could run in behind defenders, latching on to through balls, in order to score goals. Hardly a match made in heaven, but the pair managed to plough through the second half of the season, albeit an occasionally interrupted one for Hughes, as he would still find himself on the bench from time to time, despite the manager's lack of attacking options.

Andrei Kanchelskis

Relations between Alex Ferguson and the Ukrainian winger Andrei Kanchelskis had frequently been strained during the wide man's four years at the club. It still didn't take away from the shock at his eventual departure in the summer of 1995, after being arguably one of the more consistent performers during that season.

Kanchelskis was a big hit with the fans and offered the side balance, with a right-footed player on the right-hand side of the pitch, long before the idea of an inverted winger became fashionable. In many ways, though, with his ability to cut inside and strike with either foot, he was arguably Cristiano Ronaldo a decade in advance. His ability to score goals was recognised by United supporters, but also by his manager, despite their occasional differences. However, Ferguson was becoming increasingly aware of external influences surrounding the Ukrainian, and money was at the centre of the issue. Kanchelskis had a clause in his contract that entitled him to a third of any upcoming transfer fee, which was bound to turn the head of even the wealthiest footballer, particularly as his valued soared towards £6m.

What was to come was to shape the futures of Ince, Hughes and Kanchelskis, as well as the club and an array of young talent. It would also propel Ferguson to even greater heights. Once again, the theme of setbacks is crucial in the decisions that were about to be made.

West Ham United 1 Manchester United 1

Despite what had been a troubled campaign, Manchester United went into the last match of the season still in with a chance of winning the title, though they knew only victory would suffice. Nevertheless, one slip from title rivals Blackburn Rovers would be enough if Ferguson's men could grab all three points from their last game.

Ferguson was encouraged by what he viewed as faltering opponents, perhaps seeing echoes of what had occurred to both himself and his side in the failed challenge of 1992. 'It is my habit to pay attention to post-match interviews with the managers of teams who are in close competition with us,' Ferguson said, with a keen eye on Blackburn boss Kenny Dalglish. Ferguson and his opposite number go back a long way. In fact, all the way to a reserve match in 1969 between Rangers and Celtic, with Ferguson playing as a centre-forward for the blue half of Glasgow, and Dalglish representing the Hoops.

Both tough Glaswegians, Ferguson was keen to get one over his long-standing rival from across town as the 1994/95 season entered the final straight. So much so he watched every second of Dalglish's post-match interviews, paying particular scrutiny to his body language, rather than what he was actually saying. 'The words a man utters don't interest me much,' Ferguson said. 'It is the face that I search and I thought I discerned quite a change in Kenny Dalglish from earlier in the season. Kenny was singing all the right songs but he didn't seem to be enjoying them.'

He may have been right. United whittled away at Blackburn's advantage in the run-in, meaning a victory against familiar foes West Ham on the last day, coupled with a slip from Blackburn at Anfield against Liverpool, would see the Premier League trophy residing at Old Trafford for the third season running.

Liverpool away was always going to be a tricky fixture for Rovers, and Ferguson quickly dismissed any favours Blackburn manager Dalglish could expect from his former club. That was 'foolish talk', according to the United manager, despite Dalglish being 'the most admired player in Liverpool's history. There was no doubt that Blackburn would have a tough time on Merseyside. I knew that and so did Kenny.'

But United were going to be in for a tricky match of their own at Upton Park against a West Ham side who, just like in 1992, had nothing to play for. This time, however, the Hammers were well clear of relegation in 13th place. Just like three years previously, though, the West Ham players were fired up as if their lives depended on it, rather than a meaningless fixture that would determine where in mid-table they would finish.

Ferguson made a brave call in leaving out striker Mark Hughes in the belief that the Welshman could do damage later in the game as the Hammers began to tire. When told he would be a substitute, Hughes didn't take it well. Ferguson later said he regretted not starting the 31-year-old.

West Ham took the lead on the half-hour mark through a Hughes of their own, midfielder Michael, who scored a neatly taken goal to leave United on the ropes.

United almost struck back immediately when Andy Cole did everything right, except score, as he saw his smart effort come back off the post with goalkeeper Luděk Mikloško gratefully looking on.

The West Ham crowd began to sing 'there's only one Alan Shearer', taunting opposition fans after United failed to land the Blackburn striker. They did so in the knowledge that Shearer's first-half strike at Anfield had given Rovers a seemingly unassailable advantage at the top of the table. Blackburn led by five points as the United players trudged off at half-time.

Ferguson's introduction of Hughes for midfielder Nicky Butt at the interval was a clear sign of attacking intent. The away side's urgency was immediately apparent. Within a minute of the restart, Mikloško pulled off a miraculous save from a Lee Sharpe header.

Shortly afterwards, Paul Ince, hitherto quiet, unlike the crowd who booed every touch of their former player, went on a driving run forward, before possession was lost. Tellingly, once West Ham had the ball, Ince seemed in no hurry to return to defensive duties. Once he did get back to the centre of the park, he stood with his hands on his hips, seemingly out of breath from his previous foray into enemy territory.

Despite Ince's travails, United were provided with a lifeline on 52 minutes thanks to a Brian McClair header which made the score 1-1. The Scotsman could have, and possibly should have, made a hero of himself a few minutes later, but he volleyed over from just six yards with the goal at his mercy.

A few minutes later, John Barnes equalised for Liverpool at Anfield, meaning that United were now within one goal of glory. News of Barnes's goal soon filtered through to Upton Park to cheers among the away support. Ferguson rose from the bench as if he now felt momentum was with his side. He kept urging his team forward and gesturing to his players with one finger on each hand, indicating the score at Anfield.

Scrambles followed in and around West Ham's penalty area as the 'excitement became unbearable', Ferguson later wrote in his autobiography. 'But the ball just wouldn't go in.'

The last 30 minutes at Upton Park turned into the Luděk Mikloško show. First he kept out a goal-bound header from Hughes. Next up the Czech goalkeeper thwarted Andy Cole with the former Newcastle striker through on goal. Just minutes later he saved from point-blank range, and once again it was Cole who was the goalkeeper's prey. Indeed, Mikloško is so synonymous with frustrating Manchester United, having done so in 1992 and 1995, that if you begin to write his name in Google, you will see an association with the Old Trafford club before the team he represented so distinctly in blowing Ferguson's team off their title paths.

When the final whistle went, news came through that Liverpool had actually beaten Blackburn but it mattered not. The title was heading to Ewood Park.

Ferguson was quick to usher his players towards the dressing room, perhaps fearful of some overly jubilant home support causing trouble.[20] Whatever it was, he soon told his players how proud he was of their achievements, particularly

---

20 His response to the final day title loss to Manchester City in 2012 could not have been more different. That day, at Sunderland's Stadium of Light, Ferguson was keen for his players to go and acknowledge the away support. Upton Park was a far more vociferous and intimidating arena than the new home of Sunderland.

as he had to pick them up ahead of the FA Cup Final against Everton which lay just six days ahead.

Everton 1 Manchester United 0

A couple of hours before kick-off at Wembley, an exhibition match took place between legends of both Everton and Manchester United. The oldest player on the pitch was former Old Trafford stalwart Bill Foulkes, who was strutting his stuff at the age of 63. Foulkes, who passed away in 2013, is fourth in the all-time list of appearances for Manchester United. But his place in the hearts of supporters comes mainly from being a part of the Busby Babes side of the 1950s, and with it, a survivor of the Munich air crash that saw 23 people lose their lives, including eight players.

Everton won the exhibition match 1-0. It turned out to be an indicator of what was to follow.

The modern day version of the team in blue was described by Ferguson as 'ordinary' while Everton's cup final song was a rehash of The Farm's 'All Together Now,' almost as if they knew only a strong sense of team spirit would enable them to defy the odds at Wembley.

Ferguson was desperate for his players to show that kind of togetherness, safe in the knowledge he had the better group at his disposal, but he was about to be let down by one of his key henchmen.

As Paul Ince picked up the ball deep in the attacking third and with Denis Irwin in acres of space on the left, the midfielder lost the ball to Everton defender Dave Watson, much to the frustration of his manager. Unfortunately for Ince, Everton took full advantage of regaining possession. Anders Limpar collected the ball and with Ince stranded, the lush green space in front of the impish winger must have seemed too good to be true. Ferguson lamented, 'I could feel the threat as Limpar attacked our two central defenders, with Paul not remotely in touch or looking like getting back.'

The Swedish international laid the ball off to his overlapping full-back, Matt Jackson, who cut inside. This was all too easy, and Everton were now into United's penalty area. Jackson teed up Graham Stuart, who struck the bar. The respite lasted just seconds, though, as Paul Rideout nodded home the rebound for what was to be the only goal of the game.

While Everton goalkeeper Neville Southall rightly earned praise for his performance between the sticks, Ferguson's men had fallen short of the high standards he demanded of them – and he let them know in no uncertain terms in the dressing room afterwards. He said losing 'to a team as ordinary as Everton is just not acceptable. If some players had let their team-mates down, on or off the field, they would not be at Old Trafford much longer.'

Nevertheless, this season's end didn't have the same kind of depressive feel as 1992. Sure, it was United's first without a trophy in six years, but fans were still optimistic about the future, citing the absence of Cantona as the key factor in the club's failure to land silverware. He would be back, alongside all the other great players, such as Ince, Hughes and Kanchelskis. Ferguson, however, had other ideas.

The decision to sell Ince was in fact made four days before the cup final loss to Everton, to the dismay of the United board as Ferguson made his intentions clear. Ince had become popular among fans, unaware that he was not following his manager's instructions. He was an England regular and would go on to attract a £6m fee as Inter Milan nabbed the player many supporters thought would be the fulcrum of the United side for a number of years to come.

Hughes wanted to leave for pastures new, despite having seemingly committed his future to the club just months before. He was an Old Trafford legend, but because of his age, and the signing of Cole in the January, his departure was more understandable. It didn't prevent the feeling of sadness engulfing supporters, though, and the manager's purchase of Cole could be seen as an indirect forcing of Hughes's hand.

On the sales of Ince and Hughes, as a Red himself, Gary Neville was unequivocal which of the two he was more surprised to see let go. 'When Ince finally left in 1995, plenty of people wondered what the boss was doing. After the disastrous conclusion to the previous campaign, he'd wielded the axe. But the big shock was Sparky [Mark Hughes]. I was in my car when I heard on the radio that he'd left for Chelsea. I was as stunned as any Stretford Ender.'

There was one player, perhaps even more than Cantona, who was sorely missed towards the end of the 1994/95 season, and that was top scorer and supporters' player of the year Andrei Kanchelskis. The Ukrainian had struck 15 goals, including a hat-trick against Manchester City, in 32 games, before succumbing to a hernia injury that meant he was absent for the last two months of the campaign. His final appearance came in a 3-0 victory at home to Arsenal on 22 March. Fittingly he was on the scoresheet, though few fans had any clue it would be his last goal for United. Indeed, the Ukrainian winger has since spoken of his regret at leaving Old Trafford and the supporters were certainly sorry to see him go.

The circumstances surrounding Kanchelskis's departure were possibly the most sinister Ferguson would encounter in all his 26 and a half years at the club. The negotiations between the winger and the Old Trafford hierarchy concluded with his agent, Grigory Essaoulenko, delivering some chilling words in the direction of chairman Martin Edwards. 'If you don't sell him now, you will not be around much longer,' Ferguson recalled the agent saying in his book *Managing My Life*. 'There was no doubting the seriousness of the threat,' Ferguson wrote. 'The meeting ended shortly afterwards, much to our relief. We needed time to consider the implications of that alarming encounter. Obviously, Martin had most to think about, given the menacing words he had just heard.'

The chairman asked club solicitor Maurice Watkins what the next move should be. 'Sell him,' Watkins said unequivocally. Ferguson added, 'By now, I couldn't have agreed more.'

The fans were blissfully unaware of these goings-on and were desperately keen for Kanchelskis to stay, particularly in light of the departures of Ince and Hughes. Though David Beckham would later emerge as the right-sided player to replace the Ukrainian, even Ferguson thought he wasn't quite ready to fill Kanchelskis's boots. For the next 12 months the United manager was desperate to find a player who could fulfil that role. A failed effort to prise Darren Anderton away from Tottenham Hotspur meant Ferguson plumped for the Czech Republic winger Karel Poborský in the summer of 1996, though he never came close to matching the achievements of his Ukrainian predecessor. If there was ever an example of not buying a player based on a good tournament, Poborský would be just that. After starring for his country at Euro 96 he couldn't hit those heights at Old Trafford and was sold after just 32 appearances in a two-year spell at the club.

Ferguson had seen enough in the failings of the 1994/95 season, culminating in those disappointing results against West Ham and Everton. He felt the club had to go in a different direction. Ultimately it would prove to be both the bravest, and arguably the best, decision he ever made as United boss. He had missed out on two trophies at the death, along with the loss of his talisman, Eric Cantona, for eight months. Now he had elected to sell three of the players who had earned him so much success over the last six years. However, there is a strong argument that each and every one of these 'losses' made both the club and its manager even stronger.[21]

Not that many saw it that way at the time, as Ferguson was the first to admit in his autobiography. 'The decision to sell

---

21 For losses, read setbacks, whether that be the departures of Hughes, Ince and Kanchelskis or the failure to land a trophy.

Paul Ince was mine alone,' Ferguson wrote, and the fans knew that, which made them all the more perplexed. With Hughes, there was a semblance of reason. With Kanchelskis, though the most difficult to replace, they would, upon reflection, realise he was toying with the club and that money was at the heart of his decision to leave. But with Ince, there was no explanation until Ferguson put pen to paper four years later in his book. 'No one at Old Trafford was inclined to let me forget. There was nothing splendid about my isolation as our supporters reacted angrily to the jettisoning of a player they saw as a vital contributor to our recent successes. I agreed wholeheartedly with that assessment but felt I had to act on my conviction that the fundamental change in Paul's attitude, his insistence on trying to assume a role for which he was not equipped, had diminished his usefulness to the point where a transfer made absolute sense.'

The *Manchester Evening News* even ran a poll, asking whether Ferguson should be sacked on the back of a trophy-less season and the sales of the three crowd favourites. More than half who voted believed Ferguson's time was up, though there is a strong suspicion to this day that a number of mischievous Manchester City fans took part in the survey to skew the numbers. Nevertheless, it gives you some idea of the ill-feeling there was towards the manager at this tumultuous time.

Ferguson said at the time, 'One of the main reasons why I decided I could afford to let Ince go was because of young Nicky Butt. I believe a midfield combination of Roy Keane and Butt will be as good as anything you find throughout the Premiership. He [Butt] is still only 20 but I have no doubt that he will be in the full England team before he is much older. It wouldn't be right to block his development. His chances would have been more limited if Ince was still at the club. We also have David Beckham coming along in leaps and bounds. Of course allowing a player of Ince's qualities to leave Old Trafford is a gamble. In fact you could say I am gambling on youth.' Ferguson's love of a gamble was about to pay dividends.

4 (ii)

… to you can win anything with kids

IF THE decision to sell three of United's stars was difficult enough for fans to swallow, the inability to sign anyone in their place was seen as criminal. But Ferguson wanted to promote the talent that was coming through that he and his assistant, Brian Kidd, had been nurturing for several years. The youth team had won trophies and Ferguson felt they were ready to become first team regulars. Indeed, Gary Neville had already reached this level, joining Ryan Giggs in coming through the ranks, and becoming one of the first names on Ferguson's team-sheet. The manager now felt there were three more youngsters ready to fill the void created by the departures of Paul Ince, Mark Hughes and Andrei Kanchelskis. Step forward – Nicky Butt, Paul Scholes and David Beckham.

The intensity of doubt surrounding the manager didn't show any sign of letting up when, after losing 3-1 to Aston Villa on the opening day of the 1995/96 season, Alan Hansen decried Ferguson's transfer policy. The former Liverpool defender turned BBC pundit said, 'They've got problems. Obviously three players have departed. The trick is always – buy when you're strong. So he needs to buy players. You can't win anything with kids.'

Surprisingly, Ferguson did not entirely disagree with the sentiment. Yet while he recognised the importance of maturity, he felt it was inappropriate to accuse his team of not having old enough heads to cope with the rigours of a Premier League season. He concluded his side had bags of experience in the shape of Schmeichel, Irwin, Bruce, Pallister, Keane, McClair and the soon-to-return Cantona. Ferguson also believed the new crop of youngsters coming through would be the 'exception to the rule' regarding a lack of experience as they were a 'group of remarkable young footballers', he said.

Ferguson himself was enjoying a new lease of life seeing the youngsters emerge from the opening day defeat to go on a run of five successive victories. The manager said he gained 'immense pleasure' from Beckham, Butt, Scholes and the Neville brothers justifying his faith in them.

The season was ticking along nicely when the first day of October arrived. But this was not just the time of the year that the leaves were about to fall, it was the moment for Cantona to spring into action after an eight-month absence, albeit this time his dive towards the crowd was out of joy as he celebrated scoring the equaliser with the fans. His penalty salvaged a draw against Liverpool and kept United firmly in title contention.

However, this began to slip away as Newcastle United, under Kevin Keegan, went on a run that meant, come 21 January, the Magpies held a 12-point advantage over the team from Old Trafford with just 15 games to play. In fact, United had dropped to third after a run of poor form that included a 4-1 loss at Spurs. It was time for United and their manager to show their mettle once again, with seven 1-0 victories in the next 13 games, five of which were decided by the returning talisman Cantona. Peter Schmeichel was also justifying his tag as the best goalkeeper his manager had ever seen, particularly in a 1-0 win at St James' Park that swung the title balance in United's favour. Cantona got the crucial winner that day.

There was one blip during the closing stages of the campaign when Ferguson excused his players for a dismal first-half display against Southampton due to the colour of the kit. Ferguson and his players were so convinced that their shirts were to blame for the 3-0 half-time deficit that the team emerged for the second half in a blue and white strip, as opposed to the grey outfit they donned in the opening 45 minutes. There may have been rhyme in their reason as the team managed to pull a goal back in their new colours in what turned out to be a 3-1 defeat. But there was nothing grey about United's end-of-season form as that defeat at The Dell was the only loss the team would suffer during those final 15 games, of which they won 13.

One of the 1-0 victories came at home to Leeds, just after the Southampton debacle. The Yorkshire side were now a shadow of the team that denied United the league four years before. But Ferguson, despite the win, was outraged at the level of performance the Leeds players had shown. He accused them of 'cheating their manager' in reference to the level of effort they were prepared to put in at Old Trafford compared to other displays that season. Ferguson then challenged them to repeat that performance against Newcastle as he said, 'For some it's more important to get a result against Manchester United, to stop us winning the league, than anything else, which to me, they're cheating their manager. Of course, when they come to Newcastle, you wait to see the difference.'

Ferguson almost certainly was playing mind games, but not with the Newcastle manager Kevin Keegan. He was genuinely frustrated with the Leeds players, who he believed were not giving their all for the beleaguered Howard Wilkinson, with whom he had struck up a good friendship. He also wanted to stiffen the resolve of the Yorkshire side in the hope that they might deny the Geordies a much-needed three points in the upcoming Monday night match, to be played in front of a live audience on Sky.

Kevin Keegan was outraged by Ferguson's remarks. After the game at Elland Road, which Newcastle won 1-0 to still give themselves an outside chance of the title, he ranted to the Sky cameras, 'When you do that with footballers like he said about Leeds, and when you do things like that about a man like Stuart Pearce ... I've kept really quiet but I'll tell you something, he went down in my estimation when he said that. We have not resorted to that.'

Ferguson had also made comments about an upcoming Stuart Pearce testimonial against Keegan's team. Pearce's Nottingham Forest still had to play the Magpies in the run-in. Ferguson cheekily suggested that it may influence the level of effort the left-back and his team-mates might put into that penultimate match of the league season.[22]

What made Keegan's tirade all the more amusing is that it was conducted while wearing huge headphones, making him seem more like a backing vocalist for Band Aid than a football manager. Keegan didn't see the funny side as he concluded his rant with the famous words, 'You can tell him now, we're still fighting for this title and he's got to go to Middlesbrough and get something. And I'll tell you, honestly, I will love it if we beat them. Love it.' United went to Middlesbrough and did get something – the Premier League trophy.

For Ferguson, the stress of the previous summer was over and was made all the sweeter when he landed the FA Cup, beating Liverpool and their famous white suits in the final to win his second double in three seasons. Roy Keane was 'incredible' in what turned out to be a tactical masterclass. The Irishman broke up play consistently throughout the match and was instructed to pay close attention to Steve McManaman. Ferguson was obsessive about the danger the Liverpool midfielder posed and wanted Keane to snuff him out, which he duly did. Ferguson couldn't help but have a joke

---

22 Newcastle dropped two crucial points in that game against Forest, drawing 1-1.

at Liverpool's expense. 'The players were given a boost before a ball was kicked when our opponents turned up looking like a squad of bakers in cream-coloured suits.' United won, 1-0 of course – Eric Cantona getting the winner, who else!

For Ferguson, the summer of 1996 became largely about the pursuit of one man – Alan Shearer. The Scot loved his horses but this was a chase he would be pursuing for the last time after previous overtures proved fruitless. This time a world record fee was going to be required, £15m, but it was one the club were prepared to pay. Unfortunately for Ferguson, there were other hurdles to surmount, not least a stubborn Jack Walker. The Blackburn owner was reluctant to let his star striker leave, but if he did, Walker was adamant it would not be to Old Trafford. United chairman Martin Edwards explains, 'Shearer had been to Alex Ferguson's house, spoke to him and assured him he wanted to come. The problem, I think, was with the chairman of Blackburn, Jack Walker, who was not a great fan of Manchester United, [we were] local rivals, both Lancashire clubs. He did not want Alan Shearer to come to Manchester United. Shearer was quite close to Walker, who was like a father figure to him, and I don't think Alan wanted to upset him by coming to United. And I'm not sure Jack would have let him come anyway, whereas he was happy for Alan to go to Newcastle. I don't think that was a threat to him.'

There was a second obstacle – Shearer's desire to play for his hometown club. Nevertheless, the decision of the Blackburn number nine left Ferguson 'baffled'. As always, the manager's response was majestic. 'When I woo a player on behalf of Manchester United, I do it wholeheartedly, but rejection doesn't leave me broken-hearted. I know there may be a more fruitful relationship around the corner.' Electing the black and white of Newcastle as opposed to the red of Manchester just meant Shearer was added to a list of players who ended up not coming to Old Trafford, only for Ferguson to respond with aplomb. For the failure to land Paul Gascoigne, see the acquisition of Paul Ince. Shearer's decision to turn down the United manager first time around was quickly followed by the purchase of Eric Cantona for a third of the price. For the second rejection from Shearer, it was Ole Gunnar Solskjaer who would be bought. All of these would be followed by a hatful of trophies, almost as if you can come along for the ride if you want but if you turn down the juggernaut of success, it does not matter, the trophies will still come along, but it will be someone else collecting the medals.

For the 1996/97 season, United started where they left off, with the youngsters firing on all cylinders and Cantona conducting the orchestra. The season began with a sensational goal by David Beckham from the halfway line and the team were unbeaten going into an autumn quartet of tricky league fixtures, starting at St James' Park against Newcastle. Kevin Keegan's side thumped United 5-0, including a strike from familiar foe Alan Shearer. His assist and celebration in front of the away end increased the hostility felt between Shearer and the travelling supporters. The display from the Magpies was topped off by a cheeky chip from defender Philippe Albert that left Peter Schmeichel looking up to the sky, hoping the ball would never drop, but it did, and into his net. The Newcastle fans gleefully showed the palms of their hands and five outstretched digits to the away support, some of whom were already filing out of the stands. The ones that remained had just one middle finger to show in response.

'I always remember standing at the top of the steps as they left the ground,' wrote Kevin Keegan in his autobiography. 'One by one, they filed past, ashen-faced: Peter Schmeichel, Gary Neville, Denis Irwin, Gary Pallister, David Beckham, Paul Scholes, Nicky Butt and all the rest. The last one out stopped to look me in the eye, and I learned in those moments that Eric Cantona spoke better English than I had realised. "Fucking good team you have here," he said.'

Newcastle chairman Sir John Hall, the man who along with his bank account and Keegan had turned the club from second tier also-rans into title contenders, was giddier than most. Hall strode confidently into the post-match press conference that rainy Sunday and proudly told the assembled media, 'Gentlemen, you've seen the next champions of England.' Hall was right, but it was the losing side that would go on to be champions, not his beloved Newcastle.

Nevertheless, there were further bumps in the road to success for United. If conceding five at Newcastle could be put down as a blip, yielding six more at Southampton less than a week later meant the club was on the verge of a crisis. That 6-3 defeat at The Dell meant United had let in more goals over the space of two matches than they had in the previous 17 combined.

An equally crushing 2-1 home defeat to Chelsea, a first loss at Old Trafford in the league in almost two years, saw United lurching from one setback to the next.

Less than 48 hours later, Ferguson took his team to Norwich City for a testimonial for Bryan Gunn, who had played under him at Aberdeen. It was a chance to blood some of the youth team alongside the senior pros. Defender Steve Bruce, who had left Old Trafford the previous summer, represented United on the night, though he had also played for the Canaries earlier in his career, prior to moving to Old Trafford. Bruce was on hand to remind the young players that they had better 'make the most of it while at Manchester United, because there's nothing like it. When you leave it's the end of life as you know it.' Ferguson mused eerily in response to his former captain's words, 'One day I will understand what that means.' No one could possibly have imagined that that day was still 17 years away.

The succession of disheartening defeats meant United's 'capacity to defend the championship' was being 'called into question', according to Ferguson, who added that the 'gravediggers' were out in force. There was no such death knell for the club, though, and Ferguson must take credit for staying calm in the face of such tumultuous criticism. 'I did not believe for a second that the double-winners of the previous season had suddenly turned into punchbags,' he said.

Keeping your head when all around you are losing theirs is not a trait often associated with Ferguson, but it is an under-rated strength of the Scot's in the face of adversity. And it certainly helped the club out of this particular mire as the clouds gathered over Old Trafford in November 1996. The tenth anniversary of Ferguson's arrival came and went but with slightly less fanfare due to the sudden loss of form. However, Ferguson remained calm. 'Others might feel that our commitment to Beckham, Butt, Scholes, Giggs and the Neville brothers represented an excessive faith in youth, but I knew that those players had character as well as talent.'

For the first time in several years, confidence was low at the club, but Ferguson's belief in both himself and the team remained intact, helping the side turn the slump around.

Nevertheless, he recognised he had 'to grasp the nettle and be honest about the areas where we are failing', he recalled at the time in his diary of the season. 'This is no time to fudge issues or make excuses.' Crucially, however, he acknowledged that 'in the past' he had 'always been a better manager in adversity'.

He was proved right in the spell that followed. A dogged performance at home to a resurgent Arsenal got the team back on track. United won 1-0 after one of the scrappiest goals of the Ferguson era. The spoils were earned after the ball went in off the thigh of the unfortunate Nigel Winterburn for an own goal, not that Ferguson or his side cared about the nature of the strike. The victory was made all the sweeter as it ended new manager Arsène Wenger's unbeaten run since taking up the reins at Highbury.

Having lost three league matches on the bounce, United's brief spell in the doldrums was over, and with it a clean sheet to boot. After the shambolic defending of recent weeks, it was the character of his side, and from his youngsters in particular, that pleased the manager most. 'Having lost three in a row with an aggregate score of 13-4,' Ferguson said, 'they made a win over Arsenal the start of a 16-match unbeaten run that transformed the title race.'

Ferguson also deserves praise for his handling of the mini-crisis. Not for the first time, he battened down the hatches, encouraged a siege mentality, shored up the defence, galvanised everyone and re-energised the belief with his unwavering trust in the players. It was enough to propel United to a second successive title.

5 (i)

From Arsenal jolt ...

IN THE summer of 1997 came a bolt from the blue – the retirement of Eric Cantona.

The imperious form of the Frenchman in the 1995/96 season had begun to tail off throughout the following term, and Ferguson began to worry about the striker's body shape – a sign of waning powers and motivation. Nevertheless, the player's decision to call it a day still came as a shock.

Ferguson had to find a replacement, and do so as soon as possible. He knew that his squad was bereft in this department. With the possible exception of Paul Scholes, he didn't have anyone who could operate effectively in the hole behind the striker, and the ginger genius was beginning to develop successfully as a central midfielder.

Ferguson made his move, paying Tottenham Hotspur £3.5m for Teddy Sheringham, who was a like-for-like replacement for Cantona. Like his predecessor, you always felt Sheringham would take as much pleasure in assisting as he would in scoring. Once again, Ferguson's ability to move on from a seismic shock with aplomb became apparent, though Sheringham would take time to settle at his new club. For some periods of the 1997/98 season it seemed as though the burden of replacing United's talisman would prove too much.

He began the season by missing a penalty at his former club Spurs, and ended it on the bench after a loss of form. 'Oh Teddy, Teddy, he went to Man United and he won fuck all!' opposing fans would taunt.

Though United's inability to win a third title in a row in 1998 cannot all be placed at the feet of Sheringham, his lack of goals in the second half of the season was notable. In fact, he didn't score a league goal from 28 December in a 3-2 loss at Coventry, until the last day of the season, on 10 May, in a 2-0 win at already-relegated Barnsley.

There was a reminder of Ferguson's insatiable desire to keep standards high during that defeat to Coventry at Highfield Road. John Curtis appeared as a 63rd-minute substitute, and with the points slipping away the full-back didn't show enough haste in retrieving the ball, in the opinion of his manager. 'He gave me the hair dryer,' Curtis recalled.[23] 'The ball went out for a goal kick and I didn't sprint to get the ball out of the ball boy's hand, to throw it to Pete, to try and get a goal. Ferguson bollocked me for that. That was the kind of thing, the kind of professionalism, tiny things, attention to detail. As a young kid I wasn't focussed on the result too much, I was more concerned with my own performance. I was new to the first team. He was never focussed so much on individual performance but only on the result.'

Ferguson and his coaching staff, including Eric Harrison, the man who developed the so-called Class of '92 – David Beckham, Ryan Giggs, Paul Scholes, Nicky Butt and the Neville brothers – instilled the winning mentality that ran right through the club. It was evident that day at Highfield Road, as far as Curtis was concerned. The full-back also played under Harrison for the youth team in the mid-90s. He said,

---

23 The hair dryer was a phrase coined by Mark Hughes. He said that Ferguson would get so close to your face when he was shouting at you that it was like having a hair dryer shoved in your direction, with the recipient's ears and hair forced back from the fierce criticism he would receive.

'There are things instilled in me about standards and attention to detail still to this day. The stuff we were brainwashed or indoctrinated with, coming through the system. Eric did such a good job with that.'

Manchester United 0 Arsenal 1

When evaluating United's lack of silverware in 1997/98 it would be doing Arsenal a disservice not to recognise the imperious form they displayed in overhauling the champions. But Ferguson was left to rue a run of poor results that had seen them blow a 13-point lead they held on Boxing Day over Arsène Wenger's team.

The match where the momentum firmly swung Arsenal's way, though, came at Old Trafford in the March of that season. Going into the so-called title decider, United held a nine-point lead, albeit having played three games more than their rivals. However, with a goal difference advantage of 16, it was still very much in United's hands.

The club were renowned for performing better in the second half of the season. But this was a case of Ferguson the leader, indoctrinating players, fans and even the media. When his claim was placed under scrutiny, a different story emerges. In the seven title chases since 1991/92, and including the 1997/98 pursuit, United had a better second half on just three occasions (1992/93, 1995/96 and 1996/97). The ability to perform strongly in the second half of the season was a mantra Ferguson would frequently peddle, and rarely did anyone question it. Given his authority in both the dressing room and the press conference, few dared to consider it might not be true.

Arsenal were without striker Ian Wright, unavailable after enduring an injury-hit season, and goalkeeper David Seaman. But United had concerns of their own. Gary Pallister, Ryan Giggs and long-term absentee Roy Keane all missed the game through injury. One of the beneficiaries was 19-year-old right-back John Curtis, who discovered he was going to play the day before. 'There were a few injuries. The boss was a big believer in young players,' Curtis recalls. 'Arsenal were our big rivals, it was a huge game.'

There was a slow pace to the beginning of the match. Perhaps Arsenal's ponderous start was an example of manager Arsène Wenger's assertion that a draw would be a good result for his team.

It was not long before Arsenal winger Marc Overmars put on the afterburners though. A quick one-two with the mercurial Dennis Bergkamp and the flying winger was away, easily showing Curtis a clean pair of heels, rounding Schmeichel, and seeing his effort flash across the face of goal from a narrow angle.[24]

Arsenal dominated the opening exchanges with Overmars at the centre of everything. Only one chance of note fell United's way but it was a good one. Lee Dixon gave away possession deep in his own half, with the ball ricocheting into the path of Sheringham, whose shot was dealt with smartly by Alex Manninger.

If United were hoping for some respite from Overmars, they were out of luck. Curtis was fortunate not to give away a penalty when challenging the Dutchman in the area. 'Would have been a penalty these days, definitely,' Curtis admits. Then, moments later, Overmars was on the ball again, jinking between Curtis and Gary Neville, before hitting the side-netting.

It was getting embarrassing for the home side in terms of the number of chances Arsenal were creating. Next up it was Ray Parlour, who hit the ball over when he had only Schmeichel to beat. Andy Cole was put through on goal after a long Schmeichel kick forward found its intended target, but the striker saw his shot hit Manninger's legs instead of the back

---

24 Bergkamp was named after United legend Denis Law, albeit their first names are spelt differently.

of the net. It gave United some short-lived belief the tide may be turning, but it was a false dawn.

The second half followed a similar pattern to the first, with Overmars again the thorn in United's side. On 52 minutes, Ferguson concluded it was someone else's turn to deal with the flying Dutchman. He hauled off Curtis and sent on winger Ben Thornley in his place, prompting a reorganisation of the team. Curtis has some regrets over how he handled Arsenal's wide man. He remembers ruefully, 'Overmars was one of those players who was so quick that in hindsight I shouldn't have got tight to him. He was so fast he would run in behind you. It was a difficult afternoon. It was tough. I wasn't relieved to come off but I was disappointed in my performance.'

As a result of the change, Phil Neville switched to right-back and would be the next to suffer from Overmars's pace and trickery.

Having come on for Curtis, Thornley didn't do himself justice either. The wide man burst on to the scene in the early 1990s, being a member of the Class of '92, before a debilitating knee injury hampered his prospects. As a result, Thornley readily admits he never quite got to enjoy the career he should have, and the same could be said of his substitute appearance against Arsenal. 'It was a mental thing, I knew what sort of a player I was before the injury. I knew I should have been a lot more advanced than I was. What was soul-destroying was I knew without the injury I would have had much more of an impact. I hadn't turned into a bad player, but the half a yard of pace I lost affected me on the highest level.'

With the game entering the latter stages it was still goalless and Arsenal knew they were missing a vital chance of putting the title destiny firmly in their own hands. Nicolas Anelka came on to replace Christopher Wreh up front and the prodigious talent soon made an impact.

Ole Gunnar Solskjaer replaced the younger Neville in the 77th minute. The substitution meant another switch on the field, with the older Neville moving to right-back to become the third player on the day tasked with managing Overmars. Two minutes later a lofted pass forward from Martin Keown found the head of Anelka. The French forward out-jumped David May, who had only been on the field a matter of seconds, to flick the ball on for his Dutch team-mate. Overmars headed the ball forward to place it ideally into his path and was now bearing down on goal. This time, however, there was a distinctly different outcome to his previous efforts as he smartly placed his shot past Schmeichel. Neville put his hands to his head as the net rippled. Centre-half Henning Berg also reacted as though the title had been lost in that moment, his face a picture of anguish, throwing his arms downward like a frustrated child who had just been deprived of the sweets they so desired. The Norwegian's grievance was possibly aimed at Neville, who had been drawn to the ball, thus handing Overmars an extra yard of space before scoring. He could also have been frustrated with May for having not prevented Anelka from flicking on. Indeed, Ferguson expressed his anger towards his defenders in the dressing room afterwards, lamenting their poor communication for the goal.

If Arsenal's first goal at Old Trafford in the Premier League era felt monumental, less than 15 minutes later it felt decisive as the full-time whistle went and the away bench was all congratulatory smiles, knowing they had taken a crucial step towards wresting the title from their rivals.

The Arsenal fans' glee after taking the three points at the Theatre of Dreams was understandable. Just moments after the whistle blew on United's title challenge, one Arsenal fan, unknown Barry Ferst, screamed in sheer delight, fists clenched, curly hair vibrating with the sense that this was a championship-winning performance. Rob Smyth wrote about Ferst's 15 seconds of fame in *The Guardian*, 'In 2013, the Bleacher Report website put him second on a list of iconic facial expressions in football history, sandwiched between Paul

Gascoigne at Italia 90 and Roberto Baggio at USA 94. "There hasn't really been any downside to it," he says. "Sometimes people ask you to do the face. If I've had ten pints I might try, but it's a bit weird when you're sober." Ferst's celebration showed what it was like to see your team win the biggest game of the season. You wonder whether [nowadays] a TV director would pick him out. There is a greater focus on banners and banter; contrived passion and outrage. Ferst had no idea anyone was looking at him, never mind a million people on Sky TV. His naked passion was totally authentic.'

Thornley spoke of the atmosphere within the United squad at the time, 'The pressure was beginning to build and that was a crucial game. If we had not lost we would have gone on and won the title. But with that game, the momentum shifted, and Arsenal were in the ascendancy. You could see it was taking its toll on the United players.'

The victory was the second in a ten-game sequence where Arsenal collected maximum points, sealing the Gunners' first championship in seven years. A Premier League trophy that had hitherto looked destined to remain at Old Trafford was now heading south.

Wenger's team had highlighted some of the issues within Ferguson's squad, which he was keen to address in what was to become his biggest transfer splurge to date.

The United manager found it difficult to admit Arsenal were the superior team. But it was obvious that Wenger and his smartly assembled squad were no one-season wonder. They were here for the long haul and the Old Trafford boss would have to dig deep, both mentally and into the United coffers, to serve up a response worthy of such a threat.

5 (ii)

... to back on the perch

ONE OF the problems Alex Ferguson had to solve was the strike force of Andy Cole and Teddy Sheringham, whose relationship off the pitch had deteriorated to the extent where they were no longer on speaking terms. On it, both had good opportunities to put United ahead against Arsenal, to effectively seal the title. But the chances were squandered. The pair had sporadic moments of joy in the 1997/98 season but 24 league goals between them was significantly short of what was expected. They lacked the consistency and harmony required to win the big games, thus the season ended without a trophy.

The 'animosity' Cole had for Sheringham stems from a time when the former Newcastle striker made his England debut. Sheringham didn't shake Cole's hand as the latter came on to replace him. Cole admitted, as he waited on the touchline for his international bow, that he was 'so nervous it was frightening' and that he felt 'embarrassed and confused' by the snub. The relationship deteriorated further in February 1998. Sheringham harshly blamed his strike partner for the concession of a goal against Bolton Wanderers at Old Trafford, in a game where two crucial points were dropped.

Cole told *The Independent* in 2010, 'We played together for years. We scored a lot of goals. I never spoke a single word to him. People wonder how on earth we could function like that. Gary Pallister once said to me, "I know you don't speak to Teddy and he doesn't speak to you, but at least you play well together." We did, and I wouldn't ever cast aspersions on Sheringham's talent as a top-rate footballer for his clubs and country. I've just loathed him personally for 15 years.'[25]

Maybe Pallister and Cole were in agreement that the partnership combined well, but Ferguson knew the team had to provide more in the attacking third in the season ahead.

Other issues revolved around the thinness of the squad. This was highlighted by Roy Keane's and Ryan Giggs's absences for large parts of the campaign.

Keane was sorely missed after he ruptured his cruciate knee ligament in a challenge with Alf-Inge Håland at Leeds United in September. He was out for the best part of a year and would later seek retribution on his Norwegian counterpart. But Ferguson was aware of just how much his side missed the Irishman. Keane was back for the start of the 1998/99 season – and better than ever before.

Giggs missed crucial moments during the season, largely due to hamstring issues, giving Ferguson plenty to ponder during the off-season.

The back four were also not working as effectively as the boss would like, and with Pallister departing, a gaping hole at the heart of the defence would have to be filled.

On this occasion, Ferguson used a more conventional way of fixing the problems with the team – the transfer market. Ferguson's solution to the questions posed by Arsène Wenger was to spend. And spend big.

If it was the Scot's long-term answer then he would have been found wanting, so he can be forgiven for resorting to it on this occasion. Indeed, he eventually saw off the threat of Wenger some years later and not by splurging the cash.

---

25 Their 24-year feud was put to bed in 2019 when Sheringham revealed, 'We've made our peace.'

Two of the players Ferguson acquired that summer were hardly the greatest finds. The arrival of the sought-after defender Jaap Stam for the princely sum of £10.6m was not exactly unearthing a gem, but represented a gamble all the same. His debut in a 3-0 defeat against Arsenal in the Charity Shield meant more eyebrows were raised among onlookers, particularly in a summer when Chelsea bought the more established Marcel Desailly for less than half the price of Stam.

The second purchase of the summer was to acquire someone who could cover for Giggs in the event that his hamstrings would fail him again. Ferguson went for a tried and trusted tactic of buying a player who had performed well against his team in the past. This time it was Jesper Blomqvist, who had terrorised the United defence previously when playing for IFK Gothenburg. The price for the Swede, who was now plying his trade for Italian side Parma, was £4.4m.

The third was not so obvious and something a little closer to the unconventional signing we saw in the shape of Eric Cantona some six years before. This time it was Dwight Yorke and the chase was a little more complicated, as well as expensive, coming in at £12.6m. But the complications arose from an unexpected source. Within the club there were doubts, not least from Ferguson's assistant Brian Kidd, who thought big John Hartson would be a better alternative. Ferguson gave that notion short shrift and it also added to his doubts about the capabilities of his assistant.

Hindsight is a wonderful thing. The retrospective thoughts of commentators who all say what a good player Yorke was and that him coming to Manchester United was an obvious choice for the manager are a case of being clever after the event. No other clubs were in for Yorke that summer, and especially at that price. Many saw Yorke as a happy-go-lucky, mid-table striker who may help you win a cup, but not the kind of trophies United were aiming for.

Gary Neville explains that the players had their doubts about Yorke, too. 'When Yorkey signed, it was late on in the transfer window. The season had already started, and it was a surprise in some ways. It came out of nowhere. Obviously, we knew Dwight Yorke from Aston Villa and he was a good player. You just didn't think he was the one that was coming to United. What we didn't realise was just how good he was.'

As it turned out, overcoming Wenger's Arsenal was just one of the obstacles for Ferguson to consider. He was beginning to find Kidd more and more difficult to work with, citing his assistant's tendency to complain too much.

There was more for the manager to ponder in the shape of David Beckham. The summer was dominated by the young midfielder's dismissal against Argentina in the World Cup. The media and many England fans blamed him for the national team's failure at the tournament as a result of his red card. A concerned United manager said he feared for Beckham, 'Much of the stuff that appeared in the papers seemed to be driven by something close to blood-lust. I found it nauseating and I worried about how David would cope with the vicious hounding that went on long after the World Cup was over.' In late August there was an effigy of Beckham hanging near Upton Park and t-shirts were printed for Hammers supporters with words expressing their anger towards the player.

Ferguson must take credit for the way he handled the situation, giving Beckham the support he needed and reminding him that United were by his side. Beckham also displayed incredible mental strength in how he turned things around, typified in the opening match of the season at home to Leicester City. His perfectly struck free kick earned United a draw in a match they seemed destined to lose. It was the beginning of a season which would yield the player nine goals, four of which were free kicks. The dead-ball scenario was becoming a trademark of his and Ferguson loved this characteristic in a player. Not the ability to take a good free kick necessarily, but the keenness to take the ball when the pressure was at its highest, and it was a trait he would admire greatly in Beckham that season.

Ferguson said, 'He never shirked the challenge. He always wanted the ball and that is a measure of a great player. I remember Brian Kidd telling a story of his own days in the United shirt, of how the team had a particularly tough away game at the end of the 1966/67 season, when they were trying to close in on the championship. Some of the players were nervous and one or two had just about bottled it. But before they went out, Bobby Charlton said, "Give me the ball and we'll be all right." Brian was convinced that Bobby won United the title that season. Anybody who has watched David Beckham play knows that he is always ready to shoulder responsibility. Nobody should ever underestimate David Beckham. At times I have disagreed with decisions he has taken off the field but he has a stubbornness that can't be broken, and he will make up his own mind, whatever Alex Ferguson may think. I do like to have control of my players as they grow up but it is impossible not to admire his resolve. It has served me well on many occasions. When the chips are down on the football field, you can bet your life David won't be found wanting.' High praise indeed, and Beckham repaid his manager's faith by the bucket-load.

Ferguson's determination to bounce back from the disappointment of the previous campaign was apparent in his dealings with Beckham and in the transfer market. He would soon get to reap the rewards as United hit top gear in the autumn, scoring goals galore with Yorke more than justifying Ferguson's record outlay on the striker with 12 goals in all competitions by the end of November. Even more significantly, Yorke had built up an excellent understanding with Andy Cole, who was now playing the best and most consistent football of his United career. The pair would seem to take as much pleasure in assisting each other's goals as they would from finding the back of the net themselves.

'There was a respect between each other,' Gary Neville explained. 'The thing about those two, they didn't mind which of them scored which is quite unique sometimes. Cole was a goalscorer, and you often find they need to score in order to be happy. But they got to the point when they didn't care if either of them scored, they'd both be happy with each other.'

Where the previous season United fell short due to the occasionally malfunctioning partnership of Sheringham and Cole, they were now benefitting from a different strike pairing, and one that, this time, struck up an excellent relationship off the pitch as well as on it. Yorke and Cole would regularly socialise together.

Ferguson also emphasised the duo's importance of having a good relationship away from the playing environment, 'Dwight was a really important signing because he and Andy Cole, from the minute they got together, seemed to have a great understanding and affinity for one another.'

For once, Ferguson can take little credit for this legendary partnership as he more or less came across it by chance, when it clicked into place in a 3-0 win at bogey side Southampton at the beginning of October. Before that, Ferguson had tried a variety of combinations up front, none of which had been truly satisfactory. Until that day at The Dell, Yorke and Cole had only started once together in 11 games, across all competitions. After the pair helped destroy Southampton, with a goal each, including an assist from Cole for Yorke's opener, the two started the next 13 Premier League and Champions League games together, wreaking havoc at home and abroad. United had scored 17 goals in their opening 11 matches at an average of 1.5. The team then netted 36 times in their next 13 outings at an average of 2.8, almost doubling their output with Cole and Yorke as the regular front two.

But the partnership was not a part of Ferguson's thinking at the beginning of the season. Indeed, the manager had been keen to bring in Dutch striker Patrick Kluivert in the summer of 1998, along with Yorke. That was the front line he wanted for the upcoming campaign. But Kluivert chose to stay with Barcelona, claiming United were no longer challengers for major trophies. The rest, as they say, is history.

The partnership would go on to score 53 goals that season and arguably become the key reason for United's unprecedented success. But it almost came about by accident, as Gary Neville confirms, 'I don't know what the plan was, because I don't think him and Cole really hit it off to start with. It took maybe ten or 15 games for them to get together, and then all of a sudden … '

Even if he stumbled across the partnership, Ferguson has to take praise for his determination to sign Yorke when many were doubting its logic. Ferguson said at the time, 'Yorke and Cole were a deadly partnership. Yorke had justified my conviction that he was a front player with a remarkable range of exceptional abilities. He is effortlessly neat on the ball, can beat opponents with swift dribbles or imaginative passes and is an excellent finisher. He has the heart and bodily strength to thrive in tough company and his joyous appetite for the game shines through the smile which is nearly always on his face. There is no doubt his arrival hugely benefitted Andy Cole. They are soulmates off the field, and on it Dwight's alertness and subtlety provide opportunities for Andy to exploit his pace and his predator's instincts.'

How Ferguson must have smiled to himself about the immediate impact of Yorke. After all, it was Brian Kidd, who had been with the club in a coaching capacity for more than ten years and beside the manager on the bench for more than seven, who had been most vociferous in his concerns about the acquisition of the Trinidad and Tobago striker. Now Ferguson could raise a glass and tell his assistant, 'I told you so.' However, where the relationship between Cole and Yorke blossomed, between Ferguson and Kidd it came to an abrupt end in December 1998. Kidd chose to go into management and take up the reins at struggling Blackburn Rovers, much to Ferguson's surprise. He was 'stunned by the news', not least as the boss had never heard of his assistant's desire to be a number one.

Nevertheless, Ferguson again proved that he could overcome a blow, learn, and even improve as a result. His next assistant, Steve McClaren, would prove at least Kidd's equal on the training pitch, and perhaps even more astute in helping the team outwit wily opponents. He had developed a reputation as one of the most tactically astute coaches in the country, using modern methods such as video analysis and sports psychologists.

Moving on from the disappointment of losing his right-hand man was something Ferguson had experienced before with the sudden departure of Archie Knox in 1991. But each time, he dusted himself down and looked for a successor that could continue moving the club in the right direction.

Kidd has gone on to have a stellar coaching career, though always as an assistant rather than as a manager, where he failed dismally at Blackburn and has never been back in such a role since. With McClaren on board, United now had a coach of the highest pedigree. He would go on to have success with Middlesbrough as the main man, and even land the England manager's job, albeit one he had to relinquish after a failed campaign to qualify for Euro 2008. However, McClaren's contribution to Manchester United's treble-winning campaign cannot be underestimated and fully justified Ferguson's determination to have him by his side after an exhaustive search. 'I had instructed Eric Harrison, our former youth coach, and Les Kershaw, director of the academy, to scour England for the best candidates in terms of coaching ability and work ethic,' Ferguson mused. Interesting how his focus included work ethic, clearly an essential ingredient for the Scotsman. 'Their researches had kept coming back to Steve. When I assessed his credentials I was sure he was the right man.' In McClaren's time at the club, United won the treble in his first season, and the league title in the next two, thus he was part of a championship winning managerial team in each of his three seasons at the club. Not bad for a man who was introduced by United chairman Martin Edwards as 'Steve McClaridge', perhaps confusing him with the former Leicester City striker of a similar name.

At the beginning of 1999, as the club set out to win the FA Cup for the fourth time in the Ferguson era, the team were about to embark on a period that would personify its manager more than ever. Harking back to the FA Cup quarter-final defeat at home to Nottingham Forest a decade before, Ferguson lamented his team's lack of commitment to the cause. 'Where was the passion that was supposed to run through Alex Ferguson teams?' When he looked at his team he realised it did not mirror its manager 'in any way, shape or form'. Now, ten years on, the team he had built very much resembled its manager, particularly in its fortitude, embodied in the fourth round defeat of Liverpool at Old Trafford in the same competition. The away side took an early lead through Michael Owen and destiny seemed to be on their side. United missed chance after chance. Roy Keane struck the woodwork twice as Liverpool rode their luck. 'I told you – this is Liverpool's day,' Andy Gray said with conviction in the Sky commentary box seconds after Keane hit the post for a second time. And few could disagree with that assertion as the game entered the 88th minute. Step forward David Beckham, who struck an inviting set piece into the danger zone. On the bench, Ferguson moved his head, as if to knock the ball across goal, which is exactly what Cole did for his strike partner Yorke to tap home. And 1-1 soon became 2-1 as Ole Gunnar Solskjaer took advantage of a weary defence having come on as a substitute for Gary Neville as United chased the game. The Norwegian slotted his shot home past Liverpool goalkeeper David James. Cue delirium. It was the kind of fightback that was to epitomise not just the season but where the club was, ten years on from that dreadful defeat to Forest. Now, Ferguson had a team in his image.

'When critics of our game parade their theories about the attributes that lift certain teams above others,' Ferguson contemplated, 'I am always amused by their eagerness to concentrate almost exclusively on technical and tactical comparisons. Frequently they discuss football in abstract terms, overlooking the reality that it is played by creatures of flesh and blood and feeling. The best teams stand out because they *are* teams, because the individual members have been so truly integrated that the team functions with a single spirit. There is a constant flow of mutual support among the players, enabling them to feed off strengths and compensate for weaknesses. They depend on one another, trust one another. A manager should engender that sense of unity. He should create a bond among his players and between him and them that raises performances to heights that were unimaginable when they started out as disparate individuals. The Manchester United of 1999 had talent by the bundle but there was nothing about them that I admired or valued more than their team spirit.'

The squad unity would play a crucial role, especially for those out of the team. The importance of substitutes as the season progressed became apparent. So many goals or key contributions would come from those who began the game on the bench. On one occasion, Solskjaer entered the fray in a league match at Nottingham Forest, with the game already won. The Norwegian was told by the coaching staff to keep it tight, play it safe and not do anything silly. 'I was sitting there thinking, "4-1, I'm not coming on today." Andy and Dwight were on fire as well. But then the boss said, "Ole, come change." And Jim Ryan had some famous words, "We don't need any more goals, just keep the ball, pass it, play nice and simple.'" The striker had other ideas, such was his determination to make an impact, scoring four goals in the last ten minutes in a game United won 8-1.

By now Ferguson's team were firing on all cylinders, but it was mental fortitude as much as talent that would eventually see them over the line as the season entered a crucial phase.

That determination and mental strength was on show again in April. This time United's steely resolve would face a much stiffer test in the shape of Arsène Wenger's Arsenal, who stood in the way of Ferguson and his desire for success just like they had a year before.

It was the semi-final of the FA Cup and the tie went to what would be the last ever replay at this stage of the tournament after a drab 0-0 on the Sunday. All the disappointment from the first outing turned to drama in the second. United took the lead through an impressive long-range effort from Beckham in the 17th minute after a deft touch from Sheringham set him up. United were on top, creating the better chances. Solskjaer could have had a hat-trick but some uncharacteristically wayward finishing, as well as smart saves from David Seaman, frustrated the Norwegian.

Nevertheless, United were looking comfortable until Lady Luck shone on Arsenal midway through the second half. A Dennis Bergkamp shot deflected off fellow Dutchman Jaap Stam, evaded Schmeichel, and nestled in the back of the net to make it 1-1.

The momentum of the match had swung, seemingly decisively, in Arsenal's favour, when Nicolas Anelka rounded Schmeichel to slot home. Arsenal were jubilant but there was to be a sting in the tail. The linesman, who had the bushiest moustache you will ever see on a touchline, had flagged, and denied what appeared to be a winning goal for the Gunners. It's lucky the linesman never made it as a professional footballer as his facial hair would have been in an offside position on a permanent basis. Fur-related news aside, it took Anelka 30 seconds to realise his effort had been ruled out due to the celebrations that included being mobbed by Arsenal fans. This only added to the drama of the occasion. Upon seeing the linesman's flag, Anelka stopped in his tracks as he ran away from the euphoric supporters, and his face went from elation to despair at the sudden realisation his goal would not count.

The thrills and spills of the evening were now gathering pace. Within 60 seconds of Anelka's moment of anguish, Roy Keane was sent off for a second bookable offence. The Irishman's dismissal made a United victory all the more improbable.

In the dying moments of the game a mistimed tackle from Phil Neville brought down Ray Parlour in the penalty area. Referee David Elleray immediately pointed to the spot and Neville instantly put his head in his hands, knowing full well it was as clear a penalty as you will ever see.

'I would have had my house on Dennis Bergkamp scoring the penalty,' Parlour later said. 'I remember asking the referee David Elleray how long was left and he said, "This is the last kick of the game."'

Parlour was clearly unaware of Schmeichel's penalty record since arriving at Old Trafford in 1991. If he had have been, he would have put more than just his house on Bergkamp scoring. The Danish international had only saved one penalty in eight years at the club, and none in normal regulation time. His only save came in the 1992 UEFA Cup penalty shoot-out loss to Torpedo Moscow.[26]

To add further weight to the certainty of the outcome, seven years prior, Bergkamp had scored past Schmeichel in a shoot-out at Euro 92. This time, however, the United goalkeeper defied the odds and was equal to Bergkamp's effort, palming the ball away to his left, giving Ferguson's team a lifeline.

---

26 Not including Charity Shields.

Phil Neville was the most relieved person in the ground. 'I honestly thought my Manchester United career was over. It was the last minute, I was tired, I'd played really well in the game as well, and I literally just collapsed on the floor and brought down Ray Parlour. I just thought "that's it – it's been a good career", and then he saved it. I owe him everything.'

Despite Parlour's assertion that the referee said it would be the last kick, it clearly wasn't and Schmeichel knew that more than anyone. Any player who wanted to congratulate the Dane on his heroics was shoved away, and urged forward, particularly as there was the prospect of an immediate counter-attack to consider. Beckham was the one who seemed particularly ecstatic, and Schmeichel gave him an almighty push. The United number seven responded by immediately sprinting as though his life depended on it. Alas, the final whistle went, and now United had to go again. And go again they did, despite the weariness of their manager. 'The following 30 minutes exhausted me,' Ferguson recalled, 'and probably everyone else in the ground. If ever a tie could be described as epic it was this one.'

But Arsenal were tiring too, despite their numerical advantage in terms of personnel. That fatigue was evident in the wayward Patrick Vieira pass that handed substitute Ryan Giggs possession after exactly 108 minutes of intensive football. But there seemed little immediate danger given that the careless pass had occurred deep in United's half. Vieira tried to atone for his error but the Welshman evaded him easily, before twisting Lee Dixon inside and out. He then squeezed through between Dixon and Martin Keown before firing into the roof of the net – cue pandemonium. Some United fans came on to the pitch to embrace the now bare-chested Giggs, who had celebrated his breathtaking goal by taking his shirt off while on the run, whirling it around his head like a Catherine wheel. Sparks had flown. Martin Tyler in the Sky commentary box described the goal as, 'Sensational. He's cut Arsenal to ribbons.'

United were in the final thanks to Giggs's wonder goal, to the dismay of their opponents, as Keown remarked, 'I still can't believe we didn't win that game.'

It also gave United added momentum in the league in their fight against Wenger's team. Ferguson's side held a one-point lead over the Gunners going into the last match of the season. Once again, mid-game changes from the bench made all the difference.

On that final day, with the title still up for grabs, United faced Arsenal's arch-rivals Tottenham Hotspur, adding a little spice to the occasion. No doubt there were some visiting fans hoping they would not gift the title to their bitter rivals by denying Ferguson's team the much-needed three points.

United began well enough but found themselves behind midway through the first half when Les Ferdinand scooped a shot over Schmeichel. The Dane had enjoyed a difficult first half to what was going to be his last campaign at the club but improved after a mid-season break.[27] Now his form was dipping at just the wrong time. Once again, though, the home side found the resolve to turn a losing situation around. Beckham has to take a lot of the credit for that, especially in the first half. It was his drive and skill that got United level just before half-time. During the break, the decisive change occurred – Cole replacing nemesis Sheringham. Two minutes after coming on, Cole collected an incisive ball from Gary Neville (yes, Gary Neville!). One touch to bring it under control, a second to tee it up, and a third – a delightful, as well as decisive, lob over Spurs goalkeeper Ian Walker. It proved to be the winner. The title had been wrenched back from Arsenal in what was the beginning of ten glorious days, and the first time the championship had been sealed in front of the home fans in the Ferguson era.

Substitutions were certainly the name of the game at the campaign's crescendo. A week later at Wembley, in the FA Cup

---

27 Schmeichel was given a mid-term break by his boss after a difficult first half of the season where the goalkeeper made a few errors that led to crucial goals. The Dane went on holiday to Barbados to recharge his batteries.

Final against Newcastle United, an early switch would turn out to be crucial, albeit one forced upon Ferguson. Sheringham was this time the substitute, rather than the one being replaced. The forward came on for the injured Roy Keane and turned in a man-of-the-match performance, scoring the opening goal just 90 seconds after entering the fray. He then assisted the second in a comfortable 2-0 win. Sheringham for Keane was not a like-for-like replacement, a number ten for a box-to-box midfielder, and Ferguson must take some of the plaudits for such a bold move after just eight minutes with the game at 0-0. The adjustment was seamless, the substitution inspired.

Nevertheless, when observing the United bench and noticing there were no central midfielders available, maybe the manager had little choice.[28] As a result of the change, Ole Gunnar Solskjaer moved to the right and Beckham switched to central midfield, a decision that would have ramifications for the Champions League Final four days later. Beckham's performance in the middle of the park at Wembley was of such a high calibre that Ferguson decided to play him there against Bayern Munich at the Camp Nou. But for now, the second leg of the treble could be enjoyed in relative comfort. The sight of a disconsolate Alan Shearer applauding through gritted teeth as the United players collected the trophy was a sight to behold for the red following. Three years previously, Shearer had chosen Newcastle over Manchester United. What was going through his head at the time, as the United players collected trophy after trophy, is difficult to know, but he wouldn't have been human if there wasn't an element of regret over his decision.

In-match switches were about to play an even more significant role, four days after the cup final, in the club's biggest game in more than three decades.

---

28 Nicky Butt was left out of the cup final squad entirely as Ferguson wanted him to rest ahead of the Champions League Final, in the knowledge he would be needed due to the suspensions of fellow midfielders Roy Keane and Paul Scholes.

6 (i)

From welcome to Hell...

TO TRULY understand what occurred in the Camp Nou against Bayern Munich on that famous night in May 1999, just days after United had won the Premier League and the FA Cup, we need to go back almost four decades and the beginning of Ferguson's obsession with ruling Europe.

The 1960 European Cup Final took place in Glasgow. An enthralling match ended with the great Real Madrid side of the time vanquishing Eintracht Frankfurt 7-3. Among the 127,621 in attendance that day was an 18-year-old Ferguson. 'The first thing to remember,' Ferguson recalled, 'was that Eintracht Frankfurt beat Rangers 12-4 on aggregate in the semi-final and, being a Rangers fan at the time, we thought those guys were gods. They were the best team I'd ever seen in my life, and then they got slaughtered 7-3 in the final! That put into perspective how good Real Madrid really were. Real lost the first goal as well but what was incredible was that Ferenc Puskás scored four and Alfredo Di Stéfano scored three – two players scoring seven goals between them in a European Cup Final![29] I was starting out at Queen's Park at the time so I had got a ticket in the Schoolboy Enclosure, because Hampden was

---

29 Ferenc Puskás is still to this day the only player to score four goals in a European Cup Final.

Queen's Park's ground. When the final whistle went, I ran to get my bus back to Govan – I always used to run back to the bus terminus rather than queue up with all the crowds outside Hampden. When the bus came round, it was still empty and I couldn't understand it, then I realised the whole crowd had stayed in the ground to watch the celebrations. I missed the laps of honour by that brilliant Madrid side just to be able to get my bus home!'

The cast had been set and United's path to the Camp Nou, Solskjaer and the Promised Land had been laid out.

The next stop on Ferguson's journey was the summer of 1967 and the crowning glory of Jock Stein's Celtic side, winning the European Cup Final against Inter Milan. Once again, Ferguson was a keen observer of their progress, albeit this time as a listener on the radio. He was impressed as Celtic overcame the odds, defeating their Italian opponents with a team that all came from within 30 miles of their own stadium. Ferguson would go on to describe it as 'the greatest feat in football'. But it was Stein who he was in awe of, and even to this day, the merest mention of the former Celtic boss will light up Ferguson's face.

Another manager who holds similar reverence in his heart is Sir Matt Busby, Manchester United boss from 1945 to 1969, and another legendary Scotsman. Busby would also enhance the esteem with which the European Cup was held, for both Manchester United and Ferguson.

Tragedy struck Busby and the club in 1958 when British European Airways Flight 609 crashed on its third attempt to take off from a slush-covered runway at Munich-Riem Airport. On the plane was the team, nicknamed the Busby Babes, along with supporters and journalists. Twenty on board died at the scene. Busby was among the injured and was taken to the Rechts der Isar Hospital in Munich where three more of the passengers died, resulting in 23 fatalities in total.

In the immediate aftermath, Busby's life hung in the balance. A devout Roman Catholic, he was given the last rites on two separate occasions while in hospital over the next two days. However, he would recover and remarkably return to Old Trafford just 71 days after the crash.

The Busby Babes killed instantly in the disaster were Geoff Bent (25), captain Roger Byrne (28), Eddie Colman (21), Mark Jones (24), David Pegg (22), Tommy Taylor (26), and Liam Whelan (22). Duncan Edwards died two weeks later in hospital. He was 21.

Walter Crickmer, the club secretary, first-team trainer Tom Curry and coach Bert Whalley also lost their lives in the disaster.

Eight journalists – Alf Clarke, Don Davies, George Follows, Tom Jackson, Archie Ledbrooke, Henry Rose, Frank Swift (who was also a goalkeeper for Manchester City until 1949) and Eric Thompson – perished in the crash, as did co-pilot Kenneth Rayment, travel agent Bela Miklos, supporter Willie Satinoff and air steward Tom Cable.

The backdrop to the tragedy involved the team returning from a European Cup match in Belgrade, having eliminated Red Star Belgrade to advance to the semi-finals of the continent's premier competition. The flight stopped to refuel in Munich because a non-stop flight from Belgrade to Manchester was beyond the plane's range.

The hierarchy at the Football League had taken a dim view of Manchester United's participation in European competition. The organisation was not keen on the champions of England competing in what it regarded as a distraction to domestic football. Previously, the Football League prohibited Chelsea from taking part in the inaugural European Cup in the season 1955/56. United became the first English entrant a year later.

Busby would ultimately lead his side, including Munich survivor Bobby Charlton, to the final in 1968, where they overcame Benfica, 4-1, in a memorable final at Wembley.

It was this achievement that Ferguson hoped to mirror as he embarked on his first campaign in the newly branded

Champions League, formerly known as the European Cup, in September 1993.

Galatasaray 3-3, 0-0 (United went out on away goals)

Having comfortably seen off the challenge posed by Kispest Honvéd of Hungary in the first round, Alex Ferguson had to pit his wits against German Reiner Hollmann, who was the manager of United's next opponents, Galatasaray.

United dominated the opening exchanges of the first leg at Old Trafford and surged into a 2-0 lead in the opening 15 minutes. However, Ferguson described what followed as a 'nightmare' as the team 'self-destructed, replacing controlled aggression with self-indulgence'. A two-goal advantage became a one-goal deficit before Eric Cantona spared the team's blushes with a late equaliser. But a 3-3 draw at Old Trafford made the away leg particularly difficult. Almost certainly only victory would suffice in Istanbul, given the concession of three away goals.

The complacency United showed in that first leg was also the narrative in Turkey prior to the game. Galatasaray were angered by suggestions they would just roll over for their more esteemed opponents. The Turkish club certainly proved they were anything but a pushover. If they were stylish as well as stubborn opposition in Manchester, they were an even more daunting proposition in their own back yard. Indeed, it was this perceived arrogance from the English champions that prompted the unsavoury welcome the United players received upon arrival in Istanbul.

During the foray into the city that straddles Europe and Asia, United were 'exposed to as much harassment and hostility as I have ever known on a football expedition', Ferguson recalled.

The feisty trip began with Turkish fans greeting the English champions at the airport in Istanbul with banners saying 'Welcome to Hell' and Paul Parker having 'You will die!' screamed in his face. Gary Pallister said it made a trip to Anfield seem 'like a tea party'. The defender said in his autobiography, 'It was a terrifying business which had nothing to do with sport and can be categorised objectively as an absolute disgrace.'

Several United players were assaulted by police; Steve Bruce was almost maimed by a flying brick while he sat on the team bus and the game ended with Eric Cantona being struck by a police officer as United crashed out of Europe, drawing the away leg 0-0 and exiting the competition on away goals.

At the final whistle, after informing Swiss referee Kurt Röthlisberger of what he thought of his performance, Cantona was given a red card. Some say the enigmatic forward didn't say a word to Röthlisberger, who was a French teacher, although his gestures probably made things clear enough.

Other reports suggested Cantona accused Röthlisberger of being corrupt. The Swiss official was banned from refereeing for life in 1997 after being found guilty of bribery and though there have been subsequent allegations about this game, nothing has ever been proved.

However, as Rob Smyth put it in *The Guardian*, 'The reality is that Terry Christian could have refereed the game and Galatasaray would probably still have gone through.'[30]

The Turkish champions were the better side throughout in Istanbul, dominating proceedings with only impressive goalkeeping from Peter Schmeichel keeping them at bay.

In the United dressing room after the game, it was eerily silent. 'Sometimes if you don't talk at all it has more of an impact. It was one of these nights. We were all sick [to go out of the competition],' Ferguson said.

If the United players were numb, the reaction from Galatasaray was one of euphoria. Players were held aloft by the hordes of home supporters as if they had won the

---

30 Terry Christian is a much-publicised Manchester United fan and former host of the Channel 4 television series *The Word*.

European Cup, the World Cup and the Eurovision Song Contest, all at once. Their reaction was understandable. Until this match, the Turkish national team and its clubs were relative minnows in world football. England had beaten Turkey 8-0 less than six years previously as they continued to toil on the international stage, not qualifying for a major tournament since 1954.

Furthermore, the country's club sides rarely threatened European football's elite. Nobody had given Galatasaray a chance against United and to shed further light into the Turkish footballing soul, there was a much-used phrase at the time to describe a narrow loss as an honour, 'at least we weren't humiliated' being the mantra, according to Turkish football expert Emre Sarıgül. Now, however, it was exhilaration the fans were feeling, not humiliation. If losing narrowly was seen as a success, you can imagine what going through to the last eight of the Champions League meant to everyone associated with the club.

A commentator on the pitch reacted to the victory as though he had just seen a UFO and was telling a disbelieving audience to come quick. He screamed his questions excitedly in the direction of Galatasaray vice-president Adnan Polat just after the final whistle, and the club official responded, 'This victory is for Turkey, not just Galatasaray.' With pandemonium around him, Polat calmly reiterated, 'It was for the whole nation.'

Legendary Galatasaray defender Bülent Korkmaz echoed these sentiments when he said, 'We delivered this victory to the nation. What can I say? I'm just so happy for the whole country.' The centre-back's surname translates as fearless, an attribute that could hardly be said of their opponents.

Midfielder Suat Kaya was seen holding his head in disbelief as fans jubilantly greeted him. He was almost on the verge of fainting as he told the reporter, 'I just want to be with my family.' He was looking forward to celebrating with his loved ones, but you sensed it could also have been rooted in wanting a safe haven from the hysterical fans.

Tugay Kerimoğlu, who would go on to play for Blackburn Rovers, was in tears as he sat on the shoulders of supporters. They were tears of happiness, though, as he said, 'Galatasaray are the biggest, Galatasaray are the best. But we love Beşiktaş fans. We love Fenerbahçe fans. We love Trabzonspor as well.' These are incredible words given the animosity between the country's most successful clubs. And with that, the reporter kissed him on the head while United went away to lick their wounds.

To put even more perspective on the dire performance of United in that season's competition, Galatasaray had peaked. They went out limply in the next round, a group stage that involved six matches, with the Turkish side winning none of them.

Meanwhile, the inquest in England was just beginning.

United had crashed out, leaving Ferguson crushed with disappointment, though he would cite the scenes throughout the trip to Istanbul as a significant factor behind their ejection from the competition. But as Rob Hughes wrote in *The Times,* the furore surrounding the match was all a 'violent smokescreen to a more horrid truth' – that United, and English football, were out of their depth in the European Cup.

Hugh McIlvanney, Ferguson's friend and ghostwriter for his first autobiography, was even more withering in *The Observer*, 'After more than three decades of reporting British involvement in the European Cup, it is difficult to remember another occasion when genuinely outstanding challengers from this country fell so pathetically short of their true standards on a foreign ground.'

Rob Smyth in *The Guardian* was keen to emphasise the learning curve had begun. 'The horror movie of 1993,' he wrote, 'became a vital part of United's European education. Gary Neville, who was brought on for the last few minutes to deliver some long throws, said he "learned more in ten minutes than I had in the previous two years".

It was not only the inexperienced who picked up new tricks; the whole club learned about man-to-man marking, the need for central midfield discipline, not to mention the alien environments they would encounter on their quest to lift the giant trophy. United didn't only go to hell; they also went to school. But you'd have been a brave man to accentuate the positive in the United dressing room on the night of 3 November 1993.'

Since first entering the European Cup in 1956, United had never failed to reach the semi-finals until the Galatasaray humiliation. Ferguson knew he would have to up his game. His resolve strengthened with every excruciating defeat. The fire had been lit, but as yet there were no sparks.

Onwards and upwards – the journey to the Promised Land

The following season, 1994/95, things wouldn't get much better as United continued to suffer from the 'three-foreigner' rule imposed by UEFA. Ferguson expressed his frustration when the regulation was eventually abandoned a couple of years later. He was both pleased and embittered at the change as he believed the '94 side were capable of even greater things. 'It's come two years late for us,' he said, 'because we'd have had a chance of winning the European Cup in 1994 otherwise.'

He had a point. The team had heaps of talent in the shape of Schmeichel, Irwin, McClair, Keane, Giggs, Kanchelskis, Cantona and Hughes, but only a maximum of three could play, plus two 'assimilated' players who had been in England for a lengthy period of time.

United began their Champions League campaign at home to IFK Gothenburg and the ITV coverage immediately began with Ferguson speaking eerily over a piece of classical music, 'When it comes to a situation like this – when you go into big games in Europe, and you look back at that '68 team, what he [Sir Matt Busby] created, particularly after Munich … it would be great to equal that, to get to that point where people can say "they also won the European Cup, they are as good as Sir Matt's team". He really set the stall out about how this club should play.' The fire continued to burn within Ferguson, but once again he would be scolded by opponents that were more streetwise.

The campaign began well enough with four points from the opening two games in the new league format. Ferguson would go on to recognise that a ten-point haul should see any team through, and United were almost halfway to that total before a tricky double header against Barcelona.

Ferguson was beginning to wise up tactically too, deploying Paul Parker as a man-marker for the ridiculously talented Romário at Old Trafford. The trick almost worked but Ferguson would lament 'two losses of concentration'. This ability to focus is a trait the manager would often preach to his players, and none more so than in Europe, where one momentary aberration can be so costly. United drew 2-2 at home before being thrashed 4-0 in the Camp Nou in a match where Barcelona swamped the English champions.

A manager often criticised for his lack of tactical analysis, Ferguson went into great detail as to what went wrong over the two matches in his first book. 'What infuriated me was that we had spent three days adjusting our zonal defending method to incorporate man-for-man marking of Romário. I wouldn't have taken such pains if I didn't think the change was necessary. I keep harping on to our lads about how imperative total concentration is in European games. Disciplined adherence to a game plan is the most important advantage continental teams tend to have over us.'

Following tactical advice was not United's only handicap as once again the foreigner rule would tie Ferguson's hands, forcing him to drop Peter Schmeichel for the 4-0 loss in the return fixture at the Camp Nou. But Ferguson was more angry with the 'naivety' his side had shown in midfield, and in particular his ire was directed at Paul Ince. His anger with the former West Ham midfielder would continue throughout the season, culminating in Ince's exit for pastures new. That defeat to Barcelona turned out to be the beginning of the end for Ince.

The defence also had a nightmare that night with centre-half and captain Steve Bruce admitting, 'It was one of the biggest games for me, and I had an absolute beast. We lost 4-0 but it could have been 14.' As Rob Smyth wrote in *The Guardian*, 'Bruce's best contribution was in the dressing room at half-time, when he and Brian Kidd separated Ferguson and Paul Ince.'

Bruce wasn't the only one to suffer. His central defensive partner Gary Pallister, usually so serene at the heart of the United back line, was also all at sea, particularly as he struggled to handle the mercurial Brazilian striker Romário. Rob Smyth, once again, takes up the story: 'The thing that struck Pallister the most was Romário's awareness. Romário was always looking over his shoulder to see where Pallister was, reversing the usual relationship between forward and defender, before slithering into a position where he could expose Pallister's high centre of gravity. "Pallister and Bruce were both auditioning for the role of Juliet: Romário, Romário, wherefore art thou Romário?" wrote David Lacey in his match report. "And nobody had a clue about Stoichkov's whereabouts." Pallister was a majestic centre-half in English football; this was the one time in his career when he walked off the pitch knowing he'd been out of his depth. In a dark corner of his subconscious, Romário owns a long-term lease.'

Despite the defence's travails it was the lack of discipline from his midfielders that really got to Ferguson and this would be a theme that the Scottish manager would return to time and again. He wanted the team to be more cautious in this area of the pitch. A gung-ho attitude would be something the team could get away with in domestic competitions, not against Europe's elite.

A lack of patience and discipline would prove to be United's undoing once more a few weeks later when they lost in Gothenburg, leading to another early exit from the Champions League.[31] It did not, however, deter the United manager. It was time to grit the teeth, and learn once more. 'Failure of this kind can either leave you in the depths of gloom or sharpen your appetite for trying again.' No prizes for guessing which of those options Ferguson chose.

The premature departure from the European stage did at least offer Ferguson the chance to blood some youngsters in the final group game, a 4-0 home win against Galatasaray that included a first goal for a 19-year-old by the name of David Beckham.

United were back in the Champions League two years later after a brief hiatus having lost the league title to Blackburn Rovers in 1995.[32]

Ferguson's desperation to do well in the competition, aligned with UEFA abandoning its restrictions on the use of foreign players, gave the team real impetus for the 1996/97 Champions League onslaught. United's transfer business had a continental feel to it too, with Norwegians Ole Gunnar Solskjaer and Ronny Johnsen joining the club, along with Czech wide player Karel Poborský, Dutch forward Jordi Cruyff, son of the great Johan, and his countryman Raimond van der Gouw, who came in as back-up goalkeeper for Peter Schmeichel.

'It's easy to dream of course,' Ferguson mused in pre-season, explaining the five-pronged transfer attack, 'especially when you're soaking up the sun, but I'm thinking more and more about the harsh realities. I've been preparing for the European

---

31 Technically, this game wasn't the killer blow, but only an unlikely scenario involving Barcelona losing at home to IFK Gothenburg when both teams knew a draw would suffice meant United's loss in Sweden proved to be fatal.

32 In 1995, only the winners of the league would qualify for the Champions League. Later it would expand to include runners-up and even teams that finished third or fourth.

challenge for some time, as I know that if you are to tackle a major project you need the right tools for the job.'

Had United managed to land long-term target Alan Shearer, as well as this group of players, it is plausible to think that they would have dominated the European scene for the next five years. Alas, the signing of Shearer didn't materialise and Ferguson would have to settle for his increasing knowhow of the continental game, garnered through some tough experiences to date, aligned with an enlarged squad of players to help his side through the rigours of a 60-game season.

Such was Ferguson's focus on conquering Europe, as well as his confidence in the club's ability to deal with the Premier League, he was beginning to use domestic fixtures to try out tactics and formations ahead of tricky European assignments.

In *A Will to Win*, a book Ferguson wrote with *Manchester Evening News* journalist David Meek documenting the 1996/97 season, the Scottish manager highlighted his keenness to try three centre-backs against Juventus for the opening round of Champions League fixtures. Two weeks prior to the trip to northern Italy, Ferguson told the players he would be trying out the new formation in the next league fixture against Derby County.

The team also arranged a practice match with the formation deployed but after the game at Derby ended in a disappointing draw, Ferguson had a change of heart and reverted to two centre-backs.

'My conclusion is that playing three central defenders against Juventus would be too big a risk,' Ferguson mused in the wake of the stalemate at the Baseball Ground. 'It's a system that could do well but perhaps just not now. We need to concentrate on it more in training, and then in the Premiership, before trying it in Europe. It's the continental style, and we must use it.'

His pursuit of Barcelona centre-half Miguel Nadal is further evidence of the manager's obsession with conquering

Europe, with his transfer policy heavily influenced by winning the club game's biggest prize. 'That's one of the reasons I have been investigating the possibility of getting Miguel Nadal from Barcelona. With him, I'd have that option. I could play Pallister with May or Johnsen but I need another player with great European experience alongside them.'[33]

The defeats to Barcelona and IFK Gothenburg a couple of years previously had clearly hurt Ferguson and had an effect on his planning for the 1996/97 European campaign. He wanted to flood the central areas, increase concentration, and hope his side had become a bit wiser after the antics of more wily opponents. The spying missions on their European adversaries intensified while the Champions League lingered in the background of almost every thought that crossed Ferguson's mind, many of which are documented in his diary of the season.

And against Leeds United, just a few days before the daunting trip to Juventus, Europe was again in Ferguson's thoughts. Not just formations, but style and team selections were influenced on the eve of the trip to Turin. At Elland Road, a 4-0 win convinced Ferguson he had found the solution to the dilemma posed by the reigning European champions. The 'experience, ability and penetration' provided by Cantona, Poborský and Cruyff had to be exploited but he always had to have at least two players in the middle of the park, meaning three would be deployed in total in central midfield to fend off the danger of swift counter-attacks.

It didn't work. Juventus dominated the first half, taking a 1-0 lead thanks to an Alen Bokšić goal on the counter, much to the chagrin of Ferguson. It was an advantage that Juventus didn't relinquish and the Italian newspaper *Corriere della Sera* was withering in its assessment of the English champions, 'If this is the Premier League's best then it's absolutely miles off.'

---

33 Miguel Nadal, nicknamed 'The Beast', is an uncle of tennis player Rafael Nadal.

But the United boss took heart from the second-half performance, feeling that after half-time his side had matched the best team in Europe in their own back yard.

At least the upcoming matches against Rapid Vienna and Fenerbahçe would offer a better chance of picking up the points required to make it through to the last eight.

Indeed, back-to-back victories at home to Rapid, and away in Turkey were evidence that United had begun to learn their lessons. The Austrian team were swept aside just 24 hours after Manchester City were beaten 1-0 in the League Cup by minnows Lincoln City. It completed an aggregate loss of 5-1 to the team from the fourth tier of the English football pyramid. The thrashing United suffered at the hands of their rivals from across town in the autumn of 1989 was but a distant memory. Oh, how the trajectories of the two sides had changed dramatically after that result. United were now dining at Europe's top table, while City were looking for scraps mired in England's second tier, as well as being humbled in the cup competitions. Still, this was no time to be looking across town as United had much bigger fish to fry.

The Old Trafford outfit were all at sea in the home fixture against Fenerbahçe, losing 1-0. But they lost more than just the match that night – they forfeited their proud unbeaten record at home in Europe, a run stretching back four decades.

United then suffered another home defeat in European competition just three weeks later as Juventus left Old Trafford triumphant. Ferguson's team seemed desperately nervous against their more experienced opponents. Panicking in possession was notable, particularly when near their own goal, and something the team had to stamp out fast as they still had one last bite at the cherry with a tricky trip to Vienna on the horizon, knowing only three points would give them a chance of progressing to the last eight.

On this occasion in the Austrian capital, United did not disappoint as goals from Ryan Giggs and Eric Cantona gave them victory. Juventus's defeat of Fenerbahçe in the Stadio delle Alpi ensured the English champions' passage into the quarter-finals for the first time under Ferguson. Though United had to rely on a favour from their Italian counterparts, their performance against Rapid Vienna was accomplished and a leap forward compared to the limp efforts away from home in previous years.

There was a lot to look forward to as United faced FC Porto in the last eight, in spite of the knowledge their Portuguese opponents had topped their group and remained unbeaten en route to the latter stages. Indeed, Ferguson was in bullish mood after the win in Vienna. 'I know that we always do well in March and April. We have won championships at that stage of the season and I predict now that the Portuguese are in for one hell of a tussle.' Big talk for a manager of a side who had just scraped through while their upcoming opponents had won five and drawn one of their six matches to date.

The United manager boldly went for the jugular against Porto, including three strikers in his starting XI – Cantona, Cole and Solskjaer. Ferguson's gamble was justified as his side put in their best performance in Europe under his stewardship to date, thrashing their opponents 4-0, effectively killing off the tie with 90 minutes still to play. The performance at Old Trafford that night had all the controlled aggression that was missing against Galatasaray in 1993, all the guile sadly lacking in all those defeats to Juventus over the years, and the speed and power that had become their trademark in the Premier League. Ferguson beamed afterwards, saying their display was 'stunning' as they 'annihilated' their opponents. The team's composure in the second leg, drawn 0-0, was yet more evidence the club's learning curve was on an upward trajectory.

Manchester United were in the semi-final of the European Cup for the first time in 28 years. All that stood in the way of a first final appearance since winning the competition in 1968 was German outfit Borussia Dortmund.

The Chemical Brothers were at number one in the UK singles charts with 'Block Rockin' Beats' but United had lost their rhythm as they succumbed 1-0 to Dortmund in the atmospheric Westfalenstadion. The goal came after a timid effort from Cantona saw him lose out in a 50-50 challenge with Paulo Sousa before René Tretschok's deflected shot gave Dortmund the advantage going into the second leg.

Cantona's form, and even his body shape, had become a concern for Ferguson and the return match at Old Trafford did little to alleviate those worries as the Frenchman failed to convert several chances. The worst of these was an opportunity blocked by Jürgen Kohler when it seemed easier for the forward to score, just three yards from a gaping goal and with the German defender on the ground.

Another moment in the first half showed that Cantona's presence was still being felt, but that his lack of pace, and maybe even confidence, were having a negative effect on the team. Andy Cole had a chance to seize possession when bearing down on goal, only to cede the space, and the ball, to the onrushing Cantona. The Frenchman, however, was not quick enough and the chance was lost. There was always a feeling that Cole somehow felt intimidated by his illustrious strike partner and here was evidence to support that theory.

United ended up losing the game after another deflected goal, this time from Lars Ricken.[34] Ferguson blamed Schmeichel for the concession of the eighth-minute goal before realising later that it had deflected off Pallister. He thereafter always wore glasses, citing his own error in castigating his goalkeeper as the reason for doing so. He reasoned that if he

---

34 Dortmund-born Ricken scored 16 seconds after coming on as a substitute in the final. The Bundesliga side beat Juventus 3-1. The German charts at the time featured a song by rapper Der Wolf entitled 'Oh Shit – Frau Schmidt' which summed up the surprising end to the 1997 Champions League. The b-side, 'Dortmund', referred to Der Wolf's favourite team, and was used by fans to celebrate the club's achievement.

was to have a go at his players, he needed to do so safe in the knowledge his eyes had not deceived him.

Ferguson said the reason his side lost was because of 'a mixture of bad luck and bad finishing'.

The defeat to the German champions proved to be the final straw for one player. One month short of his 31st birthday, Eric Cantona told Ferguson the day after the loss that he wanted to retire, having failed to fulfil the one remaining dream of his career. Ferguson reluctantly accepted the enigmatic striker's decision.

In the meantime Ferguson was still hungry for European success, having not managed to secure the prize he, like Cantona, so desperately sought.

The 1997/98 season would bring more frustration, yet also there were signs that United were inching closer. Once again Juventus would provide menacing opposition in the group stage but this time United had grown in stature. The nervousness evident in the matches the previous year was no longer an issue as Ferguson's team swept the Serie A outfit aside at Old Trafford in a classic European encounter. The Old Lady actually took the lead through an extraordinary piece of skill from Alessandro Del Piero, managing to take out both defender Henning Berg and goalkeeper Schmeichel with one touch, before slotting home.

United showed how their resolve, as well as their capabilities, had improved after defeats home and away to the Italians a year earlier. New signing Teddy Sheringham, brought in as a direct replacement for Cantona, got United back on level terms before excellently taken goals from Giggs and Scholes sealed victory, despite a late free kick from Zinedine Zidane. Once again, United had passed an exam they had previously failed.

They topped the group and managed to avoid the big guns in the last eight, where they would face AS Monaco. Sadly the impressive form United had shown in the earlier stages of the tournament eluded them when it mattered most.

This, aligned with injuries to key players such as Schmeichel, Pallister, Keane and Giggs, meant Ferguson's men fell short once more. Monaco went through on away goals after a David Trezeguet thunderbolt stunned Old Trafford into silence. Not even a Solskjaer equaliser could inspire a United comeback.

Having reached the semi-final the previous season, United were beginning to acclimatise to the Champions League. But consistency, injuries and fatigue proved their undoing against a French side containing three players who later that year would win the World Cup with their national team – Fabien Barthez, Trezeguet and a 20-year-old named Thierry Henry.

Ferguson always took going out of the competition badly. Losing in Europe, particularly when he felt his team had an outstanding opportunity, like in 1997 and 1998, was 'a real killer,' according to Ben Thornley, who made the bench for both legs against Monaco. 'The manager always had in his mind, having won the domestic league title on so many occasions, that winning the Champions League was definitely the next step. He felt United could have and should have won it during this period.'

6 (ii)

… to football, bloody hell!

AS MANCHESTER United embarked on their fifth European Cup campaign under Ferguson, ITV's Clive Tyldesley, who commentated on each of their matches in the Champions League that season, noticed that things had changed since the first effort under the Scottish manager, back in 1993. 'The team had developed a pedigree over these years. And one that was beginning to be felt in opposing dressing rooms across the corridor.'

Ferguson knew, however, that it would take more than pedigree to overcome the shortcomings that had undermined previous attempts to win the trophy. He had been frustrated with the club's lack of ambition in the transfer market that thwarted efforts to land the best players, such as Argentinian striker Gabriel Batistuta, Brazilian forward Ronaldo and French defender Marcel Desailly. But in the summer of 1998 he did spend almost £30m on Dwight Yorke, Jesper Blomqvist and Jaap Stam, all signings that would prove crucial in the season ahead.

United only qualified for the 1998/99 Champions League by virtue of the rule change a couple of years previously, meaning some nations' domestic runners-up would also qualify for the biggest club tournament in the world. Ferguson's team would have to negotiate a qualifier against ŁKS Łódź to earn the right to compete in that year's group stage. They beat the Polish outfit 2-0 on aggregate to comfortably progress to that phase.

If the route into the Champions League was fairly routine, their opponents in the group were anything but – Brøndby, Barcelona and Bayern Munich all stood in the way of United's hopes of going further in the competition.

To say the team performed well in the group phase, particularly going forward, would be an understatement, scoring 20 goals in their six matches, a Champions League record at the time. The quality of the opponents made the achievement all the more impressive. What's more, the style in which the team played, scoring scintillating goal after scintillating goal, only added to the joy of the United faithful.

An enthralling 3-3 draw at home to Barcelona was followed by a 2-2 scoreline away at Bayern Munich. In truth, they outclassed their German opponents and were only undone by a bizarre late error from Peter Schmeichel, who thought he was superman as he led with his fist while airborne, completely missing the ball, eventually bouncing off the unfortunate Teddy Sheringham's head into the net. It mattered not as United trounced Brøndby home and away, scoring 11 goals in the process against the Danish champions, before what turned out to be the standout match of the tournament so far – another 3-3 against Barcelona, this time in the Camp Nou. Once again United fell behind, once again they came back, this time with a new combination in town.

When Sonny Anderson opened the scoring after just one minute, memories of the 4-0 defeat in 1994 must have come flooding back for the manager, and players such as Denis Irwin and Roy Keane who started both games. But this United were different; they were better. Going behind, even so early on, didn't bother them, as we would see time and again on this journey. If there was a mantra during the Ferguson era of learning from defeats, then this season it was about how to come back from losing positions within a game – the team did so on 17 separate occasions across all competitions during the 1998/99 campaign. Almost half of the Champions League matches were spent recovering after going behind.

After that early shock and the initial onslaught from the Catalans, United eased themselves back into the game. Ferguson's side now had the experience and composure sorely lacking in the team in the earlier part of the decade. After 25 minutes Yorke found himself in acres of space on the edge of the box, collected the ball from Blomqvist and struck it low and with conviction for 1-1.

Schmeichel made some smart saves in the first half, but by the opening exchanges of the second period it was United who were in the ascendency. What was to follow was the announcement of the arrival of a dynamic duo. The combination play between Yorke and Cole, culminating in a smart finish from the latter, drew puffs of smoke from the Barcelona coaching staff on the bench. United were on fire, and 2-1 in front.

'Yorke and Cole was a game changer,' Clive Tyldesley explained, whose words in the commentary box would become synonymous with that season's Champions League run. Their partnership had ripped Brøndby to shreds in the two fixtures prior to the trip to the Camp Nou but this performance announced the pair as a force to be reckoned with on the greatest stage of all.

The home side equalised when a Rivaldo free kick deceived Schmeichel who, not for the first time, wrongly anticipated the flight of the ball before watching it nestle in the corner of the net. Barcelona were back on level terms but it wasn't long before United took the lead once more. Yorke scored eight goals in the Champions League that season, seven of them headers, a record for the competition. And five of those came from Beckham crosses, including one here to make it 3-2 to

United. A late equaliser from Rivaldo gave Barcelona parity once more but it didn't take the shine off what had been a brilliant performance from United, particularly as a draw at home to Bayern Munich in the final group game eased their passage into the last eight and a meeting with Inter Milan.

United had reached the latter stages of the Champions League in the two previous seasons, only to just fall short. Against Inter, that trusty combination of Beckham's right-footed crosses and Yorke's heading ability saw the club take a 2-0 advantage into the second leg at the San Siro. A 1-1 draw in Italy thanks to a late equaliser from Paul Scholes saw them through to the semi-finals.

It wasn't plain sailing against the Italians by any means, and some last-ditch interventions from Henning Berg in both legs kept Inter at bay, but there was a definite sense United were beginning to peak at the right time. Indeed, peak was very much the operative word as many of the team were entering their prime. The team had an average age of 27 while for the game at Old Trafford, Beckham was the youngest player on the pitch, and he was almost 24, so you really had the feeling the tie was between two sets of stellar, established professionals.

After United had beaten Inter, Sir Bobby Charlton, a survivor of the Munich air crash and European Cup winner ten years later, was asked about whether the club could repeat that victory of 1968. 'Well, I hope, I hope. If it's not this year, it'll be soon,' Charlton reasoned. 'But this could be our year. If we get a little bit of luck, and we stay free of injuries, we can give it a good shot.'

The club were giving it their best but next up were Juventus, the standout club in the Champions League in the latter part of the decade and an opponent Ferguson recognised as the benchmark, though he was relieved that his opposite number had changed. Marcello Lippi was no longer in the Juventus dugout having been replaced by Carlo Ancelotti just a couple of months prior to the semi-final clash. The head coach may have changed, and the Old Lady may have been struggling domestically, but the first 45 minutes at Old Trafford produced a familiar feeling – United trailed 1-0 to an Antonio Conte goal.

In the second half United picked up the pace, and after plenty of pressure on the Juventus goal, including a disallowed Teddy Sheringham effort for offside, the Italian defence was breached thanks to a late equaliser from Ryan Giggs, making it 1-1 going into the second leg. That Giggs goal preserved United's unbeaten record in all competitions which stretched back almost four months, to 19 December, when they had lost at home to Middlesbrough. At the time, after that setback, Ferguson watched a video of the 3-2 loss that stirred him into action and to deliver 'some plain words to the players', he noted in his autobiography. Time and again, Ferguson would preach the importance of maintaining focus, and this occasion was no different. 'I pointed out how a lack of concentration, unforgivable sloppiness, had cost us "joke" goals on the Saturday and I let them know that we would have to work on sorting ourselves out without delay. "There is nothing wrong with the quality in your game or the effort you put in," I told them. "So let's get the show on the road." I think it could be said that their response was adequate,' Ferguson remarked ironically, knowing full well they didn't lose another match for the rest of the season.

The 33-game unbeaten run included the scalps of Liverpool, Chelsea, Arsenal, Inter Milan, and now Juventus, after a stunning 3-2 victory in the away leg in what Ferguson described as the best performance from a United side in all his time at the club. Once again, though, his team did it the hard way, coming from 2-0 down to win 3-2 thanks to headers from Keane and Yorke, before a late winner from Andy Cole provoked commentator Clive Tyldesley into exclaiming 'full speed ahead Barcelona' in reference to the location of that year's Champions League Final.

Early on such a result seemed implausible. After going behind to a sixth-minute goal from Filippo Inzaghi there must have been concern on the away bench. Inzaghi, who Ferguson once famously said must have been born offside given the striker's propensity for straying ahead of play, then scored a second five minutes later after a wicked deflection off Stam saw the ball loop over a helpless Schmeichel. The goal was greeted on the stadium's sound system with the Blues Brothers' rendition of 'Everybody, Needs Somebody To Love'. The only thing United needed at this stage was 'a minor miracle' according to Tyldesley. United could have been forgiven for panicking. However, there was a strange calm over this team, even when enduring a setback as big as this, as Juventus midfielder Edgar Davids recalled. The Dutchman was shocked at how relaxed his opponents were, as if the jolt of conceding two early goals was nothing more than a flesh wound. United struck back in some style to leave the Old Lady floundering, setting up a final against Bayern Munich. They would go up against the Germans, however, without two of their best players. Roy Keane and Paul Scholes picked up bookings in the second leg against Juventus which ruled the pair out, leaving a gaping hole in midfield.

Keane's performance in the semi-final second leg, where he played most of the match in the knowledge he would be unavailable for the final, elicited this comment from Ferguson when he reflected on the game in his autobiography, 'I didn't think I could have a higher opinion of any footballer than I already had of the Irishman but he rose even further in my estimation in the Stadio delle Alpi. The minute he was booked and out of the final, he seemed to redouble his efforts to get the team there. It was the most emphatic display of selflessness I have seen on a football field. Pounding over every blade of grass, competing as if he would rather die of exhaustion than lose, he inspired all around him. I felt it was an honour to be associated with such a player.'

Keane responded to the compliment more than a decade later. He told ITV he felt 'offended' by the description. 'It's like praising the postman for delivering letters. What did he expect me to do? Give up?'

The absence of Keane and Scholes for the final posed a selection dilemma for Ferguson, one he tried to resolve by playing Beckham in the middle to fill the hole vacated by the suspended duo. It didn't work and Bayern dominated proceedings. Giggs looked out of place on the right of midfield and Blomqvist made little impression in the Welshman's normal spot on the left while Yorke and Cole were suffocated by the Bayern trio of Thomas Linke, Samuel Kuffour and veteran midfielder turned sweeper Lothar Matthäus. Yorke was uncharacteristically nervous, which didn't help, but the team's anxiety was aided and abetted by goalkeeper Schmeichel, who was at fault for Bayern's goal after six minutes. The Dane was once again wrong-footed by a free kick that nestled in the corner of the net. Mario Basler's strike settled any nerves the Germans may have been feeling, and made United's grow ever more. To this day, Ronny Johnsen says it wasn't a free kick in the first place when the Italian referee, Pierluigi Collina, adjudged that the Norwegian had bundled over Carsten Jancker. Johnsen's argument seems weak as he clumsily ran into the Bayern striker, taking him clean out. Either way, United had to come from behind again, just like they had so often before.

Throughout the first half Bayern were in control and never looked in any serious danger, though it was a period of few chances. At half-time Ferguson told his team some memorable words, reminding the players that if they didn't give their all, and ended up on the losing side, they would have to walk past the trophy without being able to touch it. In truth, the motivational speech did not have an immediate impact, with Bayern continuing to dictate. They were even beginning to cut through the United defence with the woodwork twice saving Ferguson's team. First, a delightful Mehmet Scholl chip left Schmeichel clasping at air as he watched the effort float over his head. The goalkeeper was relieved when the ball not only hit the post, but rebounded back into his grateful grasp. It wasn't long before the frame of the goal came to United's rescue again, this time after an attempt from Jancker.

Ferguson said when reflecting on the final many years later, 'I've always believed in, if you're down, with say 15 minutes to go, gamble. Risk has got to be a part of the club. And it's always worth risking. Some of the greatest moments in my time at United were in the last 15 minutes.'

Ferguson wanted to shuffle the pack, hoping his substitutes would have the same impact as they had had in the previous two games, when the replacements sealed the Premier League and the FA Cup. First of all, Sheringham came on for the disappointing Blomqvist.[35] Then, the baby-faced assassin, Ole Gunnar Solskjaer, replaced Cole. Finally United were beginning to look more like themselves, but time was running out with less than ten minutes remaining. They were 'now creating chances for fun', Clive Tyldesley told viewers on ITV. However, the score remained 1-0 as the final went into three minutes of injury time and with United looking desperate.

In the 91st minute, right-back Gary Neville collected possession on the left wing, in a sign of the haphazard nature of the team's attacks. What happened next must live with Stefan Effenberg to this day. Having bossed the midfield so splendidly throughout the match, he flung a tired leg at the ball and seemed content to only concede a corner. If he had shown the composure he had illustrated over the previous 90 minutes, and just controlled the ball, Bayern would surely have won, and United would never have reached the Promised Land. However, he panicked, and United had an opportunity.

Schmeichel, in one last throw of the dice, raced upfield for the set piece as he had done on so many occasions before

---

35 The Swede never played for United again, after injury kept him out for the next two years before he was sold to Everton in 2001.

whenever United were chasing a late equaliser. It was to be the Dane's last game for the club he had represented for the best part of a decade, and he got his last touch in a United jersey as the ball scraped his head and fell into the path of Yorke, who nodded it back across goal. In another moment of panic, Thorsten Fink, who had come on for Matthäus ten minutes before, mis-hit his clearance, and the ball fell to Ryan Giggs on the edge of the Bayern area. The Welshman then joined the party of scuffs, using his weaker right foot to strike the ball. At least it was still heading towards goal, albeit off target, before Sheringham redirected it, swinging a right boot, to help it on into the net with Oliver Kahn stranded. Matthäus looked stunned as he stared at the scene from the bench.

Substitutes played a significant role in that final, and not just the United ones. German journalist and Bayern fan Raphael Honigstein expressed his dismay at Ottmar Hitzfeld's changes, particularly the decision to replace Matthäus with Fink. He said, 'That substitution was hugely controversial for a number of reasons. First of all because Hitzfeld later said Matthäus had signalled he was injured. Matthäus then denied that. Thomas Helmer, the defender who'd won the Euros with Germany in 1996, was expected to come on for Matthäus, but didn't. Hitzfeld chose Thorsten Fink. And Fink, crucially, is the guy that mis-hits the clearance that immediately precedes United's equaliser. If he just hits the ball properly none of this happens. Which is why I still bear a bit of a grudge against Thorsten Fink.' Honigstein was not the only one bearing grudges. After the match, the aforementioned Helmer, clearly angered at not getting a chance to enter the fray, expressed his frustration by sticking his middle fingers up in the direction of his manager.

As for United, assistant manager Steve McClaren wanted the team to revert to 4-4-2 having got back into the game. Ferguson, however, had other ideas. He told McClaren to sit down and wanted United to continue to attack, at least for the remaining 90 seconds of injury time.

Ferguson remembered the incident with the clarity you would expect from the British game's most successful manager, 'I thought that was it. I thought we were a certainty after that. Steve McClaren said, "Right, extra time, we'll go back to 4-4-2," and I said, "This won't go to extra time."'

And he was right. Deciding to twist, when it was more obvious to stick, proved to be a masterstroke as 100 seconds later the ball was in the Bayern net once more. A Beckham corner again, Sheringham flicked on, Solskjaer instinctively flicked out a boot, and it was 2-1.

Solskjaer said that at 1-1 he 'was thrilled to get to play an extra 30 minutes in a Champions League Final. I was going to learn from that experience. Obviously that didn't happen, and I only have myself to blame for that.'

John Curtis, who travelled to Barcelona but didn't make the matchday squad, sat beside Jordi Cruyff up in the heavens in Europe's largest stadium. He had left his seat along with Cruyff just seconds before the 90 minutes were up. The pair were keen to get to the United dressing room to 'commiserate' with the team.

'Jordi and I missed both goals,' Curtis said. 'We were in the gods. Jordi knows the stadium, obviously he played there, and his dad, so we were on our way down to the changing room to commiserate with the boys when we heard the first goal go in. We went to have a look when we heard that goal, to see who'd scored. We then realised it was us so headed down to the pitch for extra time. Then we were in the tunnel when the second goal went in. By the time we got to the pitch the final whistle went 30 seconds later. We left our seats thinking we'd lost and by the time we got to pitch level, we'd won.'

'The noise when those two goals were being scored,' Bayern fan Honigstein remembers, 'followed by the third noise of the game being finished is still to this day, one of the most moving, but in a horrible way, atmospheres and noises I have ever heard in a stadium.'

Referee Pierluigi Collina said the noise as Solskjaer's strike hit the back of the net was like 'a lion's roar'.

Collina was seen trying to pick the crestfallen Bayern players up off the ground for the restart, with around 30 seconds still to play. They didn't seem to want to get up, though. Defender Kuffour was seen punching the ground over and over again, and at the final whistle Jancker was in tears. 'Football can be so cruel,' said Bayern Munich president and legendary figure Franz Beckenbauer after the game.

Shortly after full time, the cameras panned around the stadium before focussing on Sir Bobby Charlton, who was teary-eyed too. Sir Bobby had survived the Munich air crash when many of his team-mates perished. He then captained the side to the European Cup triumph in 1968 and was also instrumental in bringing Alex Ferguson to the club. Now, on what would have been Sir Matt Busby's 90th birthday, he had witnessed the new crop of United youngsters, fused with the smart purchases made by Ferguson, finally lift the trophy with the big ears.

Wednesday, 26 May 1999 is the day Ferguson achieved what he had set out to do and with youngsters all over Europe buying the chart-topping song 'I Want It That Way' by the Backstreet Boys, it was his team who got it their own way, in their own inimitable style, the style of their manager. 'They never give in,' Ferguson beamed at the end as he told the ITV audience, 'Football, bloody hell!'

United won the three biggest trophies on offer in the 1998/99 season, culminating in the Champions League success. And there are a number of key factors that led to that European glory.

Ferguson's drive and passion were characterised in that final. His desperation to do well in Europe, inspired initially by that day at Hampden Park, watching on as Real Madrid tore

Eintracht Frankfurt apart to win the European Cup, cannot be discounted.

Nor can the sight of Jock Stein leading his Celtic side to European Cup success in 1967, and the lessons he learned from the great Scottish manager, as both a friend and assistant for the national team.

Ferguson used this inspiration and knowhow to guide Aberdeen to European Cup Winners' Cup success in 1983. In the final in Stockholm, Aberdeen overcame the mighty Real Madrid and it was Jock Stein who told Ferguson to buy a bottle of whisky for his opposing manager, Madrid legend Alfredo Di Stéfano, to make him 'think that we were in awe of him – that he was the big guy and little Aberdeen were already beaten'. They certainly weren't as they went on to lift the trophy, something that led United chairman Martin Edwards to earmark him for the job at Old Trafford.

The signings of the summer of 1998, prompted by the trophy-less season that came before, gave United the depth and quality needed over the final furlong. Jaap Stam was a rock at the centre of the United defence, Yorke provided crucial goals, and Blomqvist was a useful addition that meant Giggs in particular remained fresh for the run-in.

Luck, of course, cannot be ignored with twists of fate against Bayern Munich in the final going United's way, though it mustn't be forgotten who they beat en route to winning the final. As well as the German giants, United also overcame Barcelona, Inter Milan and Juventus, which is almost a who's who of European heavyweights.

But the biggest factor of all in landing club football's most prestigious prize surely lies in the learning curve. The lows Ferguson and his team suffered against Galatasaray, IFK Gothenburg and Barcelona in the mid-1990s, before the knockout blows at the hands of Borussia Dortmund and AS Monaco in '97 and '98, were instrumental in ultimately winning the Champions League.

Ferguson's problem-solving after those crushing defeats is notable and the ability to learn the lessons handed out by continental foes meant United's trajectory was upward throughout the decade.

What happened in the Camp Nou would not have occurred without the succession of setbacks the club had previously endured. David Beckham said those European defeats were 'a bit like learning football all over again'.

If there is one other example of Ferguson's ability to react positively to losing situations, in 1998/99 it was witnessed during games. That season, on no less than 17 occasions, United came from behind to earn draws or wins. They fell behind in almost half of their Champions League matches. It was often the manager's decisions on the bench that brought about those turnarounds, especially in terms of crucial substitutions, and none more so than at the Camp Nou.

Ferguson hoped, though, that the schooling the club had received in Europe was now at an end, and he was dreaming of an era of dominance in the Champions League. He wanted his team to be the teachers, and for other sides across the continent to be the pupils who would learn from the new masters of Europe – Manchester United.

However, that wish never quite came to fruition, and it would be another nine years before they were at the top of the European tree once more. In between, of course, there would be more setbacks. Each one, though, would provide the platform to inspire both Ferguson and his team to even more success.

7 (i)

From Wenger vanquished ...

'IN A lifetime's journey in football,' Alex Ferguson reminisced in his second book, simply entitled *Alex Ferguson My Autobiography*, 'you will have dips, lows, defeats and disappointments. In my years at Aberdeen and Manchester United, I decided right away that in order to build trust and loyalty with the players, I had to give it to them first. This is the starting point for the bond on which great institutions thrive. I was helped by my ability to observe. Some people walk into a room and don't notice anything. Use your eyes; it's out there. I used this skill in my assessment of players' training habits, moods and behaviour patterns.'

Someone who spent time in Ferguson's company, particularly during trips abroad when he would often joust over the knowledge of European opponents, is ITV commentator Clive Tyldesley. He was in little doubt as to what was Ferguson's greatest strength, 'His biggest talent was being able to move with the times.'

This ability would become more important with every year that passed as Ferguson grew older and the age gap to his players became greater. It became especially vital when more questions of his ability to do the job came to the surface during the fallow years between 2003 and 2007.

Upon his arrival at Arsenal, Arsène Wenger felt there was an issue with fitness among his players and went about fixing it, giving the Gunners' famous back line a resurgent last few years. Wenger also transformed a team renowned for grinding out results into one that would play breathtaking football.

The wily Frenchman had an uncanny knack of unearthing gems from around Europe, particularly his homeland. Importantly, these players were ready for the fast-paced rough and tumble rigours of the English game.

Mourinho, meanwhile, turned FC Porto, Chelsea and Inter Milan into serial winners and was an excellent problem-solver during a match.

But where both Mourinho and Wenger failed, and Ferguson prevailed, was in the deep-rooted problems that would appear during, rather than at the beginning of their tenures. The ability to save a sinking ship, when all seemed lost, was something neither Wenger nor Mourinho were capable of. The ability to bounce back by solving a longer-term problem – in these departments, Wenger and Mourinho were found wanting while Ferguson shone. When age eventually caught up with Arsenal's back four and goalkeeper, and midfielders such as Patrick Vieira and Emmanuel Petit needed replacing, Wenger was unable to find a solution. He also wasn't up to the task of outwitting Mourinho and had no answers to both the challenge Chelsea offered thanks to Roman Abramovich's wealth, nor the questions posed by Europe's elite.

As for Mourinho, when success dried up and things began to go wrong, particularly inside the dressing room, the Special One had no answer. Also, when new challenges were provided by opposing managers, once again the enigmatic coach couldn't rise to the challenge. Where Ferguson could deal with bigger issues, and ones that went right to the core of the club, such as the out-of-control drinking culture among players the fans adored or when the club were suffering from heavy defeats or painful title losses, he would thrive, both in terms of galvanising himself and the team, and by making calculated, correct decisions.

Arsène Wenger

From when Wenger first arrived at Arsenal in September 1996 until the end of the 2004 season, when his team went the entire league campaign undefeated, the Frenchman was a constant threat to Ferguson's domestic ambitions. Eight years into his reign, Wenger seemed to be emerging on top in the duel. Over the next decade however, there was only one winner – and that was the Scot. So what happened?

Everything Wenger did seemed to irk Ferguson during the Frenchman's first eight years in the Premier League. There is little doubt this frustration is rooted in the fact Wenger appeared to have his counterpart's number, particularly after snatching the 1998 title from under United's noses. There was a new kid in town and he threatened to usurp Ferguson and his team from the perch they were sat on for most of the 1990s.

Some of the remarks Ferguson would fire in Wenger's direction had smatterings of desperation about them, and the Arsenal manager's ripostes seemed to be smarter. Whether it was the fact he was a bespectacled Frenchman, or because his team were exerting an authority over United not seen since the Old Trafford outfit's ascent to the top of English football, Wenger always appeared to have an answer to the grenades Ferguson would throw his way.

Arsenal vice-chairman David Dein said of Wenger, 'He influenced dramatically, not just Arsenal, but the rest of English football.'

His influence on Ferguson was obvious.

'Whenever Sir Alex started mentioning opposition managers, opposition teams, you knew they were becoming a threat,' Phil Neville mused.

Mention is an understatement. 'He's just arrived from Japan, what does he know about it?' Ferguson spouted following a dispute over the fixture list not long after Wenger's arrival.

In another moment, also during Wenger's first season at Highbury, Ferguson said, 'Arsène Wenger's had plenty to say. Maybe he should concentrate on Ian Wright's tackles rather than talk about Manchester United.'

Wenger's impact was immediate. His team was playing stylish football from the get-go, not something the Arsenal fans were accustomed to after the turgid football of George Graham and the coaches who followed. Wenger revolutionised the brand, playing some quick touch interplay, with strength, pace and skill, that had commentators purring. The Frenchman led Arsenal to third in his first season, and by the end of his second, the Gunners were league and cup winners, firmly putting Ferguson and his team in the shade.

By this stage the handshakes between the pair had become awkward on the occasions the two teams played each other. And if there was a psychological one-upmanship to be recognised from the exchange, it always appeared as though Ferguson wanted a friendship more than Wenger. The Frenchman would look the other way while Ferguson appeared a bit keener for eye contact to occur. The Scot wanted to drink wine together. Wenger would stand him up, leaving Ferguson like a jilted partner at the altar.

Most importantly, though, Wenger's team were winning on the pitch, and in style. At least when Leeds and Blackburn had brief moments at the top of the tree, the way in which those two clubs won their titles was less pleasing on the eye. What really must have grated Ferguson was the plaudits Arsenal received from anyone who didn't have an association with Old Trafford.

Nevertheless, the battle between the two managers ebbed and flowed. First, Ferguson held the upper hand. Then Wenger made his mark, before the United manager exerted his authority once more in the wake of that treble success of 1999.

In the two years that followed, the Red Devils stole a march on their rivals, finishing 18 points ahead of Arsenal in 2000 and ten points clear of the Gunners a year later. A 6-1 United victory at Old Trafford in February 2001 seemed to illustrate the chasm between the two teams and was particularly galling for Wenger. By the summer of 2001 the dispiriting nature of that defeat, coupled with a splurge in the transfer market from Ferguson, appeared to suggest the disparity between the clubs was only going to become greater.

Ferguson seemed to be at his strongest, and announced he would be retiring at the end of the 2001/02 season. He brought in Juan Sebastián Verón and Ruud van Nistelrooy at a cost of almost £50m. United were putting their rivals in the shade on the pitch, and now the daunting prospect of these two coming along prompted David Beckham to predict that the side would go the whole season unbeaten. Surprisingly, however, the balance of power was about to swing back towards Arsenal.

United stumbled from one defeat to another through the first half of 2001/02. Ferguson eventually blamed the poor form on announcing his retirement one year in advance. He eventually reversed that decision on Christmas Day, at the behest of his family, and said he would never give such lengthy notice when he finally did decide to step down.

Whereas in the past this change of heart may have propelled United to title glory, this time they were up against a much-improved Arsenal.

The final nail in United's title coffin that season came at Old Trafford, of all places, as Arsenal won 1-0, sealing the Premier League crown on opposition turf. After three seasons in the shade, Wenger and his team were now in the ascendency. This humiliation on home territory, aligned with splashing the cash the previous summer while Wenger remained prudent, only made Ferguson look more foolish. Verón, in particular, was a flop, and coming in at great expense. Whereas Wenger's buys over the last three years, such as Thierry Henry, Robert

Pires and Sylvain Wiltord, who scored the winner at Old Trafford to seal the title, were all proving far better value. These three combined cost a fraction more than Verón. More importantly, the French trio's impact was significantly greater.

Manchester City 3 Manchester United 1

The 2002/03 season began with more of the same and United looked like they were going to see an opposition team win the title for two consecutive years for the first time in the Ferguson era, which would have signalled a real shift in the balance of power. The turning point, however, was brought about by another crushing defeat – this time at the hands of rivals Manchester City, United's first in the derby since the 5-1 thrashing of 1989. The 3-1 margin of defeat wasn't so great but a strong reaction was required all the same. United were well off the pace, both in that game and in terms of the title race, as they witnessed Arsenal galloping ahead, and even Liverpool eight points in front. Ferguson had to act.

Daniel Taylor wrote in *The Guardian* after the bitterly disappointing defeat, 'Ferguson's players had their noses bloodied in the 127th Manchester derby because City passed the ball better when it mattered, played with greater cohesion and showed the sleeves-up mentality that was so lacking from those in red. Every United defeat is enough these days to prompt talk of a crisis but in this case the most galling aspect for Ferguson was that it was not totally unexpected.'

Taylor continued in his assessment, 'The reaction it provoked from Ferguson, usually such a fierce protector of his own, epitomised his sense of helplessness. "I've given them a bollocking, and quite rightly. You can't accept that. I just feel sorry for the fans. I wish I could let them into the dressing room so the players would know what they are thinking." The inquest will be tortuous and torturous.'

ITV's Clive Tyldesley spoke to Ferguson after that game and recalled his mindset, particularly in the wake of such a significant defeat. 'He made that comment about letting the fans in to remind them of how they should be feeling after a derby defeat, and I often felt with Ferguson, he knew exactly what he was going to say, no matter what I asked him. I could have asked him what the capital of Ecuador was and he still would have ranted about letting the fans remind the players of what it's like to lose a derby.'

Ferguson's biographer, Paul Hayward, backed this up. He said, 'His idea was always that this is *my* press conference, not *your* press conference. He always wanted to be in control of the discussion. Often he would turn up with an idea he wanted to get across.'

Gary Neville reflected on Ferguson's reaction to his first derby defeat in 13 years, 'The boss was steaming. You could see him looking around, ready to explode. Then Ruud walked in with a City shirt slung over his shoulder. He'd been asked to swap on the way off and hadn't thought anything of it. But the manager did. "You don't give those shirts away. Ever. If I see anyone giving a shirt away they won't be playing for me again."'

It was to be the season's nadir for Ferguson and his team. He got the reaction he wanted, with his team coming from behind in the title race to eventually win the league with a week to spare.

A 2-2 draw at Highbury as the season entered the final stretch was particularly significant and felt even more so when Ferguson took to the pitch at the end of the match, repeatedly punching the air, as if his team had won, rather than drawn.

Wenger, though, was not done yet, and this title win for United was to be their last for four years, an age by Ferguson's standards.

The summer of 2003 was dominated by one story – David Beckham's future at Manchester United. Having sealed the title, and with Beckham scoring in the final two games of the season, the speculation of an impending departure was frequently dismissed by those in the know. But the relationship between the midfielder and Ferguson had been deteriorating throughout the season, despite Beckham having only signed a new contract a year before.

'In his final season with us,' Ferguson wrote in his autobiography, 'we were aware that David's work-rate was dropping and we had heard rumours of a flirtation with Real Madrid.'

The frayed relationship was summed up by one infamous incident, also following a defeat. To make matters worse, that loss came against Arsène Wenger's Arsenal in the FA Cup.

Ferguson was livid with his team, and none more so than Beckham, who he thought was careless in his inability to track back, failing to stem the twin threats of Arsenal left-back Ashley Cole and winger Sylvain Wiltord. Beckham took umbrage in the dressing room to the criticism, an attitude that was becoming all too familiar according to Ferguson. Beckham swore in the manager's direction and Ferguson's reaction was to kick a football boot that caught the midfielder just above the eye, leaving a gaping wound. It was a 'freakish incident', according to Ferguson. 'If I'd tried it a million times, it wouldn't happen again. If it did, I would carry on playing.'

Nevertheless, it was the beginning of the end for Beckham and United. Ferguson tried to explain to the midfielder why he had been so frustrated with his display, but his complaints fell on deaf ears. Ferguson felt as though his authority had been challenged sufficiently, and sold Beckham to Real Madrid for £24.5m.

Dismissing the challenge posed by Wenger would not be so easy and in many ways the boot incident summed up where the two managers were at the time. Wenger was playing his reserves against most of United's first team in that cup match, yet still the French manager's side came out on top. While Ferguson reacted angrily, Wenger seemed cool.

At that stage, it looked like there would only be one winner in their duel.[36]

Wenger was also up for the challenge after United's title win of 2003. The following season, boiling point in the rivalry was soon reached. By September, in fact, with a match that became known as 'The Battle of Old Trafford'. Ferguson certainly wanted it to be a fight, thinking he had found a chink in Wenger's Arsenal – a soft centre.

'It's funny,' Paul Scholes said. 'In team talks against Arsenal, the ball was rarely mentioned. We knew we had to get about them. We had to tackle them. The manager always put that into us, he revved us up.'

He would eventually expose that weakness, albeit not on that September day.

It was a cantankerous game with six bookings in total, plus a red card for Patrick Vieira, much to the annoyance of his Arsenal team-mates who were convinced Ruud van Nistelrooy had conned the referee to get the French international sent off. When the Dutch striker earned and missed a last-minute penalty, the Arsenal players couldn't restrain their delight.

Arsenal's Martin Keown said, 'When the player missed, I just give it to him, as you might do in the playground.'[37] Keown jumped up and struck the back of Van Nistelrooy's head as the defender came back down to earth in a mixture of rage and ecstasy. Other Arsenal players joined in with the pushing of the Dutchman, and the incident ended up earning the London outfit a £175,000 fine, the largest ever given to a club by the FA. In addition to the already dismissed Vieira, defenders Lauren and Keown, and midfielder Ray Parlour, all earned suspensions for their actions.

---

36 In the game that followed the cup defeat to Arsenal, with United and Ferguson seemingly on the floor, the club managed to respond in emphatic fashion, winning 3-0 away to Juventus.

37 Keown cannot even bring himself to mention Van Nistelrooy by name.

'They went over the top,' Scholes said. 'It wasn't a nice thing to see.' But nor was the fact that Arsenal remained top – and unbeaten, something they would maintain throughout the campaign to become the only English top flight side to not lose a league match in a 38-game season.[38] And to think, they were centimetres from having that run broken at Old Trafford. United would end up finishing a distant third and it was time for Ferguson to go back to the drawing board and devise a plan to overcome his nemesis.

Arsenal, by virtue of their record-breaking campaign, won the title at a canter and an ungracious Ferguson complained that their achievement was tainted by too many draws. But the facts didn't lie. United ended up 15 points behind Arsenal.

'You could see his mind thinking, what we were thinking – these are better than us and we need to improve,' Phil Neville recalled. 'You could see him planning. How do I topple these because this is probably going to be my biggest challenge as Manchester United manager.'

Neville continued, 'It was chipping away at us every day, with little things. It wasn't a big Winston Churchill speech, it was every single day "everyone loves Arsenal, look at the football they're playing, everyone's praising them", and it was hurting us every single day.'

But Ferguson was up for the fight. 'The gaffer loved the challenge,' his former assistant Steve McClaren mused. 'He had to have someone to fight, someone to complain about. Arsenal! Arsenal! Arsenal! Wenger!'

There was an FA Cup semi-final success in 2004 over the Gunners that suggested Ferguson was coming close to a formula to beat his counterpart. Arsenal's unbeaten stretch in

---

38 The Invincibles was a nickname given to the Preston North End team of the 1888/89 season, as well as the Arsenal side of 2003/04. Preston earned the name after completing an entire season undefeated in league and cup (27 games), while Arsenal were undefeated in the league (38 games). The original nickname of the Preston team was the Old Invincibles.

the league, however, continued well into the 2004/05 season. It had reached 49 games when the two teams met once more at Old Trafford in what turned out to be 'The Battle of the Buffet'.

'When you hear Wenger now talk about his greatest achievement he talks about the 49 games unbeaten. And the fact United were so desperate to stop it I think says a lot about the mindset of Ferguson,' journalist Sam Wallace said.

The United boss had spent every minute of the previous two weeks plotting the downfall of Wenger's Arsenal in that October 2004 clash. United kicked their opponents off the park, and in particular José Antonio Reyes, who endured some pretty ugly challenges from Gary Neville. Having missed under the same circumstances a year before, it was ironic that it was a Van Nistelrooy penalty midway through the second half that sparked the end of Arsenal's unbeaten run. Rooney made victory certain with a late tap-in.

The Gunners were fuming once again, because of what they deemed to be rough treatment from Ferguson's team, but they were also aggrieved at a couple of key decisions from the referee. Firstly, Rio Ferdinand was fortunate not to see red in the first half when he took out Freddie Ljungberg when the Swede was through on goal. And then there was the perceived foul from Sol Campbell on Wayne Rooney that led to the crucial spot-kick converted by Van Nistelrooy. The Arsenal players felt the Englishman had gone down too easily to earn the penalty. The Battle of the Buffet nickname for the occasion came from what followed the match. 'There was a bit of commotion,' Arsenal vice-chairman David Dein recalled. 'And then right in front of my eyes I saw a pizza winging its way, just flying in the air, and unfortunately landing on Sir Alex.'

Cesc Fàbregas remembers the incident clearly. He said, 'We felt so upset about that day. How it happened. It was the end of the unbeaten run of 49 games, the end of the invincible era. The way it happened – Wayne Rooney diving, the referee letting them do whatever they wanted, Gary Neville kicking José Antonio Reyes all over the park. Even the second free kick he should have been sent off. He kept going and going. I wasn't even playing that game, I was about to come on when they scored the second goal. After that I was one of the first ones to run into the tunnel. And I had a pizza in my hand. In the olden days we had pizza in the changing room. So I took it, and I was eating it and I remember Edu coming in, Robert Pires coming in. And then we start hearing shouting. All of a sudden the players went out, and I was the last one to go out. I was 17 and skinny, and the Old Trafford tunnel is so tiny, I could see Rio Ferdinand, Thierry Henry, Patrick Vieira, Roy Keane, Sol Campbell, and I was at the back, I couldn't do anything from there. I was upset, and took the pizza ... and I didn't even know where it fell. I promise. I was meant to hit someone on the other side. After that they told me that it hit Ferguson on the face which obviously I apologised for 10,000 times. He was very upset, I heard. But it was not directed at him.' And the topping? 'A Margherita.'

But in the long term, Arsenal were 'rattled' according to Phil Neville. Indeed, Ferguson thinks that single defeat 'scrambled Arsène's brain' to such a degree it affected him permanently. Arsenal never won another league title under Wenger, and rarely threatened to do so, whereas a period of dominance would return to Old Trafford in the not-too-distant future. Ferguson knew how to respond to a defeat while his opposite number was less adept, certainly over the long haul.

Now the insults being fired were coming from Wenger towards Ferguson, in another sign the power was shifting back towards the Scot. 'Ferguson's out of order. He has lost all sense of reality,' was one jibe directed from Wenger at his opposite number. It got worse. Wenger later said of Ferguson, 'I will never talk about THAT man again.'

In the return match a few months later, things began to kick off between the two teams before a ball had even been kicked. United captain Roy Keane had a go at Arsenal skipper Patrick Vieira over some comments the French international made in the direction of Gary Neville in the pre-match warm-up. More significantly, United played Arsenal off the park that evening, winning 4-2 at Highbury, including a marvellous goal late on from John O'Shea that sealed victory. O'Shea looked as surprised as anyone at how he had scored such a sublime effort. The tide had turned.

Wenger enjoyed a fortuitous win over United on penalties in that season's FA Cup Final in a match Ferguson's side dominated. But the result was a one-off. Indeed, the FA Cup in 2005 was the last trophy Wenger would win in the remaining eight years Ferguson was United manager.

The evidence is clear when analysing the records of the two managers when their teams played each other. From Wenger's arrival in 1996 to the summer of 2005, the Arsenal manager had a 41 per cent win ratio, compared with Ferguson's 38 per cent. Post 2005, until the Scot's eventual retirement in 2013, Wenger's win ratio plummeted to 20 per cent. Ferguson, meanwhile, saw his win ratio shoot up to 60 per cent.

Ironically, the pair went up against each other 49 times, including Charity or Community Shields, with Ferguson victorious on 23 occasions to Wenger's 16, with the rest ending in draws. More importantly, Ferguson won the Premier League on ten occasions while Wenger was Arsenal manager, with the Frenchman sealing three league titles.

So what changed? Though Ferguson eventually overcame Wenger in the head to heads thanks to tactical and physical masterplans, there was a lot more to how he eventually prevailed over his French rival.

For a start, Wenger stole an initial march in his deep knowledge of the European market, something Ferguson counteracted by improved scouting, which even included successful raids on the Latin American markets. That would bring shrewd purchases such as the Brazilian twins Rafael and

Fábio da Silva, as well as Mexican striker Javier 'Chicharito' Hernández. But the stepping up of the European scouting missions, as well as the appointment of Carlos Quieroz as assistant manager, helped United secure Cristiano Ronaldo at the expense of Arsenal in 2003.

There was more. Losing the titles of 1998, 2002 and 2004 hurt Ferguson. He had to respond. The manager would often use defeats or title losses to inspire the club to greater things and this time was no different. It was also something Wenger was ultimately unable to achieve over a sustained period of time. 'Football brings out the best and worst in people,' Ferguson said, 'because the emotional stakes are so high. In a high-stakes game, a player can lose his nerve for a minute and he can lose his temper too. And you're left regretting it. Arsenal had a lot of those moments, but Arsène struggled to believe that internal failings and weaknesses can sometimes cause you to lose. The explanation is sometimes within.'

When United lost, Ferguson would eventually find an answer, at least privately, whereas his opposite number would find an excuse. Queiroz returned to the club in 2004, after a year managing Real Madrid, and was largely left responsible for training, as well as tactical work regarding opponents, particularly in Europe. He would also prove invaluable in helping Ronaldo settle in, mainly thanks to both being native Portuguese speakers. The pair's relationship annoyed Ruud van Nistelrooy who, after an altercation with Ronaldo during training, told the winger, 'What are you going to do? Complain to your daddy?' It was a clear reference to how the Dutch striker viewed the bond between Ronaldo and Queiroz. It also prompted Ferguson to sell Van Nistelrooy, on the basis that the striker was proving more trouble than he was worth. A by-product of that decision was the improvement of the manager's rapport with Ronaldo. To this day, Ronaldo still speaks in glowing terms of his former boss.

Even though Queiroz left in 2008, Ferguson could move on, promoting both Mike Phelan and René Meulensteen from his backroom staff to offset the loss of his right-hand man. The domestic juggernaut continued. Herein lies Ferguson's biggest advantage over Wenger. Whether it be losing matches, players or assistant coaches, the Scot would always bounce back, often higher than ever before. Once Wenger lost his legendary defence and goalkeeper, or his French midfield stalwarts of Petit and Vieira, he struggled to find adequate replacements. In addition, he was unable to respond with the same authority and vigour when losing big matches.

By 2011, due to the chasm in quality on the pitch between the two clubs, there was a warmth in the relationship between the two managers that would have been unheard of a decade before. Ferguson clearly felt his opposite number was no longer a threat. Worse than that, during the 8-2 humiliation of Wenger's Arsenal at Old Trafford in the August of that year, Ferguson felt so sorry for the Frenchman that 'it actually reached the point where I felt – "please, no more goals"'.

Wenger, once the master at plucking talent from around Europe, was no longer demonstrating such prowess in the transfer market, according to Ferguson. Yet the Scot was showing he was now adept at achieving sustained success on a budget. In his last four years at the club Ferguson had a net transfer spend of just £47.8m.[39] This figure pales into insignificance when compared with the net spend of rivals Chelsea and Manchester City over the same period. Chelsea's in those four years was more than £250m while City's exceeded £300m. Even Liverpool outspent United between 2009 and 2013, with a total net spend of roughly £80m. And even though Wenger spent less than Ferguson during this time, making a small profit for his club, the performances of his team reflected one that needed major surgery.

---

39 Not including the £11.75m outlay for Wilfried Zaha who was a Ferguson signing but joined the club after his retirement.

Wenger's training methods, so revered when he first arrived at the club, became dated. When Robin van Persie arrived at Old Trafford in the summer of 2012 he described the training as very different to what he had left behind.

The Dutch striker said, 'It just clicked, with the sessions we had with Ferguson and Meulensteen [first-team coach]. It was very focussed on the next opponent. Every week we had different kinds of sessions. For example, if we played against Chelsea, the whole week we were training on going over their left side, so our right side, getting a wide low cross, because we needed a low finish against Petr Čech, because Čech is very tall and has difficulties in going down. That detail, that is what I really liked.'

In the game Van Persie was referring to against Chelsea in October 2012, United won 3-2 with all three goals coming as a result of low crosses from the right. Arsenal finished fourth that season, 16 points behind United, who reclaimed the title they had lost to Manchester City the previous season. Though Van Persie is only talking about how it was at United, you sense he is also referring to how this didn't take place at his previous club. Many former Arsenal players spoke of how the training would rarely consider opponents.

Wenger had just one assistant, Pat Rice, in all but one of the years he came up against his Scottish foe. Ferguson, meanwhile, had six in the same period, each one gaining more trust and responsibility as the boss spent more time focussing on other tasks while the club continued to expand. Ferguson once said an ability to delegate was crucial to his success, something Wenger struggled to do, remaining heavily involved in training sessions right up until he too rode off into the sunset of retirement in the summer of 2018. He did so, however, in the knowledge that having won a few initial battles against Ferguson, he had been resoundingly beaten in the war of attrition.

7 (ii)

... to Mourinho outlasted

ANOTHER PROBLEM Wenger endured was his inability to deal with the new kid in town – José Mourinho, who arrived in 2004, just after Arsenal last won the title under the Frenchman.

The 2004/05 season began for United with defeat to the Special One and his team at Stamford Bridge. That opening day loss and numerous others during the first two years of Mourinho's Chelsea reign also gave Sir Alex Ferguson food for thought. How could he combat this new threat, one that was bankrolled by Roman Abramovich's millions?

Armed with this injection of cash and under the leadership of Mourinho, Chelsea hit the front early and eased to a first Premier League crown. Their first away game after clinching the title at Bolton was a trip to Old Trafford.

One thing Ferguson wanted to instil in his players was the pain and humiliation involved in defeat, which is why he was fully supportive of holding a guard of honour to mark the London club's first league title in half a century.[40]

---

40 Fun fact: Guards of honour are not exclusive to the modern era, and occurred as far back as 1955 when Manchester United provided one for Chelsea to mark the club's first ever league title.

'I remember at Old Trafford we had to do a guard of honour on our own patch for Chelsea and it was almost like Sir Alex enjoyed it,' according to Phil Neville. 'It was like, "This is going to hurt, seeing a team that has got your title come out at your stadium and you have to applaud them."'

'In the period from August 2004 to May 2006,' Ferguson wrote in his second autobiography, 'we won one trophy: the 2006 League Cup. Chelsea and José won the Premier League in both those campaigns. As Arsenal dropped away, Abramovich's wealth and José's managerial ability became the biggest obstacle to our rebuilding. Traditionally, our preparation for a new season had emphasised the second half of the 38-game programme. We always finished strongly. There was science as well as spirit behind our talent for winning games in the months that really mattered.'

Ferguson continued, 'José was fresh in town, working for an employer with stacks of money, and with hype clearing his path. In the autumn of 2004 he needed to make a strong start in his first few weeks at Stamford Bridge.' Indeed, he did just that, including beating Ferguson's United in his first game in charge of Chelsea. Ferguson took note. 'Chelsea skated to a six-point lead and we could never make it up. Once they hit the front in the title race, José made sure they won plenty of games narrowly. It was all one- and two-nil victories.'

Mourinho's Chelsea won the 2005/06 Premier League in similar fashion, with United a distant second.

In those fallow years, a number of United fans would scream 'Attack! Attack! Attack!' Supporters sensed a more cautious approach from players who seemed short on confidence. Few fans would outright mention anything to do with Ferguson's dismissal, though undoubtedly some were thinking of the notion privately.

It got worse. A spat between star players Cristiano Ronaldo and Wayne Rooney at the 2006 World Cup threatened to spill over into Old Trafford affairs. It is difficult to imagine most managers dealing with the issue with the aplomb that Ferguson did, least of all Mourinho, who once faced with a problem in the dressing room, would only be weeks away from losing his job. Think 'palpable discord' and Mourinho and you immediately think of the end of the Portuguese manager's spells at Chelsea (twice), Real Madrid and finally Manchester United a few years after Ferguson retired. Think dressing room bust-ups and Ferguson, and you immediately think that there will only be one winner.

'The interesting thing about you is that you brought on all these incredible star players – Keane, Beckham, Van Nistelrooy – and yet you fell out with all of them,' Channel 4's Jon Snow highlighted in an interview with Ferguson shortly after his retirement. But with each fall-out, United got better. Out went Beckham, in came Ronaldo. Out went an ageing and disruptive Keane, in came Michael Carrick to give a calm authority to the midfield, as well as excellent ball-retention skills, perhaps even better than the Irishman's. Ferguson also got rid of Van Nistelrooy the same summer that Carrick arrived due to the Dutch striker's attitude and it proved to be a masterstroke, enabling Ronaldo to become the scoring machine that would take him to another level even the manager could scarcely believe. As for the spat between Rooney and Ronaldo, it was soon forgotten, with the pair functioning in tandem upon their return to the club after their World Cup exploits.

The Scot delivered a blueprint for success, claiming 'comprehensive control' was vital, and he never ceded it during his time as manager of Manchester United. But like with Rooney and Ronaldo, he could also ease tensions, as well as simply jettison a player he thought was disruptive.

Think of how Mourinho would have handled Eric Cantona or even the Van Nistelrooy and Ronaldo fracas, and you wonder if the Portuguese manager would have been the Special One at dealing with such delicate matters. The sale of Van Nistelrooy, followed by the solitary purchase of

Michael Carrick, left United fans pretty underwhelmed as they headed into the 2006/07 season. Little did they know that Ferguson had learned from his previous mistakes in the transfer market.

There had been plenty of long-term planning to see off both Wenger and Mourinho and it was about to come to fruition. It had included a change in transfer policy. From buying what Ferguson believed was ready-made talent, now the club had a more long-term strategy. The earlier purchases of World Cup winners Fabien Barthez and Kléberson were examples of that. Neither cut the mustard at Old Trafford so instead, teenagers Wayne Rooney and Cristiano Ronaldo were signed with one eye on the future, albeit after failed pursuits of Ronaldinho and Arjen Robben. Signing that duo would have almost certainly meant Rooney and Ronaldo would never have joined United and history may well have been very different. As good as Ronaldinho and Robben were, given how their careers panned out, United may have only got a couple of years out of them rather than six from Ronaldo and more than a decade from Rooney.

The January 2006 purchases of Patrice Evra and Nemanja Vidić were not immediately successful. The defenders endured a nightmare start to their United careers, but ultimately proved to be two of Ferguson's best signings. Both players enjoyed eight and a half years at the club, winning the game's biggest prizes.

Finally in this period, Ferguson managed to solve his goalkeeping conundrum. Mark Bosnich, Massimo Taibi, Fabien Barthez, Tim Howard and Roy Carroll had all failed to varying degrees to fill the gloves of Peter Schmeichel. However, in the summer of 2005, Edwin van der Sar arrived with the presence, as well as talent, to fulfil the position to distinction over the next six years. Interestingly, what impressed Ferguson most about Schmeichel and Van der Sar was their ability to bounce back from errors, a trait that helped the Scot stay in the job for 26 and a half years.

The lightning starts of Mourinho's teams was something Ferguson successfully managed to emulate. He altered his training methods with the help of his assistants. United had been slow out of the blocks for the first two years of the Mourinho era. That had to change as there would no longer be surging second halves to seasons to reel in opponents like they had in 1996 with Kevin Keegan's Newcastle or Wenger's Arsenal in 2003. Now United had to be ready from the off. Training would begin earlier, and would be more intense, so that by the 2006/07 season Ferguson's team got off to a flyer, winning their first four league matches and only dropping seven points from the first 54 available. United's promising first half of the season propelled the club to their first championship in four years in one of the sweetest Premier League titles of the Ferguson era.

The rapport Ferguson enjoyed with his players would bear early fruit, but the Scot could maintain them and see them develop into vintage wines, whereas Mourinho's relationships would eventually go stale. Although it could be argued that the ownership style of Roman Abramovich didn't allow a manager to think long-term, either with recruitment, promotion of youth, or even how he treated the players, the way Mourinho suffered in every environment he worked in suggested he didn't have the man-management skills or the ability to move with the times that Ferguson undoubtedly possessed.

Today, it is often argued that Mourinho's struggles with the modern game have been down to his inability to evolve, something Ferguson was always able to do. Even as a septuagenarian he was still capable of getting the best out of players, some of whom were more than 50 years his junior. He adapted, and managed to stay contemporary, embracing new styles, fresh coaching methods and sports science.

When it was put to him by DJ Spoony on a BBC radio interview in 2012 that 'the most successful people in life are the people that adapt to change the best and the quickest',

Ferguson's response was clear-cut, 'Absolutely. It's the same with management.'

Ferguson treated players differently in the latter years to how he did when he first entered management. Commentator Clive Tyldesley, who had monitored Ferguson's behaviour closely during his time at United, said, 'The way he treated Ronaldo, for instance, was very different to how he was with the younger players in the late '80s, early '90s.'

But Ferguson revelled in the challenge, often saying how working with young players kept the age off him. You often wonder if Mourinho had the same ability. His post-match rhetoric is still very similar today to what it was almost two decades ago. His teams play in a similar style and his relationships with players seem full of passion and positive intensity at first, but frayed and on the verge of burn-out at the end.

There was another key factor for Ferguson in overcoming Wenger, and Mourinho in particular, and that was in choosing Carlos Queiroz as his assistant in 2002.

The role of Ferguson's henchman cannot be under-estimated, in keeping both himself and his team fresh with new approaches and novel ideas. With his success at Aberdeen and the early progress at Manchester United, it couldn't have been achieved without Archie Knox. Brian Kidd was essential in bringing the youth through in the 1990s and Steve McClaren was a massive influence in both the treble-winning season and the league title wins in the two years that followed before he departed to manage Middlesbrough in 2001.

With each assistant, Ferguson made a step forward and when he appointed Queiroz, he had reached a peak. The Mozambique-born coach was hired for his tactical acumen but also due to his understanding of multiple languages and cultures, a must in a United dressing room where different nationalities numbered 21 at one point. Patrice Evra backed that up, praising Queiroz's influence in helping him settle in at Old Trafford. He told ITV in 2018, 'When I joined he was the only one speaking French so he helped me a lot to adapt to Manchester United.'

But it was still Ferguson's man-management that was held in the highest possible regard, as Nani, who played along the United touchline during Ferguson's last six years in charge, recognised. He said, 'He's a man who knows how to manage all the characters, all the different ages, personalities. My personality was not easy, I know. I learned a lot, and I changed a lot.'

Queiroz had two stints at Old Trafford. The first lasted for just one season, 2002/03, and United won the league. More importantly, it was on Queiroz's advice, as well as his Portuguese connections, that United landed Cristiano Ronaldo, who was fundamental in Ferguson's return to form, both in the Premier League and the Champions League, at a time when Chelsea under Mourinho looked set to dominate. It was therefore important that Ferguson could continually revitalise and reassess, both himself and his team. Queiroz was arguably the most influential of all his assistants. Ferguson mentions the one-time Real Madrid boss on 25 separate pages of his second autobiography, which is the same amount as Archie Knox, Brian Kidd, Steve McClaren and Mike Phelan put together. More importantly, Ferguson is positively gushing in his praise of Queiroz, whereas he was not afraid of pointing out the shortcomings of others, especially Kidd.

It is no coincidence that during Queiroz's second stint at the club, between 2004 and 2008, United managed to re-emerge on the European stage, ultimately winning the club game's biggest prize in his last year. It was just a few weeks into the 2007/08 season that Mourinho was shown the door by Roman Abramovich, largely because of his inability to maintain good relations with the players, as well as not reaching a Champions League Final while in the Stamford Bridge hot seat. Ferguson, thanks to Queiroz, achieved both, even cutting his captain

Roy Keane adrift after a bust-up with his trusted assistant in order to maintain harmony within the squad. With this act, Ferguson could move the club forward.

United were in the midst of a rebuilding job when Mourinho arrived. When there was a dearth of top managers in England's top division, in the early to mid-1990s, Ferguson could still challenge for, and often win Premier League titles during a transitional period. With the arrival of Wenger and then Mourinho, he was unable to cover the cracks so easily.

Stellar players in United's history, such as Roy Keane, Ruud van Nistelrooy, Phil Neville and Nicky Butt, were all ushered, or shoved, out of the door in the mid-2000s. Ferguson saw it through, however, and was to emerge on the other side, winning the league title in 2007. Mourinho's Chelsea came second but rarely threatened top spot. It was the first of three successive championships for United, and it was enough to see off the Portuguese manager.

Mourinho would never get far enough along the line to warrant a reconstruction of a team. Ferguson did it on many occasions, and doing so held no fears for him. 'Rebuilding held no terrors for me,' he said. 'It was second nature. A football club is like family. Sometimes people leave. In football, sometimes they have to, sometimes you want them to, sometimes there is no choice for either side, when age or injury intervene.'

The loss of a player, like a football match, was all part of the game for Ferguson. Sometimes a bitter pill to swallow, always a lesson to be learned.

8 (i)

From treble retreat ...

AFTER WINNING the Champions League in 1999, Alex Ferguson wanted to build a dynasty at Manchester United – one founded on a period of sustained European success. This meant back-to-back triumphs, like the great Ajax, Bayern Munich, Real Madrid and Liverpool sides had done. What he didn't expect was that it would take a series of painful lessons over the next nine years to help him reach the pinnacle of club football once more.

In the 1999/2000 season United cruised through to the last eight where they came up against European heavyweights Real Madrid. It was to prove a pivotal two-legged affair, and one that would alter Ferguson's approach to the competition forever. It would also inspire him to take the decisions that would eventually lead the club to success in Moscow in 2008.

Where such an encounter would have left Ferguson a little intimidated or starry-eyed in the past, he was now much more confident on the biggest stage of all, invigorated by the previous year's dramatic success at the Camp Nou. However, a 0-0 in the Bernabéu prompted the worries to return, particularly due to his team's inability to score an away goal. If that concerned him, what happened at Old Trafford left him distraught.

'It was one of those nights when just about everything that could possibly go wrong for us did so in spades,' Ferguson said. It started with a Roy Keane own goal and the death knell on United's European campaign was delivered when Madrid struck twice more on the counter to give them an unassailable lead. United were needlessly throwing men forward with still 40 minutes left on the clock and the second Madrid goal, smartly executed by Raúl, exposed that carelessness. Shortly afterwards, Keane missed an excellent opportunity to get his team back in the tie with the goal at his mercy. It would prove costly as just moments later, the Spanish outfit scored a third. The goal that killed off the match included an incredible back-heel nutmeg on Henning Berg from Fernando Redondo, which left the Norwegian halfway up a fjord while the Argentinian went downstream to the touchline, before assisting Raúl for his second of the night. United clawed back some of the deficit to make the final score 3-2 to Real Madrid but were left to rue missed chances as well as over-ambitious attacking, flooding forward and chasing the game at a time when patience was required.

As much as losing meant learning lessons, captain Keane wanted to raise the bar in the wake of this excruciating defeat. He said, 'This was the standard we had to aim for, world-class. A number of features of Real's play struck me. The incredible first touch. The economy of movement, no daft running, every move purposeful. Raúl's cunning, waiting like a panther to pounce on any half-chance. And burying it when it came.' Journalist Rob Smyth argued that this match was the single most cataclysmic defeat of the Ferguson era in his assessment of the quarter-final in a 2011 article he penned for *The Blizzard*, 'It continues to impact 11 years on; every time Manchester United line up for a big game at home or in Europe, their tactics are a direct consequence of that chastening experience against Madrid. [Vicente] Del Bosque spoke of United's "tactical anarchy" that night, and Ferguson ensured such suggestions could never be made again. Put simply, up until that game his teams tried to score one more than the opposition; ever since they have tried to concede one fewer. Something died in the United team that night. And something certainly died in Ferguson: his faith in the power of swash and buckle.'

This match punctured the club's previously unshakeable self-belief and prompted Ferguson to look for alternative tactical options. 'One of the forceful reminders delivered by that defeat was that consistent success in Europe would be more readily achieved if we improved our capacity to defend against the counter-attack,' the United boss said.

His opinion was shared by Italian manager Arrigo Sacchi, a legend of the game, not least for his guidance of AC Milan to consecutive European Cups. 'Manchester are a very good side,' he said after the game. 'But their win last season was exceptional. Madrid, I believe, are more likely to win the Champions League on a regular basis. Their style of play, alone, means they are better equipped to dominate Europe.'

'You can't keep giving yourselves mountains to climb, especially against the top teams,' said Keane after the quarter-final. 'But it is the way we play and I think it will be hard for us to change.' So it proved. This United side struggled to win knockout ties, never mind multiple Champions Leagues. After 1999 they only saw off one opponent in the knockout phase until 2007.[41]

In 2000/01 Ferguson kept the same personnel and system, but United were much more cautious in their approach to European games. Nevertheless, they ultimately succumbed at the quarter-final stage again, this time to the team they vanquished in 1999, Bayern Munich.

The 3-1 loss on aggregate to the Bavarians spelt the end for United's traditional 4-4-2 formation that had flying wingers as a fundamental part. It also was the final throw of the dice for the remarkable treble-winning team. Henning Berg had

---

41 Deportivo La Coruña in 2002.

departed six months prior to the Bayern defeat while Jaap Stam, Andy Cole, Dwight Yorke and Teddy Sheringham all made their final Champions League appearances for United in the second leg at the Olympic Stadium.

The summer of 2001 saw an overhaul of the squad, including the incomings of Laurent Blanc, Ruud van Nistelrooy and Juan Sebastián Verón. The latter's arrival was pivotal as Ferguson sought a new path to European success after the failures of the previous two seasons.

The losses to Bayern and in particular Madrid hurt Ferguson. Commentator Clive Tyldesley, who was working for ITV on both those nights in Bavaria and at Old Trafford, said, 'Ferguson struggled to get over that defeat against Real Madrid in 2000. He couldn't get over how open they were, and he changed his style somewhat in the subsequent years.'

Verón was key to that change. Gone was the open, swashbuckling style epitomised by attacking wide players, two central midfielders, and a front-two combination, such as Yorke and Cole. Verón was bought with Europe firmly in mind.

'The team was altering,' Ferguson wrote in his second book, released shortly after his retirement. 'Verón was a superb footballer with immense stamina.' But there was a problem that meant this experiment ultimately failed. 'We couldn't find a position in which to play him. If we played him in the centre of midfield he would end up at centre-forward, or wide right, or wide left. He just hunted the ball.'

The plan was to use Verón in a midfield three along with Scholes and Keane. Quite simply it would add another body in the middle of the park, making sucker-punch goals like the ones conceded against Madrid in 2000 less likely. Of course, he was an incredible player too. 'There were moments when he'd take you to the heavens,' Ferguson recalled. He could also keep the ball, as well as create. He had played in Italy for the five years prior to his arrival at Old Trafford so it is safe to assume Ferguson must have had some confidence in the Argentinian's ability to be tactically disciplined, something Serie A is renowned for.

As the manager struggled domestically at the beginning of 2001/02, he began tweaking with the formation, and with Verón's position. The Argentine was essentially a central midfielder with Paul Scholes playing slightly further forward. However, after a run of poor form, Ferguson switched the pair. The system still didn't function properly. It is arguable that the experiment failed as much because of Scholes's inability to perform as a number ten, a role he seemed perfect for, as much as Verón's failure to adapt. Either way, the tactical discipline Ferguson so craved after the crushing defeats since 1999 meant the Scot's tactical brainwave didn't work and the fall-guy was the player nicknamed La Brujita – The Little Witch. 'He went wherever he liked,' Ferguson said of his wayward nature on the pitch. Though it happened a year before his eventual departure, perhaps the standout moment in Verón's demise didn't come during a game, but in the pre-match line-up prior to that season's Champions League semi-final second leg.

United were tantalisingly close to a final once more and as the players lined up in the pre-match ritual, captain Roy Keane noticed something, 'As we stood for the UEFA anthem before the second leg of the Champions League semi-final with Bayer Leverkusen, one of our players was shaking. He was afraid. Played for his country, won championships, big star – afraid of taking the step up.' Keane played alongside Verón in midfield that night and the Argentinian's performance was timid. If there was any doubt who Keane was referring to, it was resolved when a fracas between the two midfielders occurred after the game.

Rio Ferdinand thinks Verón may have thrived without Keane's intimidating influence, 'He was an unbelievable player, great passer. The only thing I think that killed him was Roy Keane was probably a bit more of a dominant personality and was picking the ball up in his positions. You have to remember Verón came from Lazio, Parma where he was the main man, the whole game went through him. He came to United, that's what Roy Keane did. Keane came and got it off the defenders, passed it through to the midfielders and attackers, and got in positions and was very vocal, like "Yeah, give me the ball! Give me the ball!" I honestly think without Roy Keane there he might have flourished in a Man United shirt. Keane was his problem. And it wasn't Roy Keane's fault, it's just that his personality was bigger and more overpowering.'

Either way, the night in Leverkusen ended in another crushing exit, this time on away goals. A final flourish at Hampden Park, scene of that famous match that Ferguson had attended in 1960 between Real Madrid and Eintracht Frankfurt, was now a dream that lay in tatters. United had led the home leg twice before being held to a 2-2 draw. They were in front again in the second leg but once more Leverkusen pegged them back and the tie finished 3-3 on aggregate, with the Germans progressing because of the goals they scored at Old Trafford.

Commentator Clive Tyldesley recalled the tie, and in particular the away leg in Germany, 'They should have won that game. Bayer Leverkusen had some good players, but United were better. I know that defeat really rankled with Roy Keane, so it must have with Ferguson too.'

It was to be as close as Keane would ever get to a final, having been suspended for the 1999 showpiece. It would be the furthest the club would progress in the competition for another five years, during which time there would be some other equally depressing defeats.

In 2003 United were outclassed by Real Madrid's Galácticos. The second leg of that quarter-final will be remembered predominantly for the Brazilian Ronaldo's hat-trick and the unprecedented standing ovation the striker received from the Old Trafford faithful. It also became the game that persuaded Roman Abramovich to invest in English football, albeit with Chelsea.

But there were other consequences to the defeat. David Beckham was sold a few months later, in part because of his flirtation with the Spanish side during the trip to Madrid in the first leg, but also for his style of play. For all the talk of the off-field distractions, there were footballing reasons behind Ferguson's decision to sell Beckham and buy Cristiano Ronaldo for half the price. Ferguson noted how Madrid's Luís Figo, Zinedine Zidane and Ronaldo could beat players, thus taking opposition defenders out of the game, which was almost worth a one-man advantage when it came to attacks. And those forays were far more likely to be on the counter, with a slightly more cautious approach to European games now very much a part of the agenda. Ferguson didn't feel this was a part of Beckham's capabilities and didn't believe it ever would be.

In the immediate aftermath of the 2003 Premier League triumph, Ferguson was interviewed on television and despite his obvious glee at securing the championship, the failure to win Europe's greatest prize still grated on him. He spoke of his disappointment at that aspect of the season and said he wanted to tweak the style of play, largely based on that quarter-final defeat to Real Madrid. Selling Beckham and buying Cristiano Ronaldo was the consequence. Though the Portuguese would go on to become a phenomenal goalscorer, initially it was his ability to beat players that took Ferguson's breath away and gave him added optimism that he could eventually win the Champions League again.

The decision to buy the Sporting Lisbon winger was also laced with the hallmarks of a classic Fergie signing – Ronaldo had impressed against his team. In a friendly against the outfit from the Portuguese capital in August 2003 Ferguson shouted at John O'Shea, 'Get close to him, Sheasy.' The Irish full-back replied simply, 'I can't.' There were already moves being made to bring the winger to Old Trafford but that match, aligned with interest from other clubs in Europe, including Arsenal, sped up the process. Within days Ronaldo was a Manchester United player.

Ronaldo is not the only player to sign for United after impressing against them. His arrival was another example of how a painful encounter would persuade Ferguson to improve the team. Louis Saha is one such instance. Ferguson said, 'Every time he [Saha] played against us he gave us a doing.' Ferguson promptly brought the French striker to Old Trafford for £12m.

From Ronaldo tearing O'Shea a new one to Saha ripping Wes Brown to shreds, there are numerous examples of how Ferguson would see a footballer cause damage to his team, and then go and buy said player. Eric Cantona is someone who falls into this category after impressing during a league fixture in September 1992. An overhead kick from the Frenchman, which Schmeichel did well to save, was a particular highlight from a match that United still won. Two months later he had swapped the white of Leeds for the red of Manchester. Jesper Blomqvist is another on the list having terrorised the United defence in the mid-1990s when playing for IFK Gothenburg. He was embedded in Ferguson's mind, though it would be four more years before the Scot brought him to Old Trafford. Blomqvist subsequently helped Ferguson win his first Champions League, playing in the final in the Camp Nou nine months after signing.

The 2003/04 assault on the Champions League would be United's most short-lived in almost a decade as they failed to make it beyond the last 16. It would be easy to come to the conclusion at this juncture that Ferguson's more cautious approach to European matches and his decision to change the dynamic of the team, by selling Beckham and buying Ronaldo, had failed, but that would be ignoring certain circumstances surrounding their exit.

Firstly, the Beckham–Ronaldo move was based largely on the latter's ability to beat players by using pace, strength and skill. Those attributes led to him frequently beating his opposite number in the last-16 clash with José Mourinho's FC Porto. On one such occasion, with just a couple of minutes remaining of the second leg at Old Trafford, he was 'chopped down' according to Ferguson, but the referee waved play on. There was no advantage for United to gain, though, especially as the clock was ticking and the home team were leading the tie by the narrowest of margins. Porto promptly went up the other end of the pitch and scored, knocking United out, and leading to Mourinho going on his now-infamous sprint down the Old Trafford touchline to celebrate with his players.

This game also contained a perfectly legitimate goal from Paul Scholes that was wrongly chalked off for offside. On fine margins Champions Leagues are won and lost. Indeed, even careers are made on such tiny fractions, as Mourinho himself can testify. Arguably this match changed his path forever.

Nevertheless, there can be few excuses for United's inability once again to even reach the quarter-final of Europe's premier competition a year later, as they were thoroughly outclassed by AC Milan. The match gets two lines in Ferguson's second book, a mark of how far off the pace the team were, and how far off the Scot's radar the game was for analysis.

If not making the last eight was bad enough two years in a row, in 2005/06 United slumped even further and didn't even make it beyond the group stage. It was Ferguson's worst moment since the winter of discontent in 1989. For some, it was even lower than that period, given how far the club had fallen since the dizzy heights of winning the treble in 1999. The team were now also-rans in Europe. They went out in the group phase after losing to Benfica, and there were now serious questions being asked about Ferguson's future.

The Scot was particularly hurt by this defeat and his frustration was only added to by suggestions that some journalists ordered champagne on the flight back from Lisbon. He also didn't like the accusations that his team's demise was related to the fact he was getting older, a suggestion Ferguson described as 'disgusting'.

Nevertheless, Ferguson needed to respond. What was crucial, though, was to decipher what went wrong, and not to over-react. Ferguson kept his head, and his faith in the young players. At that stage, Ronaldo had never scored a goal in the Champions League and Rooney hadn't done so for 15 months.[42] But this was not the time to panic.

Only one United player who started that match in the Portuguese capital would not be in the squad the following season. For the first goal that United conceded, it was Ruud van Nistelrooy who carelessly lost possession in the middle of the park prior to Benfica scoring. It should have been meat and drink for the Dutch striker but was another sign of his decline in Ferguson's eyes. He was sold to Real Madrid six months later.

Ferguson was 'sure the scouting structure was strong' and that it wouldn't be long before 'players would be found to take us back to our natural level'. First on the agenda was the defence. A poor showing in Europe meant reinforcements were required and within weeks of losing to Benfica, Patrice Evra and Nemanja Vidić were signed.

Roy Keane left for Celtic a couple of weeks before the trip to Portugal, again Ferguson wielding the axe on a player he thought had become more trouble than he was worth. A lot has been said regarding the division between Keane and Ferguson, but Edwin van der Sar and Gary Neville both felt it was necessary for the Irishman to seek pastures new, particularly in the wake of his critical comments about his team-mates on MUTV.

---

42 Excluding the qualifying round before the group stage.

After the Benfica debacle, the team went on to have a relatively good domestic season in comparison with their European travails, winning the League Cup and coming second in the league – a significant improvement on the previous two campaigns.

United bought Michael Carrick in the summer of 2006 in another piece of business that also helped put them on the right path to both domestic and European success.

However, it was the transformation of Ronaldo that same off-season that made the biggest difference to their European trajectory. The Portuguese winger went from fragile and inconsistent to powerful and machine-like in his scoring prowess. There was more. At the beginning of Ronaldo's United career he would 'showboat a lot' in the words of Ferguson, but the manager's assistant, Carlos Queiroz, helped immensely in his fellow native Portuguese speaker's development. 'Carlos worked hard' on Ronaldo's propensity to do too much showing off, too many unnecessary step-overs. Despite this habit, Ronaldo also had a characteristic that Ferguson loved in a footballer – courage. Ferguson uses this word time and again when talking about some of his favourite players. Courage in many senses. Courage to receive the ball when under pressure. Courage to take the ball or a set piece when the team are desperate for a goal, and 70,000 fans are demanding it. And most of all – courage to ride tough tackles, of which there were plenty coming Ronaldo's way in the English Premier League.

But it was in Europe that Ronaldo knew he would have to perform if he was to elevate himself to the Ballon d'Or-winning levels he yearned for. In 2006/07 he made a leap in that direction, helping United comfortably emerge from their Champions League group, although it wasn't until the quarter-final that he finally got on the scoresheet in that year's competition. But he got off the mark in fine style, netting twice in the 7-1 demolition of AS Roma in what was easily United's best performance in Europe since the treble in 1999.

They were majestic, after Ferguson had made a surprise choice in his starting XI. Alan Smith was chosen to lead the line after the manager had a hunch about starting the former Leeds striker. His gut instinct proved to be a masterstroke. Smith was excellent, scoring United's second goal. Roma didn't know what hit them, particularly for that strike, when he rounded off a move that involved four one-touch passes before finishing it off with a first-time shot that flew past goalkeeper Doni.

Stellar performances from Carrick, Giggs and Rooney propelled United to the semi-finals but Ronaldo's game really took the eye and moved him a step closer to the world number one status he so craved.

In the last four United faced AC Milan, who had out-classed them two years before, but this side had improved immensely since then and showed it by winning the first leg 3-2 thanks to a dramatic late winner from Wayne Rooney. United's form was their most electrifying in eight years and it was a delight to behold. However, they would eventually be undone by the absences of key players, especially at the back. An already thin squad was stretched by an injury to Rio Ferdinand in a draw with Middlesbrough just three days before the first leg. It meant United had just one of their regular back four, Evra, going into that game. Between the two legs Ferguson's team played in an energy-sapping Premier League match against Everton, which also didn't help their fitness levels in Milan. By the second leg in northern Italy, Vidić had been rushed back when barely fit and this was evident when he was slow to react for the Italians' first goal, scored by Kaká. The Serbian also didn't quite seem to have the same bite in his tackle immediately prior to the home side's second goal, scored by Clarence Seedorf.[43] The match ended up 3-0 to Milan and

---

43 Seedorf is currently the only player to have won the Champions League with three different clubs – once with Ajax in 1995, once with Real Madrid in 1998 and twice with Milan, in 2003 and 2007.

Ferguson lamented United's preparation, by which he meant a gruelling set of fixtures and injuries that illustrated the paucity of his options.

Ferguson said their opponents were 'a fantastic team' but one that had benefitted significantly from being able to 'rest eight players the Saturday before they played us. If we'd had better energy we would have been through.' Nevertheless, the manager knew his team were improving and that they were edging closer to matching the European exploits of 1999.

8 (ii)

... to Red Square delight

SIR ALEX Ferguson wanted to add extra depth to his squad to avoid a repeat of the shortfalls that were evident against AC Milan. Anderson and Nani were signed, largely on the recommendation of assistant manager Carlos Queiroz. The pair were seen as squad players at the outset but both were young enough to eventually emerge as first-teamers. Ferguson also wanted to add two players who would immediately improve his first-choice XI. Owen Hargreaves had been a long-term target and was seen as someone who could make the midfield trio of himself, Carrick and Scholes arguably the strongest in Europe at the time, though it wouldn't be long before Barcelona would take that tag.

For now, though, Ferguson had a midfield that had a better balance than the one he had initially formulated in 2001. Back then the erratic Juan Sebastián Verón undermined the work of Keane, and pushed Scholes out of his comfort zone.

With Carrick, Hargreaves and Scholes, there were three players who would comfortably sit deep if necessary, almost always leaving two to negate the counter-attacking threat of Europe's best. Ferguson still wanted one more player – a forward, particularly with injuries beginning to plague the otherwise brilliant Louis Saha. The manager had eyes for just one man, and it was someone who had been the scourge of his side at the end of the 2006/07 season – Carlos Tévez. The Argentine would dovetail perfectly with Rooney and Ronaldo, Ferguson felt, particularly as all three had the tactical flexibility to interchange with each other. Each of them could play wide-left, wide-right or through the middle.

With the team now looking much stronger there would also be the increased knowhow and experience among his players that would stand them in good stead, especially at the back, where Nemanja Vidić and Rio Ferdinand had built up an understanding not seen at Old Trafford since the mid-1990s pairing of Steve Bruce and Gary Pallister. The dynamic in defence was complemented by the calming influence of Edwin van der Sar. The Dutchman was a very different goalkeeper both in terms of the way he played, and his character, to the previous United legend between the sticks – Peter Schmeichel – but he was no less effective. Van der Sar made fewer mistakes than the Dane, though perhaps he didn't quite make the same incredible saves that Schmeichel did, or ever have games where he seemed like a brick wall. Schmeichel's performance against Newcastle United in 1996 certainly springs to mind. Nevertheless, the former Danish international would be responsible for the concession of around half a dozen or more goals a season, a higher proportion than Van der Sar, who was more consistent. And Schmeichel's propensity for a clanger was particularly evident during the Champions League campaign that would end in eventual triumph at the Camp Nou. United conceded 16 goals en route to eventually lifting the trophy with Schmeichel culpable for at least four. In contrast, Van der Sar conceded just four goals in the 2007/08 Champions League campaign.[44]

---

44 Van der Sar didn't play in the 2-1 home win against Sporting Lisbon. He also didn't play in a 1-1 draw at AS Roma. So the Dutchman let in four in total, with Tomasz Kuszczak conceding two.

The full-back situation was fairly settled with Wes Brown excelling at right-back and Patrice Evra continuing to impress on the other side. With Park Ji-sung, Louis Saha (when fit), Darren Fletcher, John O'Shea and Ryan Giggs also playing significant roles, United were ready for their most significant assault on the Champions League in almost a decade. Fans knew it too. So did Ferguson and his backroom staff, including René Meulensteen, who also played a prominent role in the development of Cristiano Ronaldo. The Portuguese winger was about to embark on a life-changing season, one even more remarkable than his outstanding 2006/07.

Ronaldo was sent off against Portsmouth in a league match early on in the campaign, giving Meulensteen the opportunity to have some extra one-to-one sessions with a player who was soon to become the world's best. Once again, a negative – Ronaldo being banned for three games – was turned into a positive – a chance to improve the team's best player.

'At that time I had been brought closer to the first team as Ferguson had seen the benefits of my work with quite a few players individually, helping them develop,' Meulensteen said. 'If the players didn't travel to games, I would work with the players who stayed behind. In this case, Cristiano stayed behind because of his suspension. I thought this was a great opportunity for me to tap into an area where I thought there was a lot to gain, in the finishing side of his game, and other aspects. He was suspended for three games which meant I had about three days in a row training him, really good quality contact time.

'There was a process that had two key components. Firstly, about bringing Cristiano from awareness to understanding, with regards for himself and what we wanted to achieve with him as a player. Secondly, it was about tactically and practically working with him on his finishing.'

But first Meulensteen wanted to understand the player better, to find out what his motivations were with regards to the season ahead. 'I asked him what his targets were for the season. It is important to have a purpose, an aim or a goal.' The Dutch coach wanted to drum it into Ronaldo. 'Goals! Goals! Goals! If you look at Gary Lineker, Alan Shearer, Michael Owen, Ruud van Nistelrooy. Their hunger for goals was insatiable.'

The Dutch coach then recalled the specifics of their conversation.

RM, 'How many goals did you score last season?'

CR, 'Twenty-three.'

RM, 'Great, I assume you want to get better. If you want progression you need to set yourself a target. What's your target for this season?'

CR, 'Okay, 30.'

At this stage Meulensteen cracked into a smile.

CR, 'Why are you smiling? What do you think?'

RM, 'I think 40.'

CR, 'Forty?! That's nearly double!'

RM, 'Yeah, that's correct. The reason I'm saying 40 is because we haven't really worked on the process of making you a better finisher, which we need to do on and off the field.'

Meulensteen then made a video of about six minutes long of some of United's best goalscorers in recent years. Dwight Yorke, Andy Cole, Ole Gunnar Solskjaer, Teddy Sheringham and Ruud van Nistelrooy all featured heavily. After watching the video, the pair picked up from where they had left off.

RM, 'What did you see?'

CR, 'A lot of goals.'

RM, 'Yeah, I know.'

CR, 'Some beautiful goals.'

RM, 'But what did you see?'

CR, 'What do you mean?'

RM, 'I'm not going to tell you. There's no point in telling you. I want you to see it.'

The pair watched the footage once more. Afterwards, the exchange continued.

RM, 'What did you see now?'

CR, 'I saw a lot of variety of goals. Shots, volleys, headers, tap-ins, inside foot, outside foot, left foot, right foot.'

RM, 'What else did you see?'

CR, 'Most of the goals were one or two touches.'

RM, 'Correct. And that's what we're going to work on.'

The focus turned to Ronaldo becoming more prolific with an insatiable desire to score, increasing the variety of goals, concentrating on the zones and areas of the goal with which to aim the ball, and scoring with one- and two-touch finishes.

The penny had dropped – 42 goals later Ronaldo was the best player in the world.

Meulensteen also made a DVD, summarising what the pair had worked on. He called the footage *Ronaldo – From Good to Great*. It seemed to do the trick.

United once again cruised through the Champions League group stage and squeezed past Lyon in the last 16 with strong defensive performances home and away, very much a hallmark of the Ferguson Mark II European Cup side. A similarly stoic performance in the quarter-final against AS Roma, who they had already played in the group phase, saw them go through 3-0 on aggregate, setting up a semi-final tie with Barcelona.

Preparation for this clash was arguably more intense than for any other Champions League tie in the Ferguson era, such was the focus and determination to make the final.

A Carlos Queiroz-inspired training ground session took place on the eve of the first leg. 'We were playing relentless games because of the league and the Champions League,' Michael Carrick said. 'We didn't really have time to train physically and do a lot of work, but Carlos Queiroz led the session and he's brought two gym mats out on to the pitch. We'd normally do sit-ups on them, but he's put them on the pitch and slung them down. It was me and Scholesy in midfield and I think Rio and Wes Brown were centre-halves, and he's put these two mats in between us, we're thinking, "What's he up to here?" For about five minutes he's just said don't let the ball get on those mats, so straight away you switch on and you're blocking that space off. That's where Barcelona, around the edge of the box, that's where they wanted to get into, that space, that was how they played at the time.'

Queiroz and Ferguson were so determined to restrict Barcelona's 'passing carousel' – a phrase Ferguson used to describe their midfield – that they went through an unprecedented level of tactical groundwork. The gym mats were just one element of how this evolved version of United in Europe wanted to strangle the central areas, remaining as compact as possible, and become familiar with parking themselves around the edge of their own box.

In 360 minutes of knockout football, United had conceded just one goal having deployed a 4-5-1 formation with a solid midfield three.[45] On paper it looks like a 4-4-2 was used for the two legs against Barcelona, but the reality was very different. Due to injuries, United had to stray from the usual three recognised central midfielders. Owen Hargreaves played at right-back with Wes Brown, in the absence of Nemanja Vidić, partnering Rio Ferdinand in the centre of defence. Under normal circumstances Hargreaves, a quick defensive midfielder, would have been an ideal addition to repel attacks through the middle. The other important caveat to remember is that the system often had wide player Park Ji-sung tucking in, making it a midfield three. United's strike pair, which in the first leg was Wayne Rooney and Carlos Tévez, had defensive responsibilities too. The Argentinian had to harry the Barcelona defenders in his own inimitable style, while

---

45 Against Roma, at home, for parts it was 4-4-1-1, but still pretty close to a five across the middle, especially when out of possession. The only goal United had conceded in the knockout stages was a Karim Benzema strike in the 1-1 draw away to Lyon.

Rooney, as so often in Europe, would have to drift wide, often filling the void that Park would leave behind. Rooney's role was largely defensive in the Camp Nou and only Ronaldo had the opportunity to roam, without too many defensive duties.

One of the most significant differences from this Barcelona team to the incarnation that would go on to dominate European football under Pep Guardiola was the summer 2008 addition of Dani Alves. The marauding right-back would mean the team would also pose a threat in wide areas.

But that was still to come. For now it was Frank Rijkaard's Barcelona standing between Ferguson and his first Champions League Final in nine years. The two legs were the clearest indication yet of how Ferguson's United had evolved from the swashbuckling team that won the treble before succumbing to Real Madrid a year later, primarily because of this attitude to pile forward. The team were now much more defensive, focussing on solidity over flamboyance, particularly in the midfield areas. Assistant coach Carlos Queiroz was significant in this tactical shift but it was something Ferguson had hoped for from his team even as far back as the mid-90s as he decried the performances of Paul Ince in the United engine room.

Wes Brown emphasised the philosophy that was to be deployed in the first leg at the Camp Nou. 'We knew it was going to be difficult. The thinking was if we can get a draw then great, if we can nick one then perfect. "Whatever happens, we have to be tight. We can't be letting one, two, three goals in and then coming back to Old Trafford and trying to get a result. That would be hard. They could easily pick us off then." Our focus was on just being tight. We knew that we had the ability to counter-attack. For that game, that's how it was. "Be tight, everyone defend. We know we can defend. We know we're not pushovers." I'm guessing they knew it was going to be hard as well – the respect between the two teams is legendary and they're not stupid – but of course they're going to try to win this first game to get a lead, as you would at home.'

Neither Brown nor Ferguson could believe the chance to sneak a goal would come so early in the game – a penalty to United after just one minute. But Ronaldo missed. Even United's top scorer was feeling the pressure. After a promising start, United just 'retreated' to their own box, Ferguson later admitted. The game was one of few chances and ended 0-0, meaning it was all to play for in the second leg.

The lack of freshness that the team suffered from in the defeat to AC Milan at the same stage the year previously was not going to be an excuse this time. Such was Ferguson's obsession with securing a second Champions League, four players were rested for a crucial Premier League clash that was sandwiched between the two legs of the Barcelona tie. Cristiano Ronaldo, Paul Scholes, Patrice Evra and Carlos Tévez were all left out of the starting XI for the top-of-the-table encounter at Chelsea, mindful of what had occurred 12 months before in a gruelling match against Everton, between the two semi-final legs against Milan. Ferguson felt that game at Goodison Park scuppered his team's chances in the second leg at the San Siro, which United lost 3-0 as they went crashing out with the final just one step away.

'Time and time again I said this club should have more success in Europe,' Ferguson said in his attempts to justify his decision to leave the four key players out against Chelsea. It also illustrated his regret at a lack of success on club football's biggest stage.

Going into the second leg against Barcelona, the match was finely poised. Wes Brown and co. just had the unenviable task of stopping Lionel Messi for the second time in a week. The Argentinian magician was beginning to emerge as a candidate for the Ballon d'Or. He would go on to become a serial winner of the game's top individual prize, but at this point in time his mind-boggling career was still in its infancy. Indeed, the Ronaldo–Messi duel was a mere twinkle in a football fan's eye.

Prior to kick-off, United supporters held up banners to celebrate the club's previous two successes in Europe's premier competition, in 1968 and 1999, while fans on the eastern side of the stadium brandished a mosaic with the single word 'Believe' etched in white around a sea of red as the Old Trafford decision-makers decided to add an extra stir of emotion to an already fervent affair. United were in their traditional red while Barcelona, who have had an array of garish away kits down the years, kept up this unusual tradition by wearing turquoise.

Brown, once again, takes up the story as he describes the opening exchanges of that nervous night at Old Trafford. 'Less than 30 seconds in, there's a loose pass towards me. Messi's there, I go for the ball, he does me a little bit and he's gone. "It's okay, Scholesy's there." I can still see it now. Scholesy comes across and dives in, brings him down right on the edge of the area. It's not a pen, but it's close. It's a free kick on the edge of the box, we clear it and we can settle down and start again. That was probably a good reminder of what could happen against Messi, looking back. Usually, if the ball was there to be won, I would win it, or try to, but this was a different player. It wasn't the day for that. "Stick to the plan. Don't. Dive. In,"' Brown recalled, referencing the drilling the team had received in the build-up to the match. The game's defining moment came with 15 minutes on the clock. Ronaldo was dispossessed on the edge of the Barcelona box but defender Gianluca Zambrotta immediately gifted possession back to United and the ball broke to Paul Scholes some 25 yards from goal. The usually prolific midfielder hadn't scored in more than eight months but showed no lack of confidence as he pulled the trigger. His strike of the bouncing ball was so sweet that it evaded Víctor Valdés in the Barcelona goal by some distance. To say Valdés had no chance would be an understatement.

What was to follow was the most nervous 75 minutes of football that the majority of United fans had experienced in their lives. On many occasions they had witnessed their team chasing games having gone behind, which brings about an anxiety of a certain kind. But hanging on knowing one goal would knock the team out is nervousness cranked up to a level most had never witnessed before. That's not to say United didn't have their chances and they did penetrate the Barcelona back line a few times, often with shots flashing across Valdés's goal. Over the 90 minutes they probably just about deserved to go through having created slightly more than the Catalans. However, as the second half progressed, United once again were on the retreat. The last 15 minutes seemed like Ferguson's men were permanently camped in their own half and there were a few heart-stopping moments, most notably when substitute Thierry Henry headed straight into the grateful arms of Edwin van der Sar. With 96 minutes on the clock a free kick was flung into the United box. It was cleared and the German referee Herbert Fandel blew for full time, sparking delirium and hugs all round. United were heading to Moscow.

Ferguson's team went to the Russian capital to play Chelsea after Avram Grant's side had knocked out Liverpool in the other semi-final, much to the relief of United fans, who were averse to the prospect of playing their bitterest rival for fear of losing. United had pipped Chelsea to the league that season but knew it would count for nothing in Moscow.

Ahead of the match, Ryan Giggs was keen to extol the virtues of the bad experiences United had suffered from in Europe, suggesting they might spur the current group on, 'Hopefully, players learn from their disappointments, like last year in Milan.' In Ferguson's mind, there would also have been the defeats to Real Madrid in 2000 and 2003, as well as the Bayer Leverkusen semi-final loss of 2002. Some of those defeats shaped this current United side. Then there would have been the memories of injustice, like against Porto in 2004, or the real low of Benfica in December 2005, when it seemed as though Ferguson might be nearing the end of his tenure. But now Ferguson and United had risen from the flames, and were ready to extinguish Chelsea's hopes in the backyard of their esteemed owner – Russian billionaire Roman Abramovich.

United coach René Meulensteen made it clear that there was a weakness in the opposition's starting XI and that Ferguson and his staff had highlighted it as a key area to exploit. Michael Essien, traditionally a box-to-box midfielder of immense power, would be deployed at right-back, a position he was less adept at. It therefore became a no-brainer to play Ronaldo on the left wing in direct opposition to Essien. It would also mean the Portuguese number seven would avoid coming up against Ashley Cole, who had regularly done a good job in taming him. 'That was definitely a part of the plan, with Cristiano on the left,' Meulensteen recalled.

Another element the coaching staff were keen to emphasise was that when the ball broke on the right of the United attack, Ronaldo would move in a little, taking Essien with him, and into a position where he could impose himself upon his out-of-position opponent, often using his superior ability in the air. 'That was something we talked about before the game,' Meulensteen said. 'If we do get through on the right-hand side and Cristiano's popping up, he would have a fantastic opportunity in the air.'

Ferguson had made the decision to play Ronaldo on the left a few weeks before the Moscow showdown, having seen Essien play at right-back in Chelsea's semi-final. 'I decided while watching Avram Grant's team that Ronaldo would play wide left to make life uncomfortable for Essien, a midfielder by trade,' he said.

But United had concerns of their own. Ferguson was wary of the danger posed by a potential penalty shoot-out should the two teams still be level after 120 minutes. It was a prospect he was dreading. 'I was the reluctant holder of possibly the worst record in penalty shoot-outs,' he said in his second autobiography. 'I had lost two semi-finals at Aberdeen, a European tie at Aberdeen, an FA Cup tie at Old Trafford against Southampton, an FA Cup Final against Arsenal and a European tie in Moscow through penalty shoot-outs.[46]

Meulensteen said the team were determined to reverse that trend if it came to a battle of nerves from 12 yards. 'The team had practised penalties and the sequence was clear,' he explained.

There was a lot for Ferguson to be bullish about going into that final, not least his conviction that this was his best side, ahead of the 1994 team and even the treble winners of 1999. In the immediate aftermath of winning the Premier League at Wigan Athletic in the final league game of the season in 2008 he told interviewer Geoff Shreeves that he believed this to be his greatest team of all. But he was aware they had to win in Moscow to make the claim more legitimate. After arriving in the Russian capital, Ferguson told the media it was the options at his disposal that impressed him the most about his current group of players. 'Last year we had played so many games with the same 11 or 12 players and we had no real reserves to change the game,' said Ferguson. 'This year we have. That will make the difference.

'The hardest part is not picking the team but leaving players out of the bench. We had 26 players at Wigan. Keeper Ben Foster is not registered for Europe, but that still leaves us 25 for Moscow. And that means seven of them can't even sit on the bench.' The players who ended up not making the matchday squad were Louis Saha, who was injured just before the final, Gary Neville, Gerard Piqué, and most regretfully as far as Ferguson was concerned, Park Ji-sung, who had played such a prominent role in the semi-final victory over Barcelona.

Just over a week before the final in Moscow, Giggs said, 'The players will be kicking lumps out of each other over the

---

46 Ferguson is choosing to discount the relevance of Charity Shield victories, courtesy of winning shoot-outs. In 1993, 1997 and 2003, United won in this manner in the season's curtain-raiser. Perhaps more importantly, they also saw off Chelsea in 2007, by virtue of a penalty shoot-out.

next week to try to get into the team. We'll all be eager to get picked and to play well.'

It is therefore not a surprise that Saha picked up an injury given the intensity of the training. 'They all seem so hungry for success,' Ferguson said at the time. 'And that is the thing that pleases you the most. Some Friday mornings, before a game, the training sessions are so competitive and I say to Carlos Queiroz, "Come on, stop this now," because they are really at it and I'm frightened there is going to be an injury. But that is just a measure of their desire to do well all the time. So, we are very fortunate. Good boys, good desire, good talent – combine all that and it gives you a good chance.'

Owen Hargreaves agreed with his manager's assessment of the team's determination. The will to win even spilt over into an altercation in training between some of the players at the Luzhniki Stadium on the eve of the big occasion. Hargreaves said, 'I remember we did a training game in the stadium in Moscow the day before and we almost had a fight amongst the two teams because the training game was so intense. One team lost and everybody was moaning at each other and Sir Alex had to come in and break it up. That's how it was. Everybody was so competitive about winning. Even in a training game, you'd think people didn't want to get injured but that wasn't the case. Everybody was just on it. Everybody was so excited for that game.'

Whereas United had recognised weaknesses in Chelsea's starting XI, it was far more difficult to find any in their own. Edwin van der Sar was one of the world's most consistent goalkeepers; Wes Brown had made the right-back berth his own in the absence of Gary Neville and would go on to have arguably his best game in a United shirt in the final; Patrice Evra was on a par with Ashley Cole, whom many considered to be the best left-back in Europe; Rio Ferdinand and Nemanja Vidić at the centre of United's defence were outstanding, and by many judgements the best defensive pairing in the history of the club; the midfield trio of Paul Scholes, Michael Carrick and Owen Hargreaves gave the side a perfect balance between bite and guile, though Hargreaves would play the first part of the final on the right of midfield; and the forward trident of Wayne Rooney, Carlos Tévez and Cristiano Ronaldo were three of the best in their position in the world.

This was undoubtedly the club's first 11 from the moment the transfer splurge of the previous summer had been completed. Curiously, it was the first and only time they would ever start together. Ferguson must have wished he could have played them together before, but form and injuries had precluded him from doing so. Within months, Hargreaves's injury-blighted career meant he barely played for United again. He was just 27 years of age going into that Moscow final. At that time, however, he was doing a sterling job in United's midfield, albeit he later confessed that he was often playing through the pain barrier, though you would not have noticed it in the Russian capital such was the level of his performance.

The pitch in Moscow was getting plenty of negative press. After England had played their European Championship qualifier in the stadium towards the end of 2007, the synthetic surface had been ripped up and a grass one was laid especially for the final. Less than a month prior to European club football's big occasion, that pitch was deemed to be too bumpy, so turf from Slovakia was hastily brought in and laid at a cost of over £150,000. 'I'm totally disappointed with the whole project and what we are presenting for the final,' said English-born Matt Frost, the groundsman who had previously promised a 'Rolls-Royce' of a pitch. However, both sides trained on it the day before the final and said they were happy with it. 'The pitch is the same for both sides and if get the footwear right we will be fine,' Chelsea captain John Terry said. 'We are not worrying about that at all.'

Ferguson was exuding confidence, 'I've got the players to do the job. I trust that and will stick by that. We may not have the overall experience of Chelsea in terms of age, but they've got the nerve, they've got the courage and I think that will make some difference.'

Ferguson mentions in his second book that he never wanted to look beleaguered in front of the media, and he certainly wasn't going to be showing any signs of weakness before this showpiece. He would often take no prisoners when it came to journalists and they had certainly felt his wrath on occasion during this particular campaign, but in a sign of his good spirits, he had a more jovial message for the reporters. His final words of his pre-match press conference were in the direction of the media, 'I love you all!' he said. 'I've come to spread peace!' The journalists in attendance immediately burst out laughing. But they also knew it was peace of mind, after all of his previous European heartaches, that Ferguson sought most.

For the opening 44 minutes Ferguson's wish was his team's command as United seized control of the final with some blistering football. Ronaldo was indeed making light wind of Michael Essien's efforts to be a right-back. Time and again he would out-strip him for skill and pace.

If United had been cautious against Barcelona in the semi-final, they were anything but in that opening period against opponents they knew so well and their attacking play was rewarded after 25 minutes. A nifty interchange between Scholes and Brown down the right saw the ball eventually fall at the right-back's feet and a left-footed cross was placed perfectly for Ronaldo to head home, climbing high above the all-at-sea Essien. The Ghanaian international knew he was at fault, immediately throwing his hands down to express disappointment. 'The plan worked,' Ferguson remarked over the tactic to push Ronaldo on to Essien wherever possible. 'Our man tore him apart.'

The onslaught was just beginning as chance after chance was created and on 34 minutes United had two bites at the cherry to score. First a Tévez header from a Ronaldo cross was smartly saved by Petr Čech, quickly followed by a shot from Michael Carrick from 15 yards that the goalkeeper was equal to. Such was the threat of Ronaldo, and Essien's struggles, that Ashley Cole had gone over to the right to help out his struggling team-mate in an effort to repel that particular attack. The next chance fell to Tévez. A Rooney ball driven across the Chelsea box seemed destined to fall into the path of the Argentinian striker but he hesitated, and the ball skimmed off his left boot. Another chance had gone begging.

Despite United's supremacy, the precariousness of their one-goal advantage was laid bare in the last minute of the first half, but it needed two ricochets and a Van der Sar slip on the rainy surface to present Frank Lampard with the simple task of clipping the ball over the stricken goalkeeper. 'A dash of luck,' was Ferguson's rueful description of the equaliser. 'Our game was full of thrust and invention and we might have been three or four goals up. I started to think it might be a massacre,' he added, but 'goals can turn games upside down'. And momentum had dramatically swung Chelsea's way.

Avram Grant, who had replaced José Mourinho earlier in the season, saw his team in the ascendancy for most of the second half, peppering the United goal from distance, including a Didier Drogba effort that struck the outside of the post with Van der Sar helpless.

Ferguson, unhappy with how momentum had swung away from his team, moved Owen Hargreaves into the centre of midfield in an effort to wrest back control. United were essentially playing 4-5-1 without the ball, and breaking into a 4-3-3 when they attacked. The switch seemed to work.

Ferguson introduced Ryan Giggs three minutes from time for his 759th appearance. It meant that Giggs had surpassed Sir Bobby Charlton's all-time record for United and set up the Welshman to play a significant role in the night's proceedings. In fact, it was now well past midnight, with the game kicking off at 10.45pm local time. It is still to this day the only European Cup Final to be spread over two days.

Extra time began with Lampard striking the woodwork, again with Van der Sar stranded. But the introduction of Giggs, aligned with the decision to move Hargreaves to the centre of midfield, meant United regained control for the majority of the added 30 minutes and the next big chance fell their way. Evra cut the ball back for Giggs to poke towards the gaping goal with the outside of his left foot, when perhaps he should have side-footed with his right. The lack of conviction on the shot enabled Terry to head clear.

United made another change, Nani replacing Rooney before half-time of extra time. Then, in the 116th minute, Terry went down injured, suffering from cramp. He received the classic leg-push treatment, as a result of his travails, from team-mate Claude Makélélé. Following a brief stoppage United gave possession back to their opponents, by way of Tévez kicking the ball out, prompting Terry to leap to attention knowing his side were back in play. Tévez then screamed to his colleagues to push up, gesturing his arms in their direction. For some reason, the combination of him gifting the ball back, albeit by kicking it out of play, aligned with his motions, seemed to upset the now fully-fit Terry. He and five Chelsea players surrounded the diminutive Argentinian before several United players joined the party.

The melee culminated in Didier Drogba being sent off for slapping Nemanja Vidić across the face. Many players would have theatrically fallen to the surface in an effort to get the Chelsea striker dismissed but to his credit Vidić hardly batted an eyelid. The incident had initially escaped the attention of the referee, Ľuboš Micheľ, but not his assistant who informed the man in the middle. The final whistle went but Chelsea would have to face penalties without Drogba.

Before the moment of truth arrived from 12 yards, Ferguson and Grant both made the classic 120th-minute substitution –

the penalty taker, with Anderson coming on for United and Juliano Belletti for Chelsea.

The coin toss between captains Ferdinand and Terry provoked a curious shout from the United skipper towards his team-mates and coaching staff. 'Us first?' he screamed repeatedly, having won the toss. Ferdinand confirmed his decision to the referee. In-depth research on penalty shoot-outs has shown there is a 60 per cent chance of success for the team that goes first.

Having lost the toss, Terry and Chelsea could choose which end the penalties would be taken at. The Blues captain inexplicably chose the goal behind which the United fans were located. 'An advantage,' Ferguson wrote years later of the fact that the kicks would be taken at that end of the Luzhniki.

Ferguson's fears of a shoot-out had materialised but United scored their first two. Tévez sent Čech the wrong way, as did Carrick. Van der Sar approached each Chelsea penalty, casually strolling toward his line, delaying the process to add to the taker's tension. He would then outstretch both arms in a way to make the goal appear that little bit smaller. It didn't work for either of Chelsea's first two kicks, scored by Michael Ballack and Juliano Belletti. For the latter, you can see Tévez in the background pointing for Van der Sar to go to his right. The goalkeeper went to his right, but Belletti slotted it into the opposite corner.[47]

Next up for United was the standout player, not just of the final, but of the entire season – Cristiano Ronaldo. Ferguson's trusted assistant, Carlos Queiroz, had felt that the third penalty should be taken by the club's best option – the regular taker.[48]

---

47 It was something Tévez repeated in a league match against Liverpool a year later, and again his prediction was wrong.

48 Later in his career Ronaldo insisted on taking the fifth penalty, in the hope of sealing glory for his team, as he did in the 2016 Champions League Final for Real Madrid. He did take the fifth for Portugal against England in the 2006 World Cup, but the trend didn't begin until Euro 2012. He didn't take a kick for Portugal due to his demand. Moutinho and Alves missed, with Ronaldo an unused fifth taker.

Grant and his staff at Chelsea also felt the same, with Lampard taking their third spot-kick.

The Chelsea boffins had done their homework on Ronaldo and came to the following conclusion: He often stopped in his run-up and if he did the ball was kicked towards the right-hand side of the keeper 85 per cent of the time. It was important that Čech did not move early. When goalkeepers moved early Ronaldo always scored.

The Portuguese international kissed the ball before placing it on the spot. He stepped back to the edge of the area. Ronaldo stuttered his run halfway, a stunt he had pulled numerous times before and never missed when deploying this strategy. This time, however, his luck ran out as Čech blocked his effort, moving to the side the Chelsea analysts suggested the United number seven would go to should he pause his run-up. Coach René Meulensteen felt Ronaldo 'lost a little bit of focus for the penalty'. Whatever the reason, United were now in trouble, needing their opponents to fail. Van der Sar intentionally waited, rather than anticipated, Lampard's kick, knowing the midfielder's propensity to strike his penalties down the middle. As a result, he managed to move in the right direction, but couldn't get a strong enough hand on the ball to keep it out. Advantage Chelsea. Ferguson continued to chew on his gum. Queiroz too.

Chelsea owner Roman Abramovich could barely watch as Owen Hargreaves stepped up for United's next penalty before coolly dispatching it into the top corner with arguably the best kick of the entire shoot-out. 'I was fortunate I had never missed a penalty in any of the knockout competitions I had ever been in, with England or Bayern,' Hargreaves commented. 'And I always did the same thing – smashed it top left.' Maybe Čech was aware of this as he went the correct way, but the power and the positioning of the strike was too good for the Chelsea number one.

Van der Sar then gestured to Ashley Cole, questioning the positioning of the ball, in more kidology from the Dutchman, who seemed well-versed in the act. It mattered not. Cole scored, despite Van der Sar again getting a hand to the kick. The Chelsea left-back was clearly relieved to take his team a step closer to Champions League glory.

If ever there is a pressure penalty, it is the one where you know if you miss, it's all over. It's one of the principal reasons that taking the first spot-kick is so advantageous. Assuming all penalties are scored the team who go second will have extra pressure on their fifth kick. On this occasion, however, United had already failed with one penalty, making Nani's achievement from 12 yards all the more impressive. Many remember what was to follow, but without Nani's successful effort, it would have all been over. And it so nearly was, with Čech getting both gloves on the ball without preventing it from going in.

It meant that Terry had the simple task of scoring to secure his club's first Champions League title. Ferguson looked to the ground in the seconds leading up to the Chelsea skipper's kick and took a sharp intake of breath. Much like in the dying moments in the Camp Nou in 1999, he was mulling over what he was going to say to the players in the wake of a crushing defeat. He was prepared to tell them 'they had worked so hard to get there' and didn't deserve to lose. Terry, meanwhile, was adjusting his armband as he strode forward. Once more, Van der Sar took his time getting to his line, again arms outstretched. It was the Dutchman's third Champions League Final, having twice reached that stage with Ajax. He had faced eight penalties thus far across those finals and seen the net bulge on each occasion. Terry slipped as he struck the ball. It skimmed the post and went wide with Van der Sar going the wrong way. Centimetres from winning the Champions League, Terry was distraught. The United goalkeeper rejoiced and United were back in the game. Sudden death and Ferguson could keep on chewing.

Anderson smashed his penalty safely down the middle so the pressure fell on to the shoulders of Salomon Kalou, who coolly slotted home for 5-5.

Ryan Giggs would take United's seventh penalty of a rain-soaked evening. He had taken one penalty of note before for the club, in an FA Cup shoot-out against Southampton a mere 16 years previously. On that occasion it was saved by Tim Flowers who promptly ran like Linford Christie to celebrate. If those memories were rushing through Giggs's head all these years later, it was not evident in his kick, sending Čech the wrong way and finding the bottom corner.

Ferguson knew the players on the bench could well have a significant role to play. He said before the match, 'The substitutes you make have got to have an impact, which is why I have to give a lot of consideration to the type of player I want on the bench.

'If I have to use them I hope they make an impact and in '99, the two substitutes won it for me. I've got the players to do the job.' All three of his subs, Nani, Anderson and Giggs, took penalties that night. All three scored.

In sudden death, Chelsea knew one miss would result in instant defeat. Anelka, like Kalou before him, had to score. Again Van der Sar had his arms outstretched, except this time he gestured obviously with one, towards his left and Anelka's right. Until now, Chelsea had taken all six penalties in that direction.

According to the book *Soccernomics*, it seemed that Chelsea's strategy of going to Van der Sar's left had been rumbled by someone on the United bench, which is why the Dutch keeper pointed to that side. Now Anelka had a terrible dilemma – to stick to the strategy, or to change.[49]

---

49 Ashley Cole had actually gone against the tactic. As a left-footed player he should have gone to his 'unnatural' side, and Van der Sar's right, but he followed in the footsteps of his right-footed team-mates in electing to shoot to the keeper's left.

The Chelsea striker would later claim that he wasn't ready to take a penalty. Strangely, he cited the 21 minutes he had on the pitch as insufficient preparation for such a kick. Belletti and Anderson, who had both entered the fray specifically to take penalties, played for a minute each before successfully converting their kicks. Anelka's excuse was almost as lame as his penalty. Van der Sar ignored his own suggestion and dived to his right. Anelka broke the mould of every previous Chelsea kick, electing to go to the keeper's right. It was an ideal height and for the first time Van der Sar's hands had repelled a Champions League Final penalty at the 11th attempt.[50]

Victory was United's but Ferguson could barely rejoice in the style we had come to expect. He was exhausted, relieved and soaking wet. 'I always remember that the rain had drenched me and ruined my shoes, so I attended the victory party in my trainers, for which I took plenty of stick from the players. I knew I should have packed a spare pair,' Ferguson later recalled.

As the players celebrated in front of the United fans after Van der Sar's match-winning save, the Dutch goalkeeper and Rio Ferdinand were called over by ITV to talk about the win. 'Edwin, what a moment!' the interviewer Gabriel Clarke said. 'I know, fucking hell! Sorry!' said Van der Sar.

Clarke asked Ferdinand what he thought when Terry stepped up. 'I was thinking he's gonna score,' the United captain admitted. 'He's a great penalty taker, normally in training, it's unfortunate he slipped but for us it's great ... I can't believe it, look at the fans!'[51]

---

50 Van der Sar failed to save any of the four penalties he faced in the 1996 Champions League Final shoot-out when playing for Ajax, in addition to the first six in Moscow, not including Terry's as it was missed, rather than saved.

51 It was only years later that Ferdinand and Terry's relationship deteriorated after the Chelsea captain was accused of racially abusing Rio's brother Anton.

A rain-soaked Ferguson said, 'I'm so proud of my players. We deserved it. With the history of this club we deserved to get this trophy tonight. I think the first half we were fantastic. We should have been three or four up by half-time. Second half, I thought they were the better team. Extra time, we got better again. Then that's the first penalty shoot-out I have ever won in a big game. I won the Charity Shield that way, but that doesn't really count. The European Cup? The FA Cup? The Scottish cups? Never. I've lost three with Aberdeen and three with United, so seventh time lucky – magnificent.

'In 1999 the victory was sudden and unexpected. Here, I told myself that if we take all our penalties correctly then we win it. But once Cristiano Ronaldo missed, it became nail-biting and once it was over we all felt incredibly tired. Maybe it was fate, him missing his kick like that. I really think fate has played its hand. I said that we wouldn't let down the memory of the Busby Babes.[52] We had a cause and that was very important because people with causes are very difficult for people to barter against.' This was Ferguson as a leader, galvanising his team with a purpose.

Ryan Giggs, United's newly crowned record appearance-maker, said, 'I couldn't have done it [broken the appearance record] on a better night. To play that many games for this club is brilliant but it's about winning trophies. I have been fortunate to win a lot. Hopefully I will have more. We've won it three times now but we want to win it more.'

At the after party in Moscow, Ferdinand was keen to speak to chief executive David Gill, not to revel in the success but to ask, 'Who are we buying next year?'

The final word on the night's proceedings must go to the boss himself. 'For me the moment of euphoria was when Edwin saved that penalty. I feel very proud and sometimes you have to pinch yourself that it has happened to you. But the feelings

---

52 It was the 50th anniversary that year of the Munich air crash that took the lives of 23 people, including eight Manchester United players.

drain away quite quickly. I will soon start thinking about next season and of defending the European Cup and I couldn't tell you what kind of game this was as a final. I spoke to a few people afterwards and they said it was a great match to watch, which is pleasing because some finals have been absolutely terrible and all because of the pressure. Tomorrow morning I will be thinking about next season. It drains away very quickly – that drug, that final moment, that save, it vanishes for me. I will be thinking about the future and looking into the eyes of the players to make sure their hunger is still there. I won't be retiring.'

This is also typical Ferguson, delighting in the moment, but knowing there are future hurdles on the horizon to overcome.

But Alex Ferguson never would win another European Cup. A red and blue carrousel lay in wait, ready to mesmerise his team into submission.

9 (i)

From mesmerised by Barça …

MANCHESTER UNITED were the European Cup holders, had won the domestic league title for a third successive year in 2009 and swatted most teams aside en route to the Champions League Final. A masterful two-legged performance saw off Arsenal with ease in the semi-final. Cristiano Ronaldo was at his scintillating best, scoring one of the club's great European goals at the Emirates Stadium. A counter-attack of the highest order saw Ronaldo begin and end a nine-second move that resulted in his second, and United's third on the night.

ITV commentator Clive Tyldesley greeted the goal, saying, 'How about that?! How about that?! One end of the field to the other in the blink of an eye. Cristiano Ronaldo scores for the second time on the night and Manchester United can pack their bags for Rome.'

The night ended on a sour note with Darren Fletcher being harshly sent off for bringing down Cesc Fàbregas when the United midfielder clearly got the ball. He would be missed in the Eternal City a few weeks later.

Barcelona 2009

Barcelona, though mightily impressive that season in La Liga, had a referee-assisted passage to the final as they struggled to overcome Chelsea when the London club were denied four strong penalty claims, two of which were blatant handballs. Chelsea were no match at the time for United and so, went the theory, nor would Barcelona be. The opening ten minutes of the final reflected that. United dominated and should have scored through Park Ji-sung but once the Catalans took the lead, there was no way back as Lionel Messi and the midfield trio of Sergio Busquets, Xavi Hernández and Andrés Iniesta dominated the central areas. Ferguson felt his players, especially in the middle of the park, were mesmerised by it all, letting the occasion pass them by, at least until half-time. First-team coach René Meulensteen also said United should have been more aggressive, 'The one thing that stood out, looking back, I felt it was too soft a final. Two fantastic teams playing against each other, but there wasn't any nitty-gritty. Paul Scholes was the one, when he came on, who thought "fuck that" and got amongst them.'

Ferguson took the defeat hard. His biographer, Paul Hayward, said, 'The bigger the game, the more illustrious the occasion, the harder he found it to accept defeat.'

Ferguson wanted the players to know, in no uncertain terms, that they had let themselves down. Michael Carrick recalls in his autobiography, 'The boss was understandably angry and had a go at everyone. "You need to have a look at yourselves and see if you can play at this level," he said. Moscow was irrelevant. We were Manchester United and the expectation was relentless. "You've let a good chance slip away here," he said. The boss summed up exactly how I was feeling.' For Carrick, it was even worse. His misplaced header gifted the ball to Barcelona in the build-up to the first goal. His reaction after the loss led to something akin to depression and his form for the next two years suffered as a result. 'I just questioned myself again and again. Am I good enough?' the midfielder said. It was a period that included going to the 2010 World Cup with England where Carrick just thought to himself, 'Why am I here?' as he felt his form did not justify a place in the squad.

Ferguson said in the immediate aftermath of the final that he knew why his side had not performed, but he would not be airing those grievances at that juncture. It led many to speculate at the time that he felt as though Fletcher's absence through suspension was the chief reason. Not so, as he revealed four years later in his second autobiography. Ferguson lamented the preparations for the final, 'A major inhibiting factor in Rome was the choice of hotel. It was a shambles.' As a result, Ferguson felt two or three players were under the weather prior to the game, Ryan Giggs in particular.

For United fans and Ferguson himself, this is the one, rather than the repeat final two years later, that got away. 'I wish we could have played the Rome final again the next day. The very next day,' he said. Ferguson reckoned the 2011 version of Pep Guardiola's team was 'superior' to the 2009 crop. In the Rome final, Barcelona were beatable, and Ferguson knew it. 'To collect a runners-up medal is a painful act when you know you could have performed much better.'

Bayern Munich 2010

Having reached at least the Champions League semi-finals for three years in a row, United now had the kind of European pedigree they had attained in the late 1990s and early 2000s. They justified their reputation as they easily qualified for the knockout stages, finishing top of their group.

They overcame their AC Milan hoodoo in the next round, thrashing the Italians 7-2 on aggregate. They were feeling confident ahead of a tricky, but negotiable, quarter-final against Louis van Gaal's Bayern Munich.

United lost the first leg 2-1 in Bavaria but raced into a 3-0 lead at home before a combination of injuries, the concession of soft goals and poor decision-making left their European dream in tatters.

Wayne Rooney picked up an ankle injury in the first leg and though he played in the return at Old Trafford, he was far from 100 per cent fit. But Ferguson did not trust his other striking options in a season where own goals were United's third top scorer.

Michael Carrick's form also did not help United's cause. He was a little timid against Bayern and especially during the move for their first goal in the return leg at Old Trafford, when Ivica Olić easily brushed him off the ball before scoring. It was the concession of this goal, just before half-time, that changed the momentum of the game, according to Ferguson.

To make matters worse, right-back Rafael da Silva, now a first-team regular, made three crucial errors on the night. First, when through on goal in the first half, he elected to shoot when Rooney was far better placed. Despite his lack of fitness, the England striker would almost certainly have scored if the Brazilian had only looked up. Da Silva's second mistake was to get a careless booking, deep in Bayern's half, when frustration got the better of him. He erred for a third time when he hauled back French winger Franck Ribéry to earn himself a second yellow card. If the decision was debatable, his tempestuous nature certainly was not. Ribéry did not cover himself in glory either, flashing an imaginary card to indicate what he wanted the referee to do. The official duly obliged and the home side were down to ten men. A more vulnerable United then conceded a second. Former Ferguson transfer target Arjen Robben volleyed home spectacularly as Carrick tried to block. United won 3-2 on the night but a 4-4 aggregate scoreline meant Bayern went through on away goals.

That quarter-final defeat was compounded by what would have been United's route to glory. The prospect of playing Lyon in the semi-final and Inter Milan in the final would have held no fears for Ferguson and his team.[53]

---

53 Pep Guardiola's Barcelona, who were en route to becoming the continent's dominant force, were dumped out at the semi-final stage by José Mourinho's Inter Milan.

ITV would regularly speak to the United boss just seconds after the final whistle of a Champions League tie, and the interviews would often crystallise Ferguson's raw emotions. This time was no different. Gabriel Clarke asked him whether the key moment in the tie was Rafael's sending off. Blood reaching boiling point, the United manager said, 'No doubt about that. They never win that game if we had 11 men. Young boy, a bit inexperienced, but they got him sent off. Everyone sprinted towards the referee. Typical Germans. You can't dispute that.' It mattered not that more than half the Bayern team were not German, nor that intimidating referees had become almost a casual pastime for the Scottish manager and his players.

Barcelona 2011

In 2011, United got to the Champions League Final at Wembley thanks to the genius of Ferguson and a fortunate draw that meant they had to negotiate comfortable knockout ties against Olympique de Marseille, Chelsea and FC Schalke 04. But once in the final, they faced Barcelona, who were now even better than they had been two years previously. A United side containing Fábio da Silva, Antonio Valencia and Javier Hernández were not quite at the level required. In addition, Paul Scholes, who came off the bench, Ryan Giggs and Edwin van der Sar were all in the twilight of their careers. This set of players could not hold a candle to their opposite numbers. Ferguson admitted so afterwards as he said, 'I think we knew we were against a very good team and we planned the best we could. They do mesmerise you with their passing and we never really controlled Messi, but I think many people have said that. Great teams do go in cycles and the cycle they're in at the moment is the best in Europe, there's no question about that. It is a great moment for them, they deserve it because they play the right way and they enjoy their football.'

Playing the right way is something Ferguson wanted to do in both the 2009 and 2011 finals. In the semi-final in 2008, United had adjusted their tactics to Barcelona, playing compact, and springing into life on the counter-attack. Those matches at the Camp Nou and Old Trafford were as defensively minded as any in the Ferguson era. But in the two finals, Ferguson wanted to be more open. 'In each of those two European Cup Finals, we might have been closer to Spain's finest by playing more defensively, but by then I had reached the stage with Manchester United where it was no good us trying to win that way,' he said. 'I used those tactics to beat Barcelona in the 2008 semi-final: defended really deep, put myself through torture, put the fans through hell. I wanted a more positive outlook against them subsequently, and we were beaten partly because of that change in emphasis.'

Ferguson said winger Antonio Valencia was 'nervous as hell' in the 2011 final, but he saved his biggest criticism, as so often was the case, for Wayne Rooney, who he said was 'disappointing' and that he 'played the occasion, not the game'.

Rooney has since criticised his manager's tactics, no doubt as a tit-for-tat response to Ferguson's rebuke. Rooney said, 'We lost two Champions League Finals going toe-to-toe with Guardiola's Barcelona, by trying to press high and get round them, which was suicidal. I remember Alex Ferguson saying, "We're Man United and we're going to attack, it's in the culture of this football club," and I'm thinking, "I'm not too sure about this."'

The problem with Rooney's argument is that had his boss elected to be more cautious, it may well have been at the expense of the England striker. He would have either been dropped or asked to play a role he didn't like, out wide or in midfield, choking the space where Barcelona's maestros caused so much damage. It is difficult to imagine the Rooney of that period being tactically disciplined. Sure, in his early years at the club he would often play out of position as a sacrifice to the team. But following Ronaldo's departure to Real Madrid he tended to want to exert himself on the team in a more authoritative way.

Just six months after the disappointment at Wembley, United's European slump, post-Ronaldo, was confirmed as they exited the 2011/12 Champions League in the group stage. This time Ferguson recognised his culpability in that he took his opponents too lightly, often resting players, such was his confidence at being able to negotiate a seemingly simple group containing Basel, Benfica and ASC Oțelul Galați. Ferguson and his players were punished as they lost to Basel in the final group game, eliminating them at that stage for the first time since 2005. But even the biggest United optimist knew that this team were nowhere near good enough to go deep in the competition. Former captain Roy Keane recognised it too as he said the club 'got what they deserved', highlighting the lack of quality in the squad, much to the annoyance of Ferguson.

Real Madrid 2013

The following season was to be Ferguson's last assault on club football's greatest prize – one final chance to put his name up there with Bob Paisley, who led Liverpool to three European Cup triumphs.

Unlike the year before, the initial stage of the competition was comfortably negotiated and United, who won their group, were unfortunate to draw Real Madrid in the last 16. Madrid came second in their group to eventual runners-up Borussia Dortmund.

Nevertheless, the clash against the Spanish giants was exactly the kind of tie Ferguson relished and United got a well-earned 1-1 draw from the first leg, Ronaldo scoring for Madrid against his former club with a typical header, leaping like a salmon to tower over the diminutive Patrice Evra to equalise Danny Welbeck's opener.

Ferguson was often criticised for his lack of tactical awareness, particularly early on in his managerial career, as naysayers saw him as someone who could motivate and recognise talent but not a manager capable of strategically out-manoeuvring wily opponents. But now, here he was, seemingly at the top of his game, out-smarting the wiliest of them all – José Mourinho. From largely stifling Ronaldo to deploying Phil Jones in a holding role, Ferguson drew praise for how he set his team up in the Spanish capital in a game where United were the better side for large spells.

Ferguson decided the key to success was to stifle Madrid's creative fulcrum – Xabi Alonso. Welbeck performed the role perfectly in both legs. Rooney played out wide in Madrid and was dropped for the second leg, in further evidence of both his waning powers and of his deteriorating relationship with Ferguson.

Another tactical masterstroke was to play Ryan Giggs in the home leg on the right of a midfield three and United dominated the match at Old Trafford, largely due to the box of tricks Ferguson used to bamboozle his opponent in the opposite dugout. His side took a deserved lead on 48 minutes through a Sergio Ramos own goal after a brief onslaught on the Madrid goal. United now led 2-1 on aggregate and looked set to go through to the next round before a bizarre decision was made by referee Cüneyt Çakır.

If Ferguson's Champions League cycle began in ignominious fashion against Turkish side Galatasaray in 1993, it was brought to an end by a person from the same city, Istanbul, two decades later. Nani, who had been playing brilliantly, jumped for a high ball unaware of Álvaro Arbeloa's presence. The Portuguese winger caught his opponent as he went to control the lofted ball. In terms of the eventual decision by the official, it is important to know that Nani never took his eyes off the ball. Roy Keane argued in his role as a television pundit afterwards that it was dangerous play but if that was a reckless action from Nani then any time a player lifted their foot above waist level it could be interpreted thus. The referee, to everyone's astonishment, brandished the red card in what Ferguson would later describe as an 'appalling decision'. It changed the course of the tie with just over half an hour left.

If Ferguson had been tactically astute up until this point, in the next few minutes Mourinho would make his move to swing the game back in Real Madrid's favour, perhaps catching his opposite number on the hop, as the Scot was left reeling from the referee's decision to send off Nani. The Madrid manager brought on Luca Modrić, seizing the midfield space created by Nani's absence. Welbeck, hitherto excellent in keeping Alonso quiet, had to move left, where Nani was previously stationed. Within 13 minutes of the home side going down to ten men, Real Madrid were 2-1 in front on the night after goals from Modrić and Ronaldo. Despite a late onslaught by United, they were unable to retrieve the situation and crashed out.

René Meulensteen takes up the story of how Ferguson felt, knowing his last chance of Champions League success had been so cruelly denied, 'It must have been absolutely devastating for him because it was devastating for all of us. And I can still remember him sitting in the stadium when Nani got given the red card. He realised this was his last chance. Both Mick [Phelan] and the manager went down to the touchline. I just sat there, 76,500 people … up to that time we had played really well. So how that game panned out, and he was leaving. The one thing I remember was him thinking it was so unjust. I do remember the moment when he was sitting in the dressing room [after the game], everything must have been going through his mind "that was my last shot at winning the Champions League" so it must have hurt. It hurt all of us, but it especially hurt him.'

That night Ferguson was in no mood to do his usual press briefing, something he would never usually shy away from, even in some of his darkest moments.

Ferguson was 'distraught and that's why I'm sat here in front of you now', assistant manager Mike Phelan told the media after the match. 'It speaks volumes that I'm sat here speaking to you in this moment in time and not the manager of this magnificent football club.'

Phelan continued, 'We felt as though we had the tactics right. We felt as though we were comfortable. We scored the goal, which put us in a commanding position. After that we were in control, created a couple of chances but then the game totally changed.'

Meulensteen said Ferguson's non-appearance at the press conference was, in hindsight, a sign of the Scot's impending retirement, 'That's probably the reason why. He felt that devastated. There was something, an underlying reason in the background.'

Even the Defeats: The phrase that inspired the title of this book was used by Sir Alex Ferguson during his retirement speech after his last game at Old Trafford. Setbacks were often used to trigger success during his time as manager

The Final Piece of the Jigsaw: After losing the title to City, Ferguson responded with a fresh sense of purpose, as well as a new striker – Robin van Persie

Maine Road Massacre: The 5-1 loss at Manchester City prompted Ferguson to do plenty of soul-searching. Defeats always hit the United manager hard

The First Trophy: After three and a half trophy-less years at the helm Ferguson finally got the ball rolling, winning the FA Cup to give him some much-needed breathing space

Anfield Agony: Ryan Giggs and other United players were asked for their autographs by Liverpool fans after the defeat at Anfield in 1992. They obliged, before seeing the opposition supporters tear them up. Ferguson told the players never to forget

Title Relief: Eric Cantona was the extra dimension the United manager sought to end 26 years of hurt

Summer Sales: Paul Ince was one of three players sold in 1995 on the back of United's first season without a trophy in six years

You Can Win Anything with Kids: Ferguson trusted his young players. It's fair to say they repaid that faith, alongside senior pros such as Cantona and Keane

Arsenal Jolt: Marc Overmars struck the decisive blow in 1998 to stop United in their title tracks

Back on the Perch: Ferguson wanted his team to resemble its manager. The United of 1999 had talent by the bundle but there was nothing about them he admired more than their team spirit, epitomised in the late turnaround against Liverpool in the FA Cup

Welcome to Hell: United in Europe was like going back to school. The atmosphere in Istanbul in 1993 was particularly testing

Football, Bloody Hell: And Solskjaer has won it! Time and again United made it hard for themselves – time and again they responded

Wenger Vanquished: In the early years of their rivalry, the battle ebbed and flowed. By its end, the Arsenal manager had been sidelined

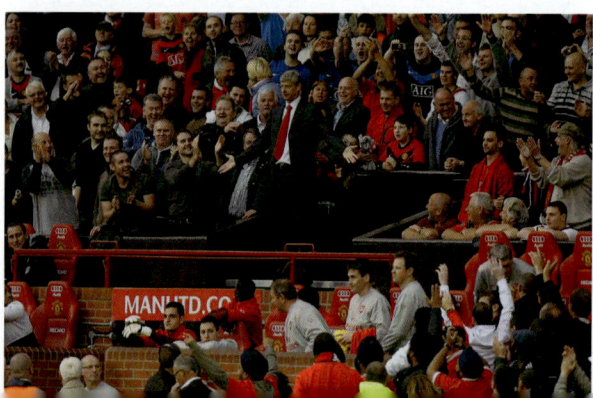

Mourinho Outlasted: The Portuguese manager posed new questions, casting doubt on the United manager's prowess. Ferguson evolved, and eventually saw off the 'Special One'

Treble Retreat: After winning the Champions League in 1999, a dynasty never materialised. Defeat to Real Madrid the following year had long-lasting ramifications for United's European approach

Red Square Delight: Ronaldo leapt like a salmon to score his 42nd goal of a remarkable season in Moscow. United reached the European summit after beating Chelsea on penalties

Mesmerised by Barça: After losing the Champions League Final in 2009 Ferguson felt the players had let themselves down

European Regrets: The United manager felt his team should have achieved more in Europe. The loss to Real Madrid in 2013 was particularly galling

Last-Minute Anguish: Ferguson and his coaching staff urge the players to recognise the United fans immediately after hearing the news of Manchester City's title-winning goal

He Did It His Way: The pain of the previous campaign only strengthened Ferguson's resolve. In winning the title in his final season, Ferguson went out on a high

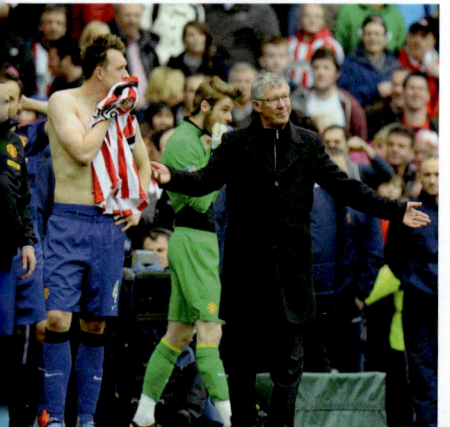

9 (ii)

... to European regrets

MANCHESTER UNITED'S attempts at winning the Champions League can be compartmentalised into four phases. The first one shows an upward trajectory, from 1993 to 1999, where every setback was another lesson learned in the gradual progression towards ecstasy at the Camp Nou. The abandonment of UEFA's rule limiting the number of foreign players also played its part in the climb towards the European summit.

The second phase is largely downward, from 1999 to 2005, as European football posed a different question. The swashbuckling nature of the treble winners was unsustainable. Ferguson went back to the drawing board. The desire to control the midfield with the Verón experiment largely failed. Domestic challenges posed by Arsenal and Chelsea also meant Ferguson took a long-term approach, resulting in an initial decline. An emphasis on youth over experience stymied United's progress in the competition in the short term, reaching rock bottom in the club's group stage exit at the hands of Benfica in December 2005. At that stage the vultures were swirling over Ferguson for the first time since the late 1980s.

The third phase, from 2005 to 2009, was Ronaldo-driven, where United's upward curve was mirrored by the soon-to-be best player in the world's trajectory. In addition, Ferguson reappointed Carlos Queiroz as his assistant, who returned to the club a year after Ronaldo's arrival. The Mozambique-born coach added a more defensive approach, notably in the two-legged victory over Barcelona en route to success in 2008. In Europe, United soon found themselves in successive Champions League finals before Ronaldo's departure in the summer of 2009.

Queiroz left in 2008 and his absence in the campaigns that followed cannot be underestimated, as Patrice Evra explains, 'His training sessions were perfect. When he left United, tactically it was not the same. We kept winning the league but ...' he said in reference to United's inability to rule the continent. The decline in Europe was obvious after Queiroz left to manage Portugal, none more so than in the way United struggled against Barcelona without the tactical nous he could provide, particularly in the build-up to a game of such magnitude. Ferguson felt he could not employ a compact, defensive approach against the Catalans like he had in the semi-final of 2008, for fear of betraying United's attacking ethos. But if his wily assistant had remained, it is likely United would have had more success against Pep Guardiola's formidable team. Maybe Ferguson didn't know if he was capable of setting the team up in the same effective manner without Queiroz at his side.

Nevertheless, the more seismic departure of Ronaldo in the summer of 2009 saw United enter the fourth and final phase of Ferguson's continental efforts. From this moment, United never quite had the star quality Ronaldo provided, save for the odd moment from Wayne Rooney, who never delivered on the big occasions like the Portuguese forward did. Rooney did not fill Ronaldo's boots in the way the 2009/10 season initially promised and, as a result, United struggled in the final period – 2009 to 2013.

United were never serious contenders once Ronaldo left. The 2011 Champions League campaign was not a real reflection of where this squad were at. United got to the final at Wembley thanks to Ferguson's improved awareness and his new-found ability to work on a strict budget. This aligned with a fortunate draw meant the performance was an outlier when really United were in decline. The European slump was more apparent in Ferguson's penultimate season in charge, with a group stage exit, as Chris Smalling, Phil Jones and Ashley Young showed they were not of the same quality as their predecessors.

The signing of Robin van Persie and astute management once again from Ferguson, who tactically was at the height of his powers, meant United had a chance of going far in what would prove to be his final assault on the Champions League in 2012/13. The Scot's tactical prowess came to the fore over two tense legs against Real Madrid. By now, the Premier League was a distant second to La Liga in attracting the world's best players and it showed in terms of how far the respective clubs were progressing in Europe. But Ferguson was able to out-wit opponents, in much the same way he himself was bamboozled by managerial counterparts earlier in his tenure. Against José Mourinho and Madrid, United were in control until an unfortunate refereeing decision undermined the manager's smart decisions.

The defeats prior to winning his first Champions League all contributed to the eventual lifting of the trophy with big ears in the Camp Nou. In the nine years that followed, the exits from the competition all had a long-lasting effect on Ferguson as a coach before a slightly more cautious approach paid dividends on that glorious night in the rain in Moscow. In the five years after victory in 2008, the defeat to Barcelona 12 months on in Rome felt like the one that got away, with his team still very much at its peak. Ferguson's team under-performed against a Barcelona side that were extremely good, but not at the level they attained at Wembley two years later.

The other thing about that final in Rome was that United still had Ronaldo. It was his last game for the club, and they never quite posed the same threat in the Champions League from the moment he left. After the Portuguese forward departed for Real Madrid, you always felt that United needed Barcelona to get knocked out to stand a chance. They could still remain competitive domestically, where Ferguson's genius at keeping them at the top, or near the top, would endure, despite relatively low spending in comparison with Chelsea, Manchester City and even Liverpool. But on the biggest stage of them all, a heavyweight like a Messi or a Ronaldo or a Lewandowski was required. And United did not quite have that level of player. Nor did they have the midfield to compete and efforts to attract players who were at or close to the level required, such as Luka Modrić, were foiled by the attraction of La Liga.

Ferguson was bitterly disappointed he could never quite build a dynasty like the great Real Madrid side of the late 1950s or the Bayern Munich or Ajax teams of the 1970s, all of whom won multiple European Cups. The Champions League in the latter years was an infinitely harder competition than its predecessor, making a succession of triumphs all the more difficult.

By increasing the participants from the strong countries, allowing the top two, then top three, then top four, to enter from England, Spain and Italy, the depth in quality meant winning the competition was more difficult than before. For instance, when Liverpool won the European Cup in 1976/77 they beat Crusaders, Trabzonspor, Saint-Étienne, FC Zürich and Borussia Mönchengladbach. The Anfield team did not face a side from England, Italy or Spain en route to winning the trophy.

A year later, it got even easier as Liverpool got a bye in the first round, meaning they eventually won the European Cup by getting past just four teams, none of which were from

England, Italy or Spain and only Benfica, in the quarter-finals, were of genuine European pedigree. Liverpool played just 16 games to win those two European Cups.

If Ferguson had one regret from his time at United, it was that he never added to those remarkable Champions League triumphs of 1999 and 2008. But to win those two tournaments they had to negotiate very different opposition in comparison with their arch rivals. For the first triumph they had three teams to overcome in the group stage, then two knockout rounds and a final. Opponents included Bayern Munich (in the group stage and the final), Barcelona, Inter Milan and Juventus.

For their second triumph in 2008, they had seven teams to overcome, including opponents from Italy, Spain and England. United played 24 games to win those two Champions Leagues.

Nevertheless, to only win it twice clearly rankled with Ferguson. 'I always said Manchester United ought to be achieving more in Europe,' he said in his second autobiography.

Three years after retiring, Ferguson gave a talk at the Stanford Graduate School of Business in California where he said, 'On some occasions we were very unlucky, some occasions we got bad decisions against us, and some occasions we didn't play well enough. We had three semi-finals we lost. The two worst were against Dortmund in 1997 and against Leverkusen in 2002.'

During this interview, conducted by Sir Michael Moritz, who worked with Ferguson on a book entitled *Leading*, it is clear that his lack of success in Europe still irritated him. The question was seemingly over when Ferguson added, 'In my last season, playing Real Madrid, that Turkish referee, he sends off Nani. The most ridiculous thing, we were in absolute control of the game. And losing a player at that time, it took us ten minutes to get over it and by that time they had scored two goals. And even at 2-1 down we still made all the chances.' Ferguson was then asked by Moritz, 'Do you feel that you should have won more?' His response was unequivocal, 'Absolutely. I think European Cups was my biggest regret.'

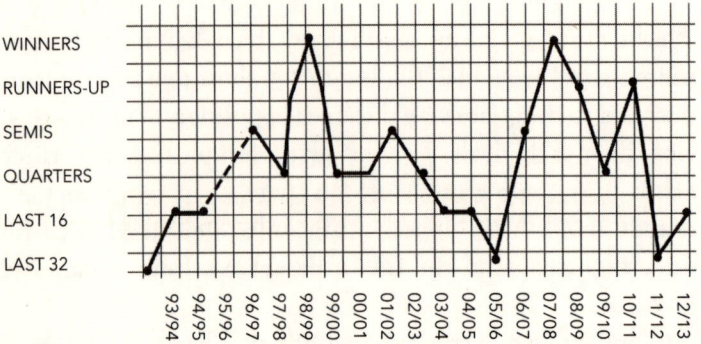

10 (i)

From last-minute anguish ...

IN 2011/12 the Premier League title was secured in scintillating style. The triumph included remarkable turnarounds and unbelievable recoveries. It culminated in a Camp Nou-style comeback with two goals in injury time to seal victory and the crown, while leaving their opponents shell-shocked – only this time United were the victims and their city rivals had performed the miracles.

Much has been said and written about the events of 13 May 2012 and they certainly hit Ferguson hard. 'Of all the setbacks I endured, nothing compared to losing the league to City,' Ferguson recalled in his second autobiography.

In the years leading up to the most dramatic end of a Premier League season, there were several key moments to consider, beginning in the summer of 2008. United acquired Dimitar Berbatov from Tottenham Hotspur, snatching him from under the noses of Manchester City, who were now a serious factor in both the transfer market and in winning trophies.

City had been acquired by Sheikh Mansour in a deal that would transform them from mid-table mediocrity to challenging for titles. From now on, they would frequently pose a threat to United.

United were weakened by the sale of Ronaldo in the summer of 2009 and by then City had had three transfer windows from which to improve. In that third transfer splurge they had lured Carlos Tévez from the red side of Manchester.[54] Following the acquisition of the Argentinian striker, a billboard was erected near Strangeways Prison and the old Boddingtons Brewery in Manchester. On it was a picture of Tévez, arms outstretched, followed by the words 'Welcome to Manchester'. Ferguson branded it 'cocky' in his press conference prior to the first clash between the two clubs since the transfer. From this comment, it is easy to draw two conclusions. Firstly, like all great leaders, it was a rallying cry to players and fans alike, showing them whose side he was on, and demanding a response from both his team and supporters. It was time to pull ranks in order to defeat this new threat. And herein lies the second prong to his attack. It was borne out of concern. When Arsène Wenger was a fly in his ointment, there would be frequent verbal attacks. By the end of the Scot's time at Old Trafford, relations had thawed so much that he had sympathy for the Frenchman's plight, such was the gap in the league table between the respective clubs. Now, here were City, firmly in Ferguson's line of fire, and they would continue to be until he retired four years later.

That derby, on 20 September 2009, just over a year after City's injection of cash, was arguably the first time the team from the blue half of Manchester had posed a serious threat on the pitch. There had been defeats in the past, but they were never more than a blip. Even the 5-1 loss at Maine Road in 1989, which forced Ferguson to shove his head under a pillow in shame, still saw United coming out on top by winning the FA Cup and finishing above their rivals come the end of the season.

---

54 Strictly speaking, Tévez was a free agent but United were in pole position and had an option to buy him. But the striker was unhappy at the amount of playing time he got at Old Trafford.

But Ferguson's nose had been put out of joint and he wanted a response, which is exactly what he got. Roared on by vociferous support, United won that derby 4-3, with a winner from Michael Owen in the sixth minute of injury time. Afterwards, Ferguson told Sky Sports, 'Sometimes you have a noisy neighbour. You cannot do anything about that. They will always be noisy. You just have to get on with your life, put your television on and turn it up a bit louder.' Oh, how the red side of the city loved it.

Though Ferguson and his team would fall short come the end of the season, with Chelsea pipping his team to the 2009/10 Premier League title, there was still another last-minute winner from Paul Scholes to enjoy in the return fixture at the Etihad as United continued to exert their authority over City.

United didn't win the league primarily because they were too heavily reliant on Wayne Rooney for goals. And when they dried up, so did their title chances. To be fair to Rooney, his loss of form towards the end of the season owed largely to an injury he picked up away to Bayern Munich, before he was rushed back too soon to play in the return leg of the Champions League quarter-final. Arguably, he would never quite reach those heights again. Ferguson seemed to back this up when he said, a couple of years later, that Rooney 'was struggling to get by people and had lost some of his old thrust. As time wore on, I felt he struggled more and more to do it for 90 minutes, and he seemed to tire in games.'

That season ended with own goals being United's third-best source of goals, prompting Ferguson to remedy the problem by signing a striker who would make up for the shortfall. Javier 'Chicharito' Hernández was acquired for a bargain £7m, and 23 goals later United had wrenched the title back from Chelsea in 2010/11. Again Ferguson proved that he still had the Midas touch in solving a problem.

City, meanwhile, were making inroads, getting ever closer to their rivals across town. In April 2011 they knocked United out of the FA Cup at the semi-final stage en route to winning their first major trophy in 35 years. Now, three years after the multi-million-pound takeover and with Roberto Mancini at the helm, they were truly ready to challenge United and Ferguson.

During the transfer windows of 2010 and 2011, City spent big. More importantly, they spent well. They strengthened their own pool of talent while also weakening domestic rivals, most notably Arsenal with the arrivals of Gaël Clichy and Samir Nasri. The purchases of Edin Džeko, Yaya Touré, Mario Balotelli and James Milner would all help City take a step forward but the acquisitions of David Silva and Sergio Agüero were the real long-term game changers.

City led the table for large parts of 2011/12 thanks mainly to their goalscoring prowess, which was ably demonstrated during a 6-1 demolition job of United at Old Trafford. Ferguson described the way his team chased the game when down to ten men as a 'farce' and 'suicidal', leading to an avalanche of late goals being conceded. He demanded a reaction, 'The impact will come from the embarrassment of the defeat. There's a lot of the boys in the dressing room today that will be feeling that. We expect an impact. Without doubt there'll be a response to that.'

As always, Ferguson called on his team to rise to the challenge posed by a crushing defeat, and they did exactly that. In the next nine league games United conceded just two goals. It was a watershed moment for the defence. Ferguson and his staff were able to plug the leak.

Firstly, they wanted to remind Rio Ferdinand of his responsibilities, dropping him for the next match against Everton. For Ferdinand, it was nothing more than a broadside, though. In the longer term, United's coaching staff wanted him to be aware he could no longer rely on his pace to get him out of trouble.

There was a subtle switch to the back line too, with Ferdinand and Nemanja Vidić switching central defensive sides. Ferdinand would play on the left of the centre-back pairing, nearer to Patrice Evra, the regular left-back. Vidić switched to the right.[55]

Finally, the midfield was stiffened, often with the use of the more defensively minded Park Ji-sung. Anderson was the biggest fall guy from the thrashing against City. His lack of due care and attention in that match contributed to him not starting another Premier League match for the rest of the season.[56] Ferguson felt the team were giving up too many chances through the centre of the pitch and the Brazilian's forays forward were not appreciated, particularly against menacing opponents.

These changes, aligned with the steely determination Ferguson demanded, provided United with the perfect platform to go on an unbeaten run of nine wins and one draw that would propel them back into the title race.

A 1-0 victory against Everton away provided the perfect response to the catastrophe against City. Ferguson knew that he was well on the way to solving the defensive issue. He commented in the wake of that success at Goodison Park, 'The fact that there have been so many chances against us recently, we had to reduce that if we are going to win the league and today we did not have any problems.'

The Ferdinand–Vidić axis was restored to play Sunderland in the next match as United chalked up another 1-0 victory and Ferguson had a stand named after him in tribute to his 25 years at Old Trafford. After a third successive clean sheet was earned against Swansea, Ferguson said, 'We didn't really look as though we were going to lose a goal. In the past when we have won titles we have won four or five games 1-0.'

---

55 Nemanja Vidić didn't play in the 6-1 loss to Manchester City. His replacement, Jonny Evans, was sent off after 47 minutes.

56 Anderson did miss large chunks of the season through injury, but wasn't trusted, either through form or fitness, to start another Premier League match for almost a year.

City dropped ten points over a crucial five-game period in March and with just six matches left, United held a commanding eight-point lead at the top of the table.

What was to occur over the next month, however, would have long-lasting ramifications. It would also have an influence on how the United manager was to eventually bow out at the club he had served for a quarter of a century. First was Wigan Athletic away, and a 1-0 defeat that gave City a chink of light as they narrowed the gap to five points. Then, with four games to play, United dropped another two points after losing two late goals to draw 4-4 at home to Everton. Some of the football from Ferguson's team that day was of the highest order, and the combination play between Rooney and Welbeck boded well for the future, though it was to prove to be a false dawn. Arguably, Rooney was in decline, and had been since the latter part of the 2009/10 season, when injuries and issues off the field began to take their toll. The magnificent bicycle kick against City in February 2011 apart, he rarely produced on the big occasion in his latter years. And even in that derby, he was having a stinker until his wonder strike.

Ferguson described the concession of two points against Everton as 'the one that killed us', especially given the careless nature of the draw. United were cruising and on 81 minutes, a Rafael cross found Evra at the far post. The Frenchman's header from two yards struck the woodwork. Just centimetres from a 5-2 lead, three minutes later United were pegged back to 4-4 after first Nikica Jelavić and then Steven Pienaar turned the match on its head. 'We've thrown it away, no question about that,' said a clearly shaken Ferguson afterwards.

With three matches to play, just three points separated United and City, but crucially the two teams still had to face each other at the Etihad and Roberto Mancini's men held a significant goal difference advantage. Ferguson said after the Everton draw, as he looked towards that next fixture, 'We've got to get a result at the Etihad Stadium. It's a derby game of amazing proportions. It's probably the most important derby in my time.'

Knowing a draw would probably be enough to seal the title, Ferguson threw caution to blanket City's wind, playing his tried and trusted man for the big occasion – Park Ji-sung. Ferguson would often play the South Korean for tricky away assignments, normally with one objective – to destroy. He famously did a job on AC Milan's Andrea Pirlo. 'Your job today is not about touching the ball, it's not about making passes, your job is Pirlo. That's all: Pirlo,' Ferguson told the South Korean international before the game at the San Siro. United knocked AC Milan out and Pirlo described his midfield nemesis as a 'guard dog' such was the close attention the tigerish midfielder paid the creative fulcrum of the Italian side.

Ferguson wanted Park Ji-sung to repeat the feat on Manchester City's dominant midfielder, Yaya Touré, as part of a five-man midfield. But the ploy did not have the same success with Ferguson citing Touré as making the 'difference'. City ran out 1-0 winners with one-time United target Vincent Kompany heading the winner. As a result, Mancini's side took over top spot on goal difference. In the space of four games there had been an eight-point swing between the two Manchester clubs. Both won their penultimate fixtures, meaning the title would go down to the final game, albeit with City as 'red-hot favourites' in Ferguson's eyes.

City knew a win at home to relegation-threatened Queens Park Rangers would mean that the volume of their television would be at an unbearable level for Ferguson and the United faithful.

It was the sixth time the Scot had led his side into the last day of the season with the title on the line, having won it on three occasions and finishing runners-up twice. Roy Keane was a part of the side that missed out under such circumstances in 1995 before winning the championship a year later on the final day when victory at Middlesbrough put an end to Newcastle

United's hopes. Keane then captained the side in the tight finish to 1998/99 where a final-day win against Tottenham Hotspur put United on the treble path.

On the morning of that crucial Sunday at the end of 2011/12, with the difference between the two Manchester clubs paper-thin, Keane had a column in the tabloid newspaper *The Sun*. The Old Trafford legend and Ferguson were, by now, no longer on speaking terms after the Irishman's acrimonious departure in 2005. Earlier that season Keane had upset Ferguson in the wake of United's Champions League exit after he had criticised the manner of the loss to Basel. Ferguson responded to the criticism by expressing his surprise at Keane's remarks, not least as they had come 'from someone we thought was on our side'.

The Irishman was anything but on Ferguson's side and seemed to be taking great pleasure from his former manager's anguish as the season entered its climatic last day. In his newspaper column, Keane wrote, 'Losing the title will haunt Manchester United players for the rest of their lives. You might think I'm exaggerating. I'm not, because I still get nightmares about losing out on the final day of the season in 1995. And if you think United losing a title to Blackburn Rovers is bad, believe me, it would be much, much worse to do it to Manchester City.'

In words that echo a lot of what this book is all about, not to mention the fact that his former manager often thought the same, Keane said, 'The titles you've lost stick with you far more than the ones you've won.' He concluded his column in jovial style, 'I expect City to be champions and that's why I'll be off to Barbados tomorrow morning to get away from their fans! Only joking.' For Ferguson, Sunday, 13 May 2012 would be no laughing matter.

A week beforehand, Ferguson said wishfully, 'Hopefully next week will be the biggest celebration of our lives,' but he knew it was a tall order. Relying on QPR to do his team a favour at the Etihad was not a position he hoped he would be in just a few weeks previously, when United held a mammoth advantage over their rivals.

The first strike of the day went to United as they took a 20th-minute lead against Sunderland. United were top of the table for 20 minutes, until Pablo Zabaleta put City ahead after a ricocheted effort spun into the air and dropped into the net. At half-time both clubs were one goal to the good, meaning City were on course to be champions for the first time in 44 years.

But the drama was just beginning. QPR equalised at the beginning of the second half through Djibril Cissé, meaning United went top once more. Seven minutes later QPR midfielder Joey Barton, who once plied his trade in the blue half of Manchester, was sent off after an altercation with ex-United striker Carlos Tévez. The momentum had seemingly swung City's way but ten minutes later QPR striker Jamie Mackie stunned the Etihad by heading Mark Hughes's team in front. Remarkable. United, still winning 1-0 at Sunderland and looking comfortable, had a three-point lead. City needed two goals and they had less than 25 minutes to get them. But the City players, like their fans, looked like they had just staggered away from a car crash, rather than a club ready to reverse a trend of almost half a century.

The next 20 minutes or so of normal time passed by and the home team could not find any cohesion. Five minutes of injury time arrived and in the first of those City forced a corner, from which Edin Džeko headed home for 2-2. United's game finished 1-0 and Ferguson had been kept abreast of the goings-on at City thanks to a member of staff at Sky Television. He was aware that his team were minutes away from being crowned champions.

Bizarrely, after City's equaliser, QPR kicked off and aimed straight for the corner flag with a punt forward. They didn't want to be there any more, having just learned of their Premier

League safety. They had been fighting relegation until those last few minutes but now knew they were staying up after Bolton Wanderers had failed to beat Stoke City. That development had filtered through to the QPR players. How much of an effect that had on proceedings, we will never know. But the kick-off suggested that they were no longer bothered. A team defending for their lives can waste a lot more time by keeping possession than just directing an aimless ball. It was almost as if they were reluctant to get involved in the title discussion.

The City players were far less reticent as Joe Hart ran to retrieve the ball. Brian Kidd, formerly Ferguson's assistant, was ushering the team forward, almost on the field of play.

Coverage on Sky Sports went split-screen momentarily as the clock ticked past 93 minutes. The right half of the television showed the United players, shirts off, applauding the crowd, shaking hands and awaiting their fate. The left half showed City piling forward. Now, United fans had their hands on their heads, begging for good news from the Etihad Stadium, unsure what else to do. 'Manchester United have done all they can, that Rooney goal was enough for the three points,' Martin Tyler said in commentary at the Etihad Stadium.

With the clock reading 93 minutes and 12 seconds, Mario Balotelli picked up possession on the edge of the QPR box. He stumbled and fell but managed to stick out a leg which poked the ball into the path of Sergio Agüero. The Argentinian took one touch to take it away from the outstretched leg of QPR defender Taye Taiwo. This was crucial, as Taiwo later admitted, 'So I just tried to stretch my leg and block him, but he hit the ball really well.' Agüero's next touch was decisive, drilling the ball past QPR goalkeeper Paddy Kenny to put his side 3-2 up.

Bedlam ensued. City were champions and United were devastated. And in 'Fergie Time' too.

As Agüero's title-winning shot hit the back of the net, Tyler famously shrieked, 'Agüerooooooooo!' Tyler, like the title race, had reached ten on the Richter scale. He added giddily with a voice somewhat hoarse from his previous exclamation, 'I swear you'll never see anything like this ever again.' United, Ferguson, and the club's supporters, certainly did not ever want to feel anything like it ever again.

QPR's manager Mark Hughes had been closely connected to both Manchester clubs during his career, as a former United player and City boss. He told Tyler the next night that it was the noisiest moment in a football ground he had ever experienced. This is particularly notable as the Welshman had been involved in football for the best part of four decades, including other spells as a player at Barcelona, Chelsea and Bayern Munich.

The sound effects felt across the city were profound as the noisy neighbours had finally reached unbearable levels. Ferguson said the day after the defeat, 'I'm a winner. When we lost the league to Leeds United in 1992 the young players came out that day and the Liverpool supporters asked for their autographs. And then they tore the autographs up. And I said to Giggs and the boys, "Remember this day." And that's exactly what I said to them yesterday. Those Sunderland fans were cheering for City. Remember the day. We won't forget that.'

United, once again, were on the path to success from the depths of despair and Ferguson was the driving force.

10 (ii)

... to he did it his way

FERGUSON WAS more determined than ever going into the 2012/13 season. The wounds from the narrow title defeat to City ran deep, but they would serve as a reminder to fuel the success that was set to follow. 'His reaction to losing the title on the last day in 2012 was very poignant and moving. He took it very badly, the whole family took it badly,' Ferguson's biographer Paul Hayward said.

The United manager's wife, Cathy, told her husband in the wake of the title defeat, 'I can't take much more of this,' before explaining her reluctance to even leave the house: 'I'm not going out. There are too many City fans in the village.'

Hayward continued, 'They had a terrible summer, reflecting on the nature of Man City's win, the last-minute drama of it.' But it would also prove to be the inspiration for the success that was set to follow for Ferguson's last season at the helm. Hayward explained, 'What was interesting about it, though, is how Sir Alex turned it round and came up with a plan to make the following season a challenge. He said he worked harder in that following season than he had for many, many years. He was never out of the video analysis room, he went back to basics, in a way, with this tremendous work ethic that he had and decided to throw absolutely everything into regaining the title from City. It was one final, mammoth effort at the end of his time at Manchester United to go out on a high. He said to Cathy, and I'm quoting, "Last season – losing the title in the last game. I can't take another one like that. I just hope we can win the league this time, and reach the Champions League or FA Cup Final. It would be a great ending."'

Hayward confirmed the evolution from the depths of despair to rising to the challenge, 'It started out as remorse but it soon turned into a mission.'

John Motson wrote an article for the BBC website, recalling how he once heard Sir Alex say 'determination separates people'. And Motson said, 'I've certainly never encountered a more determined person in all of my time working in football.' Quite a compliment given that the man behind the microphone was in the industry for half a century.

For Ferguson, that resolve went into overdrive after a setback, and there were few blows to match the one inflicted by Manchester City.

The first significant step towards wresting the title back was through the acquisition of Robin van Persie, denying City the Dutchman's services in the process. The Van Persie transfer saga started in January 2012 with Ferguson doubtful about the Arsenal striker's age and fitness. But it didn't take first-team coach René Meulensteen long to convince his boss of the benefits of signing the Dutch international.

At that point, United were heading towards a title showdown with their cross-city rivals, one they would eventually squander on goal difference. Ferguson promised that neither of these failings would happen again. To lose the title to City, and because United had not scored enough goals (they had scored four fewer which contributed to the eight-goal differential), was an affront to Ferguson. He was keen to put it right. In January 2012, Wayne Rooney's form was patchy. The England striker had off-the-pitch issues, laid bare when he came into training with a hangover that resulted in him being dropped for a 3-2 defeat at home to Blackburn Rovers. It meant Ferguson was keen to address the striker situation.

Dimitar Berbatov was nearing the end of his time at United. Having joined on the last day of the summer transfer window in 2008, amid great fanfare, the Bulgarian never quite lived up to expectations at Old Trafford. He failed to adapt to United's style of play, often wanting to slow the game down rather than speed things up. But with players like Rooney, Nani and Ronaldo at the club when he first arrived, speed of thought was imperative if you wanted to conduct this orchestra.

A phone call from Van Persie's representatives to Meulensteen would eventually herald the end of Berbatov's United career.

Meulensteen takes up the story, 'I got contacted by the company that represents Robin, basically saying, "Would Ferguson be interested?" And that was around January, and I said to them, "I'll ask him." So I walked up to his office and I knocked on his door and said, "Would you be interested in Robin van Persie?" Ferguson said, "Only if he's on a free." I told him he wasn't, but "the information I just got, and asked to run it by you, is that he's got a year left and he's not in agreement with the future plans or ambitions of Arsenal. Robin would like to stay in England and he only wants to play for one club in England and that's Manchester United, especially for you."

'I wasn't sure how genuine the interest was as sometimes players do this flirtation to get a better contract. I left it a few days and went to speak to Ferguson again at the end of the week. "Have you thought about Van Persie? It's clear he wants to come." And he said, "Ah, but he's been injured ... " and I said: "That's all behind him. Look at the stats, he's played most of the games, scored goals, assists." I also said, "Do you rate him, do you like him as a player, do you think he would fit in our team?" And he said, "Yeah, absolutely." I told him to have a word with David Gill, and some of the senior players too. Weeks went by and eventually they decided to go for it. Obviously for Robin it turned out to be a perfect match. I only worked with him for a year but it was an absolute joy.'

The affection Meulensteen has for his compatriot is clear, especially as his most treasured picture in his office is of the pair with the Premier League trophy on the pitch at Old Trafford.

Meulensteen played a big part in Van Persie's success on the pitch and also in certain decisions off it. The coach said, 'There were only two numbers available, 20 and 21. I told him to play in number 20 as "you want to win the league and if you want to win the league it will be [United's title] number 20, and you will have it on your back the whole season, reminding you why you're here."'

Meulensteen was keen to emphasise the nature of the club to Van Persie and recalled the flip-chart Ferguson once showed him. He said, 'The manager would close his eyes and imagine how United would attack, and he had it detailed in that chart. On the final page it said, "Pace. Power. Penetration. Unpredictability. Those are the four things I want you to instil in that group every single day." And those are things I obviously discussed with Robin. I spoke to him a month after he arrived at United and I asked him what he thought of the training sessions. He said it was like chalk and cheese in comparison with what he had experienced before – the tempo, the competitiveness, the purpose, so much more volume in every aspect. It was good for him, it was great.'

ITV commentator Clive Tyldesley was in no doubt that the acquisition of Van Persie was an example of Ferguson's determination to bounce back from the title anguish of the previous season. He also thought, with Ferguson traditionally buying players with the future in mind, that the signing of the Dutch striker was an indication of a short-termism that had not been apparent before; a clear indication of the need to win, and win now. 'When he bought Robin van Persie it was a statement. It wasn't a typical Ferguson signing, but it was like, "this is it, win the league" kind of signing,' Tyldesley said.

Journalist Mark Ogden, whose ties with the club were so strong at the time that it was he who first broke news of Ferguson's retirement, agreed with Tyldesley's assessment. When asked how much of an effect did the title loss to City have on the following season, Ogden said, 'It was the reason he signed Van Persie. Fergie wanted a guaranteed 20-goal-a-season striker who knew the Premier League.'

United's new £24m man also noticed some differences in his new surroundings and there were a few characteristics that took him by surprise, principally the 'toughness of everyone', he told Utd Podcast. 'Physically and mentally I was impressed. In training they were tough on each other, but everyone was okay with it. Dealing with injuries, dealing with setbacks, dealing with defeats. There was a calmness.' This echoes the thoughts of opponents, too, who would often notice how Ferguson's teams would remain calm when going behind in games. Van Persie continued on that very theme, 'The combination of the characters of the players and the staff, there was a kind of arrogance, like "it's okay, whatever happens, we got this". What I liked about Ferguson was after one defeat, I think against City, he really trained us hard in the next couple of days. But after that we had a short meeting and he said, "Listen. I had this couple of sessions with you done. Now we have to forget it. We have to look forward." And that is a very important point. If you lose, it can happen. It all depends on how you react. If you stay unhappy, if you stay disappointed then Ferguson always believed your chance of winning the next game would be smaller and I believe so too. You have to move on. You have to learn from it, but he didn't want a bad vibe for too long after a defeat.'

Once again, United's principal opponents in 2012/13 were City. Unlike United, though, City were not a wounded animal. Roberto Mancini's side were basking in the rays of success. There is no doubt their form dropped off, which was something Ferguson would never allow on his watch.

A rejuvenated Ferguson, who galvanised United after the previous season's heartache, the signing of Van Persie, and the decline of their Manchester rivals, all contributed to the title win the legendary manager enjoyed in his final season.

However, you never would have imagined that United were going to embark on a successful campaign after their opening-day defeat to Everton. Following the loss at Goodison Park, Ferguson criticised his team for not making the most of Van Persie's runs. The Dutchman made his debut in a 25-minute cameo as a substitute and Ferguson was keen to rectify the tactical error he felt his players were committing. Meulensteen explained, 'We had to create the link with the other players. Robin is a glider, he's not a sprinter. He glides behind the opponent's back. And it's that split second in which to play the ball in, like he had in the relationship with Fàbregas, at Arsenal, and we had to create the same, I told the midfielders there's a short window and that ball needs to be played.'

Five goals in Van Persie's next four games suggested the manager and his coaching staff had got the message through to the players.

United fell behind in three of that quartet of matches but crucially, they still ended up winning them all. The last of which was particularly sweet, coming at Anfield, Van Persie getting the winner with a penalty.

Next up was Tottenham Hotspur at home. Margaret Thatcher was Prime Minister and Jive Bunny was at number one in the charts the last time Spurs had won at Old Trafford. But the London club came away with all three points, ending a run that stretched back more than two decades, thanks to a 3-2 win. It was the end of September and United were third in the table. However, their ability to snatch victory after falling behind was evident again at home to Stoke City and then most dramatically when coming from 2-0 down to beat Aston

Villa. That result put United on top of the table. A week after that win at Villa Park, United lost to Norwich City, knocking Ferguson's side off top spot. On 24 November they fell behind again in a league match, this time at home to Queens Park Rangers. Again they dug deep to emerge with all three points. Remarkably, it was the sixth time the team had won a league match from a losing position in the opening 13 games of the season. It put the team on top of the table, a position they would never relinquish.

The Premier League campaign's defining game came at the Etihad against City as the season's halfway point approached. United took an early 2-0 lead thanks to a Wayne Rooney brace. But City fought back to 2-2 and the momentum was with them. However, a deflected Van Persie free kick in injury time sealed a 3-2 win for the Red Devils. MUTV commentator Stewart Gardner echoed the thoughts of every United supporter the moment the Dutchman's strike hit the back of the net. He exclaimed, 'Thank goodness he chose red over blue.' It was the fifth time in seven derbies United had won the game in added time. It gave the Old Trafford outfit a six-point cushion over their rivals.

A Champions League exit at the hands of Real Madrid and an FA Cup loss to Chelsea were the only blots on Ferguson's copybook in that last season at the helm. The former was particularly painful for the Scot, who was so distraught he didn't show up for the usual press briefing after the game, almost certainly in the knowledge that his last chance of European Cup success had slipped through his fingers.

One thing Ferguson was not going to let slip was the healthy advantage United held in the league. He said he and the players had learned from the painful lessons of the year before, when they blew an eight-point lead with six games to play. He said, 'The difference for United, as opposed to last year, we didn't anticipate the unexpected [defeat] at Wigan. That was a mistake. And when we played Everton at home, 4-2 up with seven minutes to go, we didn't anticipate a reaction from Everton coming back at us that way. That won't happen this year. It won't happen, trust me.'

And the United fans did trust their manager. After 26 years of coming back from defeats, Ferguson had earned that faith, and he repaid it one last glorious time in his final season. 'A great test of any Manchester United team is how they recover after a defeat,' Ferguson said a couple of years after his retirement. It was also a test of the manager and he passed with flying colours time and time again. The way he galvanised United to win the title, sealed thanks to a Van Persie hat-trick in a 3-0 home win against Aston Villa, was testimony to that.

When United played Chelsea on 5 May in the penultimate home game of the season, Ferguson spoke in his programme notes of how the club was in rude health, confidently predicting a bright future for both him and his young team. There was no sign of the bombshell that was about to come.

His retirement was a closely guarded secret and one Ferguson wanted to keep that way. In 2001 he announced he would be leaving football at the end of the upcoming season. The fact he revealed the news a year in advance, Ferguson felt, weakened the resolve in his team and was a significant factor behind a trophy-less campaign. He went on to reverse his decision but knew that when the day would finally come to leave the sport, it would not be made public until the last possible moment. As a result, not even Ferguson's staff were aware of his plan to retire.

On Tuesday, 7 May, two days after the home match with Chelsea, the United players had a day off and were playing golf together, but some of them had heard one or two suggestions that Ferguson was about to retire. Meulensteen explained, 'The players had a golf day and I got a message through from a staff member that played with the players. He told me some of the players were making noises about Ferguson retiring.

And he asked me if I knew anything about it, which I didn't. I then got a message later, around 1am, from my neighbour asking, "Is it true?" And I replied "What?" And he said, "Sir Alex Ferguson." And I thought, "What is he on about?" So I went downstairs and switched on the computer to check. By now there was so much smoke, there must be fire. I saw lots of camera crews standing outside Carrington the next morning. The manager's got us all in the office, me, Mick Phelan and Eric Steele, and basically he explained. First of all he apologised and said he was very disappointed with how it got out. How it got out he still didn't know exactly. He explained the reasons, the family reasons why. And he's not getting any younger, etc.'

How the story leaked remains a mystery, though there are some clues. One or two journalists had good connections with the club during the latter years of Ferguson's reign and there have been strong suggestions at how they would break stories via a mole within the dressing room. The level of the stories, such as the seismic decision for Fergie to retire, would make it highly unlikely that it was a minor member of staff. Therefore a player or coach has to be the likely source. Given that the coaching staff had no idea that Ferguson wanted to ride off into the sunset, and would be extremely unlikely to undermine the manager, they can be quickly ruled out as a possibility. It also had to be someone who had some longevity at Old Trafford, given the timespan of the stories. He probably played for the club for more than five years. Also, it was almost certainly someone who spoke English and probably had good relations with the media. Finally, it has often been said that the source was one of the English players at Old Trafford which, given the aforementioned suggestions, would make sense.

A key factor in Ferguson's decision to retire was the death of his wife's twin sister, Bridget, who had passed away in October 2012. Ferguson suggested he might have remained as manager beyond the 2012/13 campaign but for the passing of his sister-in-law and the effect it had on his wife, Lady Cathy, who had convinced him the time was right to stand down. Lady Cathy had been by his side for half a century and the United manager recognised the absence of her sister was a traumatic loss. He said, 'I saw she [Cathy] was watching television one night, and she looked up at the ceiling I knew she was isolated.'

Lady Cathy and the rest of the family had cajoled the United manager out of his decision to retire on Christmas Day a decade earlier. But on this occasion there would be no such persuasion. 'When I told her this time I was going to retire she had no objection whatsoever. I knew she wanted me to do it.'

Meulensteen also said that neither he nor Ferguson's staff had the slightest clue about the news until that Wednesday morning. 'It was strange, I had absolutely no Scooby-Doo whatsoever. I mean, we sat down in the March talking about pre-season plans, going to Australia, visiting vineyards. I had absolutely no reason to believe anything else. It came as a shock.' Meulensteen understood why Ferguson wanted no one to know. 'He obviously kept his cards close to his chest not to disrupt the team.'

Once the news of Ferguson's retirement was officially announced, the scramble for tickets for his last home game, against Swansea, became even more intense, especially as there would be a trophy presentation to witness. That Sunday, 75,572 people crammed into Old Trafford. A large percentage of those who were in attendance were not even born when Sir Alex Ferguson took over at Manchester United on 6 November 1986. An even greater portion of the ground had never known any other manager of their club by virtue of being too young to remember the Scot's predecessor – Ron Atkinson. As a result, there were many tears around the stadium as Ferguson entered to the tune of 'The Impossible Dream' by Frank Sinatra. For much of the Ferguson era, United fans felt like they were dreaming. On several occasions what they witnessed seemed implausible and, in a way, so was his parting. A day that had to come, but one that few had contemplated.

United beat Swansea 2-1 as the Manchester rain began to fall. A late winner from Rio Ferdinand, scoring his first goal in five years, sealed victory. At the game's conclusion, and as Ferguson took the microphone to say goodbye, it was not just the clouds that began to pour – so too did the tears down the cheeks of numerous onlookers.

A week later, United drew 5-5 at West Bromwich Albion in one of the craziest matches of the Ferguson era. Interestingly, in all his games as a manager, at all his clubs, and as Scotland boss, Ferguson never lost after being two goals ahead. In that match at the Hawthorns, he nearly lost that record with interest as United held a three-goal advantage on two separate occasions before clinging on for a draw.

Ultimately, the Scot went out on a high, winning his final home game, drawing his last match in a ten-goal thriller and, most importantly, guiding Manchester United to their 20th league title. Ferguson's reign could never have ended in defeat. It just couldn't. For Ferguson's opponents, that would have been an impossible dream. And what would his reaction have been to such a setback? For once, I'd rather not know.

Bibliography

Andrews, D. *Manchester United: A Thematic Study* (Hove: Psychology Press, 2004)

Arrondel, L.; Duhautois, R.; Laslier, J.-F. Decision Under Psychological Pressure: The Shooter's Anxiety at the Penalty Kick (*Journal of Economic Psychology*, ScienceDirect, 2018)

Barton, W. *King Eric – Portrait of the Artist Who Changed English Football* (London: Reach, 2020)

Barton, W. *The Man Who Kept The Red Flag Flying: Jimmy Murphy* (London: Reach, 2018)

Carrick, M. *Between the Lines: My Autobiography* (London: Bonnier Books Ltd, 2018)

Ferguson, A. with Hayward, P. *My Autobiography* (London: Hodder and Stoughton, 2013)

Ferguson, A. with McIlvanney, H. *Managing My Life, My Autobiography* (London: Hodder and Stoughton, 2000)

Ferguson, A. with Meek, D. *Six Years at United* (Edinburgh: Mainstream Publishing, 1992)

Ferguson, A. with Moritz, M. *Leading* (London: Hodder and Stoughton, 2015)

Keegan, K. *My Life in Football: The Autobiography* (London: Pan Macmillan, 2019)

Kuper, S. and Szymanski, S. *Soccernomics* (New York: Nation Books, 2009)

Lake, P. *I'm Not Really Here: A Life of Two Halves* (London: Random House UK, 2011)

Maltin, T. *101 Things You Thought You Knew About The Titanic ... But Didn't* (London: Penguin Books, 2011)

Neville, G. *Red: My Autobiography* (London: Transworld Publishers, 2012)

Pallister, G. with Ponting I. *Pally: The Autobiography of Gary Pallister* (Studley: Know the Score Books, 2008)

Pirlo, A. with Alciato, A. *I Think Therefore I Play* (Cardross: BackPage Press, 2015)

Winter, H.; Neville, P. via *The Feud Sir Alex Ferguson vs Arsene Wenger* documentary, ITV, 2018

Worrall, F. *Fergie the Greatest – The Biography of Sir Alex Ferguson* (London: John Blake Publishing, 2014)

https://www.11v11.com/league-tables/league-division-one/23-september-1989/

https://www.youtube.com/watch?v=-k34HjLuJ8U

https://www.youtube.com/watch?v=5bPnEvogGnw

https://www.youtube.com/watch?v=YdKDTfvGwyo

https://www.youtube.com/watch?v=_MrzmtVXCVo

https://www.youtube.com/watch?v=bRngvUS1BmE

https://www.youtube.com/watch?v=eNAHGZcV56c

https://www.youtube.com/watch?v=y5WNqAJCxyU&t=5s

https://www.youtube.com/watch?v=hSu5GQOeuuI

https://www.youtube.com/watch?v=OF144mbnLSk

https://www.youtube.com/watch?v=Xl5plowl8Sg&t=111s

https://www.independent.co.uk/sport/relief-at-end-of-foreigner-rule-1526032.html

https://www.sportsjoe.ie/football/alan-shearer-man-united-137764

https://www.skysports.com/football/news/11667/11962761/dwight-yorke-and-andy-cole-what-made-manchester-united-strike-partnership-so-special

https://www.manutd.com/en/news/detail/sir-alex-ferguson-and-paddy-crerand-share-memories-of-1960-real-madrid-team

https://www.theguardian.com/sport/blog/2012/sep/19/forgotten-story-manchester-united-galatasaray

https://www.youtube.com/watch?v=i5bJtXysjf8

https://www.youtube.com/watch?v=9xnctVCWKgQ

https://twitter.com/GaryLineker/status/1281580011502407682

https://therepublikofmancunia.com/carrick-reveals-what-fergie-said-after-2009-cl-final-defeat/

https://www.theguardian.com/sport/blog/2019/apr/09/the-joy-of-six-barcelona-v-manchester-united

https://www.bbc.com/sport/football/21583952

https://www.theguardian.com/football/2009/sep/18/sir-alex-ferguson-manchester-city-united

https://www.11v11.com/teams/manchester-city/tab/opposingTeams/opposition/Manchester%20United/

https://www.youtube.com/watch?v=ydz-WMJFtBc

https://www.youtube.com/watch?v=LsuT1pS0jZs

https://www.youtube.com/watch?v=Mjyoyp0evyg

https://www.youtube.com/watch?v=KQE0h6g8SR8

https://www.bbc.com/sport/football/46411576

https://www.theguardian.com/football/2014/jan/29/paul-ince-guvnor-nickname

https://www.youtube.com/watch?v=4Sl6SsYFLkw

https://www.oddsportal.com/soccer/europe/champions-league-2008-2009/barcelona-manchester-united-GSUpSzP6/

https://www.bbc.com/sport/football/13451151

https://www.independent.co.uk/sport/football/news-and-comment/the-andy-cole-column-the-real-reason-ive-hated-sheringham-for-15-years-he-refused-to-shake-my-hand-1915658.html

https://www.irishtimes.com/sport/keane-puts-veron-back-in-united-firing-line-1.1056512

https://econfix.wordpress.com/2011/03/14/game-theory-penalties-and-the-champions-league-final-2008/

https://www.theguardian.com/football/2019/nov/27/michael-knighton-manchester-united-keepie-uppies-interview

https://www.manchestereveningnews.co.uk/sport/football/football-news/manchester-united-news-today-latest-18225570